2nd Workshop on NLP for Conversational AI 2020

Online
9 July 2020

ISBN: 978-1-7138-1379-8

ACL 2020

NLP for Conversational AI

Proceedings of the 2nd Workshop

July 9, 2020

Introduction

Welcome to the ACL 2020 Workshop on **NLP for Conversational AI**.

Ever since the invention of the intelligent machine, hundreds and thousands of mathematicians, linguists, and computer scientists have dedicated their career to empowering human-machine communication in natural language. Although the idea is finally around the corner with a proliferation of virtual personal assistants such as Siri, Alexa, Google Assistant, and Cortana, the development of these conversational agents remains difficult and there still remain plenty of unanswered questions and challenges.

Conversational AI is hard because it is an interdisciplinary subject. Initiatives were started in different research communities, from Dialogue State Tracking Challenges to NIPS Conversational Intelligence Challenge live competition and the Amazon Alexa prize. However, various fields within the NLP community, such as semantic parsing, coreference resolution, sentiment analysis, question answering, and machine reading comprehension etc. have been seldom evaluated or applied in the context of conversational AI.

The goal of this workshop is to bring together NLP researchers and practitioners in different fields, alongside experts in speech and machine learning, to discuss the current state-of-the-art and new approaches, to share insights and challenges, to bridge the gap between academic research and real-world product deployment, and to shed the light on future directions. "NLP for Conversational AI" will be a one-day workshop including keynotes, spotlight talks, posters, and panel sessions. In keynote talks, senior technical leaders from industry and academia will share insights on the latest developments of the field. An open call for papers will be announced to encourage researchers and students to share their prospects and latest discoveries. The panel discussion will focus on the challenges, future directions of conversational AI research, bridging the gap in research and industrial practice, as well as audience-suggested topics.

With the increasing trend of conversational AI, NLP4ConvAI 2020 is competitive. We received 27 submissions, and after a rigorous review process, we only accept 15. There are total 13 accepted regular workshop papers and 2 cross-submissions or extended abstracts. The workshop overall acceptance rate is about 55.5%. We hope you will enjoy NLP4ConvAI 2020 at ACL and contribute to the future success of our community!

NLPConvAI 2020 Organizers
Tsung-Hsien Wen, PolyAI
Asli Celikyilmaz, Microsoft
Zhou Yu, UC Davis
Alexandros Papangelis, Uber AI
Mihail Eric, Amazon Alexa AI
Anuj Kumar, Facebook
Iñigo Casanueva, PolyAI
Rushin Shah, Google

Organizers:

Tsung-Hsien Wen, PolyAI (UK)
Asli Celikyilmaz, Microsoft (USA)
Zhou Yu, UC Davis (USA)
Alexandros Papangelis, Uber AI (USA)
Mihail Eric, Amazon Alexa AI (USA)
Anuj Kumar, Facebook (USA)
Iñigo Casanueva, PolyAI (UK)
Rushin Shah, Google (USA)

Program Committee:

Pawel Budzianowski, University of Cambridge and PolyAI
Sam Coope, PolyAI
Ondřej Dušek, Heriot Watt University
Nina Dethlefs, University of Hull
Daniela Gerz, PolyAI
Pei-Hao Su, PolyAI
Matthew Henderson, PolyAI
Simon Keizer, AI Lab, Vrije Universiteit Brussel
Ryan Lowe, McGill University
Julien Perez, Naver Labs
Marek Rei, Imperial
Gokhan Tür, Uber AI
Ivan Vulic, University of Cambridge and PolyAI
David Vandyke, Apple
Zhuoran Wang, Trio.io
Tiancheng Zhao, CMU
Alborz Geramifard, Facebook
Shane Moon, Facebook
Jinfeng Rao, Facebook
Bing Liu, Facebook
Pararth Shah, Facebook
Ahmed Mohamed, Facebook
Vikram Ramanarayanan, ETS
Rahul Goel, Google
Shachi Paul, Google
Seokhwan Kim, Amazon
Andrea Madotto, HKUST
Dian Yu, UC Davis
Piero Molino, Uber
Chandra Khatri, Uber
Yi-Chia Wang, Uber
Huaixiu Zheng, Uber
Fei Tao, Uber
Abhinav Rastogi, Google
Stefan Ultes, Daimler

José Lopes, Heriot Watt University
Behnam Hedayatnia, Amazon
Dilek Hakkani-Tür, Amazon
Ta-Chung Chi, CMU
Shang-Yu Su, NTU
Pierre Lison, NR
Ethan Selfridge, Interactions
Teruhisa Misu, HRI
Svetlana Stoyanchev, Toshiba
Ryuichiro Higashinaka, NTT
Hendrik Bushmeier, University of Bielefeld
Kai Yu, Baidu
Koichiro Yoshino, NAIST
Abigail See, Stanford University
Ming Sun, Amazon Alexa AI

Invited Speakers:

Yun-Nung Chen, National Taiwan University
Dilek Hakkani-Tür, Amazon Alexa AI
Jesse Thomason, University of Washington
Antoine Bordes, Facebook AI Research
Jacob Andreas, Massachussetts Institute of Technology
Jason Williams, Apple

Workshop Program

July 9, 2020

06:00   ***Opening Remarks***

06:10   *Invited Talk*
Yun-Nung Chen

06:40   *Invited Talk*
Antonie Bordes

07:10   *Invited Talk*
Jacob Andreas

07:40   *Using Alternate Representations of Text for Natural Language Understanding*
Venkat Varada, Charith Peris, Yangsook Park and Christopher Dipersio

07:50   *On Incorporating Structural Information to improve Dialogue Response Generation*
Nikita Moghe, Priyesh Vijayan, Balaraman Ravindran and Mitesh M. Khapra

08:00   *CopyBERT: A Unified Approach to Question Generation with Self-Attention*
Stalin Varanasi, Saadullah Amin and Guenter Neumann

08:10   *How to Tame Your Data: Data Augmentation for Dialog State Tracking*
Adam Summerville, Jordan Hashemi, James Ryan and william ferguson

08:20   *Efficient Intent Detection with Dual Sentence Encoders*
Iñigo Casanueva, Tadas Temčinas, Daniela Gerz, Matthew Henderson and Ivan Vulić

08:30   *Accelerating Natural Language Understanding in Task-Oriented Dialog*
Ojas Ahuja and Shrey Desai

08:40   *DLGNet: A Transformer-based Model for Dialogue Response Generation*
Olabiyi Oluwatobi and Erik Mueller

08:50   *Data Augmentation for Training Dialog Models Robust to Speech Recognition Errors*
Longshaokan Wang, Maryam Fazel-Zarandi, Aditya Tiwari, Spyros Matsoukas and Lazaros Polymenakos

July 9, 2020 (continued)

09:00   **Panel**

10:00   *Invited Talk*
Jesse Thomason

10:30   *Invited Talk*
Dilek Hakkani-Tür

11:00   *Invited Talk*
Jason Williams

11:30   *Automating Template Creation for Ranking-Based Dialogue Models*
Jingxiang Chen, Heba Elfardy, Simi Wang, Andrea Kahn and Jared Kramer

11:40   *From Machine Reading Comprehension to Dialogue State Tracking: Bridging the Gap*
Shuyang Gao, Sanchit Agarwal, Di Jin, Tagyoung Chung and Dilek Hakkani-Tur

11:50   *Improving Slot Filling by Utilizing Contextual Information*
Amir Pouran Ben Veyseh, Franck Dernoncourt and Thien Huu Nguyen

12:00   *Learning to Classify Intents and Slot Labels Given a Handful of Examples*
Jason Krone, Yi Zhang and Mona Diab

12:10   *MultiWOZ 2.2 : A Dialogue Dataset with Additional Annotation Corrections and State Tracking Baselines*
Xiaoxue Zang, Abhinav Rastogi and Jindong Chen

12:20   *Sketch-Fill-A-R: A Persona-Grounded Chit-Chat Generation Framework*
Michael Shum, Stephan Zheng, Wojciech Kryscinski, Caiming Xiong and Richard Socher

12:30   *Probing Neural Dialog Models for Conversational Understanding*
Abdelrhman Saleh, Tovly Deutsch, Stephen Casper, Yonatan Belinkov and Stuart Shieber

12:40   ***Closing Remarks***

Using Alternate Representations of Text for Natural Language Understanding

Venkata sai Varada, Charith Peris, Yangsook Park, Christopher DiPersio

Amazon Alexa AI, USA

{vnk, perisc, yangsoop, dipersio}@amazon.com

Abstract

One of the core components of voice assistants is the Natural Language Understanding (NLU) model. Its ability to accurately classify the user's request (or "intent") and recognize named entities in an utterance is pivotal to the success of these assistants. NLU models can be challenged in some languages by code-switching or morphological and orthographic variations. This work explores the possibility of improving the accuracy of NLU models for Indic languages via the use of alternate representations of input text for NLU, specifically ISO-15919 and IndicSOUNDEX, a custom SOUNDEX designed to work for Indic languages. We used a deep neural network based model to incorporate the information from alternate representations into the NLU model. We show that using alternate representations significantly improves the overall performance of NLU models when the amount of training data is limited.

1 Introduction

Building NLU models can be more challenging for languages that involve code-switching. Recent times have seen a significant surge of interest in voice-enabled smart assistants, such as Amazon's Alexa, Google Assistant, and Apple's Siri. These assistants are powered by several components, which include Automatic Speech Recognition (ASR) and Natural Language Understanding (NLU) models. The input to an NLU model is the text returned by the ASR model. With this input text, there are two major tasks for an NLU model: 1) Intent Classification (IC), and 2) Named Entity Recognition (NER).

Code-switching is a phenomenon in which two or more languages are interchanged within a sentence or between sentences. An example of code-switching from Hindi is 'मेरी shopping list में dove soap bar जोड़ें' ('add dove soap bar to my shopping list'). NLU models expect ASR to return the text in the above form, which matches with the transcription of the training data for NLU models. Then, NLU model would return the action as *Add Items To Shopping List*, while it also recognizes 'dove soap bar' as the actual item name to be added to the shopping list. However, ASR could inconsistently return 'मेरी shopping list में dove soap बार जोड़ें', where the English word 'bar' is recognized as a Hindi word 'बार'. Note that while the Hindi word 'बार' means something different than the English 'bar', their pronunciation is similar enough to mislead the ASR model in the context of mixed-language utterance. In this case, the NLU model should become robust against such ASR mistakes, and learn that 'dove soap बार' is equivalent to 'dove soap bar' in order to correctly recognize it as an item name. The phenomenon of code-switching is common amongst other Indic languages as well.

ASR inconsistencies can cause significant challenges for NLU models by introducing new data that the models were not trained on. Such inconsistencies can occur due to 1) code-switching in the data, especially when the input text contains more than one script (character set), 2) orthographic or morphological variations that exist in the input text, or 3) due to requirements for multilingual support. In a language such as English in the United States, where code-switching is less common, both ASR and NLU models can perform quite well, as input data tend to be more consistent. However, when it comes to Indic languages such as Hindi, where code-switching is much more common, the question arises as to which representation of the input text would work best for NLU models.

Proceedings of the 2nd Workshop on Natural Language Processing for Conversational AI, pages 1–10

July 9, 2020. ©2020 Association for Computational Linguistics

There is ongoing research on solving modeling tasks for data with code-switching. In Geetha et al. (2018), the authors explore using character and word level embeddings for NER tasks. Some of this research focuses on using alternate representations of text for NLU modeling. For example, Johnson et al. (2019) explore the use of cross-lingual transfer learning from English to Japanese for NER by romanizing Japanese input into a Latin-based character set to overcome the script differences between the language pair. Zhang and Le-Cun (2017) has shown using romanization for Japanese text for sentiment classification hurt the performance of the monolingual model.

In this paper, we explore the possibility of mitigating the problems related to ASR inconsistency and code-switching in our input data by using two alternate representations of text in our NLU model: ISO-15919 and IndicSOUNDEX. ISO-15919[1] was developed as a standardized Latin-based representation for Indic languages and scripts. SOUNDEX is an algorithm that provides phonetic-like representations of words. Most work on SOUNDEX algorithms has focused primarily on monolingual solutions. One of the best known implementations with a multilingual component is Beider-Morse Phonetic Matching Beider and Morse (2010); however, it only identifies the language in which a given word is written to choose which pronunciation rules to apply. Other attempts at multilingual SOUNDEX algorithms, particularly for Indic languages, were smaller studies focused on two Indic languages with or without English as a third language. Chaware and Rao (2012) developed a custom SOUNDEX algorithm for monolingual Hindi and Marathi word pair matching. Shah and Singh (2014) describe an actual multilingual SOUNDEX implementation designed to cover Hindi, Gujarati, and English, which, in addition to the actual algorithm implementation, was aided by a matching threshold declaring two conversions a match even if they differed in up to two characters.

In this study, we use ISO-15919 and Indic-SOUNDEX representations of text in a deep neural network (DNN) to perform multi-task modeling of IC and NER. We experiment on one high-resource Indic language (Hindi) and three low-resource Indic languages (Tamil, Marathi, Telugu). In Section 2, we describe the two alternate representations of text that we explore. In Section 3, we describe our data, model architecture, and detail our experimental setup. In Section 4, we present our results followed by our conclusions in Section 5.

2   Alternate representations of text

Using data transcribed in the original script of a language can cause problems for both monolingual and multilingual NLU models. For a monolingual model in a language where code-switching, orthographic variations, or rich morphological inflections are common, NLU models may not be able to perform well on all the variations, depending on the frequency of these variations in the training data. For multilingual models, words with similar sound and meaning across different languages (e.g., loanwords, common entities) cannot be captured if the words are written in their original script. For example, the same proper noun 'telugu' is written as 'तेलुगु' in Hindi, as 'தெலுகு' in Tamil, and as 'తెలుగు' in Telugu. Although they sound similar and mean the same thing, NLU model will see them as unrelated tokens if they are represented in their original scripts in the input data.

From the NLU point of view, a text representation that can minimize variations of the same or similar words within a language and across different languages would be beneficial for both IC and NER tasks. In this section, we explore two alternative ways of text representations for Indic languages: ISO-15919 and a SOUNDEX-based algorithm, which we call IndicSOUNDEX. Compared to using the original scripts, these two alternatives can represent the variants of the same word or root in the same way. For example, in the original Hindi script (i.e., Devanagari), the word for 'volume/voice' can be represented in two forms: 'आवाज़' and 'आवाज'. These two forms, however, are uniformly represented as 'āvāj' in ISO-15919 and as the string 'av6' in IndicSOUNDEX. Similarly, the English word 'list' may be transcribed as 'list' or as 'లిస్ట్' in Telugu; however, they map to the same Indic-SOUNDEX representation, 'ls8'.

---

[1] https://en.wikipedia.org/wiki/ISO_15919

2.1 ISO-15919

ISO-15919 is a standardized representation of Indic scripts based on Latin characters, which maps the corresponding Indic characters onto the same Latin character. For example, 'क' in Devanagari, 'క' in Telugu, and 'க' in Tamil are all represented by 'k' in the ISO-15919 standard. Consequently, ISO-15919 can be used as a neutral common representation between Indic scripts. However, ISO-15919 has some downsides. Indic scripts often rely on implicit vowels which are not represented in the orthography, which means they cannot be reliably added to a transliterated word. Additionally, Indic scripts have a character called a halant, or virama, which is used to suppress an inherent vowel. This character, although usually included orthographically in a word, does not have an ISO-15919 representation and so is lost in an exact, one-to-one conversion. Finally, it is not always the case that the same word in two different Indic scripts will have the same ISO-15919 conversion due to script-to-script and language-to-language differences and irregularities. Table 1 below shows some examples of conversion using ISO-15919.

2.2 IndicSOUNDEX

SOUNDEX algorithms provide phonetic-like representations of words that attempt to reduce spelling and other orthographic variations for the same or similarly-sounding words, mainly to increase recall in information retrieval or text search tasks. This is done by following a set of simple steps which may include removing vowels, reducing character duplication, and mapping sets of characters to a single character, based on whether they 1) sound similar or 2) are used in similar environments in similar sounding words. For example, at its most extreme, American SOUNDEX maps 'c', 'g', 'j', 'k', 'q', 's', 'x', and 'z' to the same character: '2'.

IndicSOUNDEX is a custom SOUNDEX approach designed to work on Hindi, Marathi, Telugu, Tamil, Malayalam, Punjabi, Bengali, Kannada, Gujarati, and English. Table 1 shows some examples of conversion using IndicSOUNDEX:

3 Experimental Setup

3.1 Data

For our experiments, we chose datasets from four Indic languages: Hindi, Tamil, Marathi, and Telugu. For Hindi, we use an internal large-scale real-world dataset; for the other three languages, we use relatively small datasets collected and annotated by third party vendors. We perform a series of experiments to evaluate the use of the alternate representations of text, ISO-15919 and Indic-SOUNDEX, described in Section 2.

Our Hindi training dataset consists of 6M data. We separate a portion (1%) of the data into an independent test set. We execute a stratified split on the remainder, based on intent, and choose 10% of this data for validation and the rest as training data. For the three smaller-scale datasets, we execute a stratified split with 60% for training, 20% for validation, and 20% for testing. Table 2 shows the data partitions across different languages used for our experiments.

Each of the four datasets contain code-switching. The transcription was done either in the original script of the language (for words from that language) or in the standard Latin (for words from other languages including English). However, the transcription was not always consistent, especially in the third party data, so some Indic words were transcribed in the so-called 'colloquial' Latin (i.e., a casual, non-standard way of representing Indic languages in online resources) and some English words were represented in the original script of the Indic languages (e.g., 'లిస్ట్' for the English word 'list'). See Table 3 for the total counts of tokens in each script in each of the training and test data, which reflects the use of code-switching in each training dataset. Note that Hindi and Marathi both use the same script (Devanagari) in their writing systems.

3.2 Model architecture

For our NLU models, we used a multi-task modeling framework that predicts Intent and Named Entities, given an input sentence. A schematic of our model is given in Figure 1 and Figure 2. For a given corpus, we built alternate text representations using the ISO-15919 and IndicSOUNDEX approaches mentioned in

Table 1: Examples of conversion using ISO-15919 and IndicSOUNDEX

Script	Indic Original	ISO-15919	IndicSOUNDEX
Devanagari (Hindi)	इन्दिके	indikē	i034
Devanagari (Marathi)	इतिहासाचा	itihāsācā	i8hs2
Telugu	పడినది	pḍindi	p303
Tamil	பிரவீண்	pirvīṇ	plv0

Table 2: Data partition across languages

Language	Train	Test	Valid	Total
Hindi	5.4M	600K	54K	6M
Tamil	27K	9k	9k	45K
Marathi	27K	8.5k	8.5K	42K
Telugu	27K	9K	9k	46K

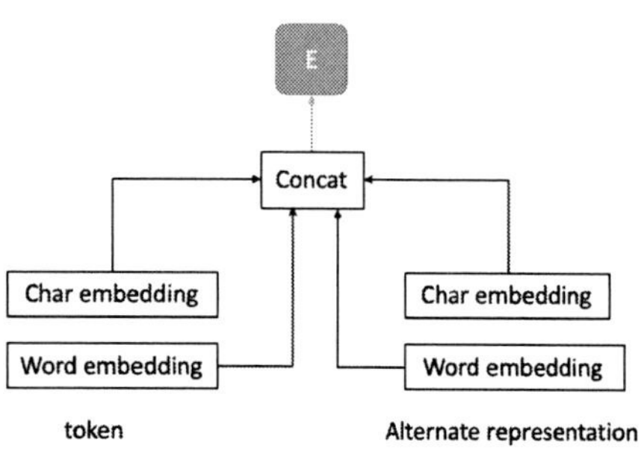

Figure 1: Embedding for a token

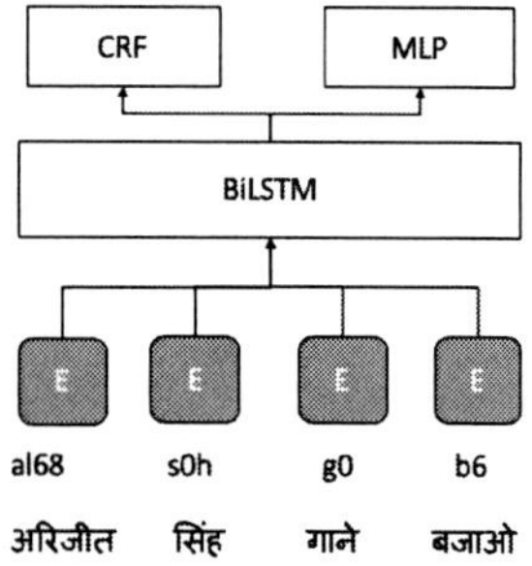

Figure 2: Modeling architecture with tokens and alternate representation (IndicSOUNDEX) as input

Section 2. We used both the original sentence as well as the alternate representations of the sentence to inform our models via added embedding layers.

First, we built a baseline model without using any alternate representations using the Baseline Embedding block architecture below. Next, we built two candidate models: the first with an embedding layer using alternate representations from IndicSOUNDEX, and the second with the alternate representations from ISO-15919. Our modeling architecture is designed as follows:

Baseline Embedding Block: For our baseline model, we designed our embedding block with two layers and concatenated the outputs. The first layer is a token embedding layer of dimension 100, while the second one is a character-based token embedding built using convolutional neural network (CNN) subsequence embedding with dimension of 16. The final embedding used in our models will be generated by concatenating these two embeddings.

Embedding block with alternate representations: For our alternate representation models, we modified the baseline embedding block to accommodate these representations. All other components, including encoder and decoder, stayed the same. The embedding block for this setting was modified to have four layers with final embedding used in our model being the concatenation of these. A schematic is shown in Figure 1 The four layers are as follows:

1. Token embedding layer of dimension 100.

2. Token embedding layer for alternate representations of tokens of dimension 100 .

3. Character embedding built using convolutional neural network (CNN) subsequence embedding with dimension of 16.

4. Alternate representations character embedding built using convolutional neural network (CNN) subsequence embedding with dimension of 16.

Eventually, we concatenated the output of the embedding layer to obtain the final word embedding.

Table 3: The number of tokens in each script within each training and test set

Script	Hindi		Tamil		Marathi		Telugu	
	Train	Test	Train	Test	Train	Test	Train	Test
Latin	13.9M	101K	22.5K	7.5K	29.1K	9.7K	40.7K	13.4K
Devanagari	15.5M	102K	0	0	110K	36K	0	0
Tamil	8	0	108K	36K	0	0	0	0
Telugu	0	0	0	0	0	0	112K	37.5K
Other	1K	0	2	0	0	0	0	0
Total	29.5M	203K	131K	43.5K	139K	46K	153K	51K

Encoder: We defined a biLSTM (bidirectional Long Short Term Memory) encoder with 5 hidden layers and a hidden dimension of 512. A schematic is given in Figure 2. In order to handle our multi-task prediction of Intent and NER, we have two output layers:

1. A multi-layer perceptron (MLP) classifier with the number of classes set to the vocabulary size of Intent.

2. A conditional random fields (CRF) sequence labeler with the number of classes set to the vocabulary size of Named Entities.

Decoder: We used a joint task decoder for our purpose. The Intent-prediction task is accomplished by single class decoder, while the label-prediction task is achieved by sequence labeling decoder. For this setup, the loss function is a multi-component loss, with cross-entropy loss for Intent and CRF-loss (Lafferty et al., 2001) for NER.

Evaluation metric: We use Semantic Error Rate (SemER) Su et al. (2018) to evaluate the performance of our models. The definition of SemER is as follows:

$$SemER = \frac{(D + I + S)}{(C + D + S)} \quad (1)$$

where D (deletion), I (insertion), S (substitution), C (correct slots).

As the Intent is treated as a slot in this metric, the Intent error is considered as a substitution.

Experimental Process: Our experimental setup consists of the following process. For each language, we build three models with the model architecture explained in model architecture section.

- Baseline model - a baseline model with architecture explained in the model architecture section using word and character embeddings from tokens.

- IndicSOUNDEX model - a model with IndicSOUNDEX alternate representations i.e., using an embedding layer with tokens, the IndicSOUNDEX representation of tokens, characters from tokens and the IndicSOUNDEX representations of characters.

- ISO-15919 model - a model with ISO-15919 alternate representations i.e., using embedding layer with tokens, the ISO-15919 representation of tokens, characters from tokens and the ISO-15919 representations of characters.

4 Results

To evaluate each model, we used our withheld test dataset and measured SemER scores associated with the three different models. To obtain confidence intervals, we bootstrapped our test dataset by sampling ten times with replacement, and evaluated our models on each of these ten datasets. Final SemER was taken as the average of all the ten iterations. We used a Student's t-test to calculate the significance of the improvements of the IndicSOUNDEX and ISO-15919 models with respect to the baseline. Here we present the results of our three models: the Baseline DNN model, IndicSOUNDEX model, and ISO-15919 model on each of the four languages.

Table 4: Comparison of ISO-15919 and IndicSOUNDEX model performance on Hindi w.r.t baseline. '+' indicates degradation, '-' indicates improvement. '*' denotes the results that are not statistically significant

Language	Model	Topics improved	Average improvement	Topics degraded	Average degradation	Overall change
Hindi	IndicSOUNDEX	3	8%	1	5%	−0.07*%
	ISO-15919	3	4%	4	9%	+1.08%

4.1 Results for a high-resource language - Hindi

Our Hindi data consisted of data from 22 topics including Music, Reminders, Alarms, Weather, Search, News, and so on. See Appendix for the full list of topics. Table 4 shows the performance on Hindi. Results revealed that, out of the 22 topics, the use of IndicSOUNDEX resulted in 3 topics showing improvement in SemER, with an average improvement of 8% and 1 topic showing 5.36% degradation. The use of ISO-15919 resulted in 3 topics showing an average improvement of 4% and 4 topics showing an average degradation of 9%. Rest of the topics showed results that are not statistically significant. We note that two topics showed improvement across both models: SmartHome and Global.

Our results show that there is no overall (i.e., across all topics together) statistically significant improvement seen for the IndicSOUNDEX model. However, we note that the improvements in 3 three topics: Global, SmartHome, and ToDoLists are significant. The one topic that showed a degradation was Shopping.

On the other hand, the ISO-15919 model shows an overall 1.08% degradation that is statistically significant. The ISO-15919 model shows statistically significant improvements in Global, Video, and SmartHome topics, and degradation in Weather, Music, QuestionAndAnswer, and Media.

In summary, for a high-resource language such as Hindi, we find that neither IndicSOUNDEX nor ISO-15919 shows an overall significant improvement. However, there are certain topics that could benefit from using these alternate representations either for IC or NER. Note that the majority of the training data for Hindi were transcribed by well-trained internal human transcribers and went through some cleaning processes for common transcription errors. Also, given the size of the training data, the NLU models were well trained on the various spelling variations represented in the original script. Owing to this relatively high consistency in transcription and the existence of various tokens with similar meaning and sound in the training data, we believe that using the alternate representations of text was not effective for improving the performance of the NLU model.

4.2 Results for low-resource languages - Tamil, Marathi, and Telugu

Unlike the case of Hindi, we see much more significant overall improvements where training data are sparse. All three languages showed significant improvement in overall performance for ISO-15919 model, whereas IndicSOUNDEX showed significant improvement for Tamil and Marathi. Within Tamil and Marathi, IndicSOUNDEX showed a larger improvement than ISO-15919.

Our data for the low-resource languages consisted of 19 different topics. Table 5 shows the performance of each language. At topic level for Tamil, we found that using the IndicSOUNDEX model improved the performance in 15 out of 19 topics with an average SemER drop of 11%. With the ISO-15919 representation, 13 out of 19 topics showed improvement with an average SemER drop of 13%. For Marathi, IndicSOUNDEX improved 7 topics with an average drop in SemER of 18%, whereas ISO-15919 improved 9 topics but with a lower average drop in SemER (10%). For Telugu, using IndicSOUNDEX or ISO-15919 improved the performance of 4 topics each with the same average drop in SemER of 15%. There were two topics that showed improvement across all three languages with the IndicSOUNDEX model: MovieTimes and Media. Furthermore, Calendar and Music topics showed significant improvement across all three languages with the ISO-15919 model.

Table 5: Comparison of ISO-15919 and IndicSOUNDEX model performance w.r.t baseline on low resource languages. '+' indicates degradation, '-' indicates improvement. '*' denotes the results that are not statistically significant

Language	Model	Topics improved	Average improvement	Topics degraded	Average degradation	Overall change
Tamil	IndicSOUNDEX	15	11%	1	7%	-7.6%
	ISO-15919	13	13%	2	2%	-6.2%
Marathi	IndicSOUNDEX	7	18%	6	8%	-2.30%
	ISO-15919	9	10%	6	11%	-1.50%
Telugu	IndicSOUNDEX	4	15%	5	7%	-0.20*%
	ISO-15919	4	15%	4	8%	-2.4%

Table 6: Percentage change in SemER for candidate models w.r.t baseline model across languages. '+' indicates degradation, '-' indicates improvement

Language	% Change in IndicSOUNDEX	% Change in ISO-15919
Hindi	-0.07%	+1.08%
Tamil	-7.6%	-6.2%
Marathi	-2.3%	-1.5%
Telugu	-0.2%	-2.4%

In Table 6, we provide the relative change in performance w.r.t baseline of all the models across high and low resource languages.

5 Conclusion

In this work, we explored the effect of using alternate representations of text for IC and NER models on a high-resource Indic language (Hindi) and three low-resource Indic languages (Tamil, Telugu, Marathi). We adopted a neural network based model architecture, where the alternate representations are incorporated in the embedding layers.

Based on the performance analysis over the baseline models, we saw that the alternate representations, while helping specific topics, do not help as much for the high-resource language overall. This is possibly due to the relatively high consistency in transcription and the existence of various tokens with similar meaning and sound in the training data. However, they helped significantly boost performance in the low-resource languages, thus creating potential applications in bootstrapping new languages quickly and cost-effectively.

In the case of the low-resource languages we saw significant improvements overall when using either ISO-15919 or IndicSOUNDEX. This suggests that smaller datasets stand to benefit from the use of alternative representations. Based on Tamil and Marathi results, where IndicSOUNDEX performed better than base-line and ISO-15919, we can conclude that the mitigation of the impact of multiple different scripts and inconsistent Latin usage accomplished by IndicSOUNDEX seems to produce better results for our NLU models. The lack of impact of IndicSOUNDEX for Telugu merits further investigation.

Our future work includes exploring different model architectures including transformer models, exploring these representations further by pre-training models with a combination of original tokens and alternate representations of tokens. We also plan to explore the use of character bigrams (of both original text and alternate representations of text) instead of unigram characters in the embedding layers.

6 Acknowledgments

We would like to thank Karolina Owczarzak for her support and invaluable discussions on this work and Wael Hamza for useful discussions. We would also like to thank our extended team mates for helpful discussions and anonymous reviewers for valuable feedback.

References

Beider, A. and Morse, S. P. (2010). Phonetic matching: A better soundex. *Association of Professional Genealogists Quarterly.*

Chaware, S. M. and Rao, S. (2012). Analysis of phonetic matching approaches for indic languages.

Geetha, P., Chandu, K., and Black, A. W. (2018). Tackling code-switched NER: Participation of cmu. In *Proceedings of the Third Workshop on Computational Approaches to Linguistic Code-Switching*, pages 126–131.

Johnson, A., Karanasou, P., Gaspers, J., and Klakow, D. (2019). Cross-lingual transfer learning for Japanese named entity recognition. In *Proceedings of the 2019 Conference of the North American Chapter of the Association for Computational Linguistics: Human Language Technologies, Volume 2 (Industry Papers)*, pages 182–189.

Lafferty, J. D., McCallum, A., and Pereira, F. C. N. (2001). Conditional random fields: Probabilistic models for segmenting and labeling sequence data. In *Proceedings of the Eighteenth International Conference on Machine Learning*, ICML '01, page 282–289, San Francisco, CA, USA. Morgan Kaufmann Publishers Inc.

Shah, R. and Singh, D. K. (2014). Improvement of soundex algorithm for indian languages based on phonetic matching. *International Journal of Computer Science, Engineering and Applications*, 4(3).

Su, C., Gupta, R., Ananthakrishnan, S., and Matsoukas, S. (2018). A re-ranker scheme for integrating large scale nlu models. *2018 IEEE Spoken Language Technology Workshop (SLT)*, pages 670–676.

Zhang, X. and LeCun, Y. (2017). Which encoding is the best for text classification in chinese, english, japanese and korean? *CoRR*.

A   Appendix A. Results across different topics on all languages

Table 7: Results for Hindi. Relative change in performance w.r.t baseline on the average of ten boot-strapped test data sets. '+' indicates degradation, '-' indicates improvement

Topic	% Change in IndicSOUNDEX	Is Significant	% Change in ISO-15919	Is Significant
Reservations	-1.64%	NO	-0.65%	NO
Books	-0.43%	NO	-5.18%	NO
Calendar	-7.59%	NO	-7.05%	NO
CallingAndMessaging	-4.36%	NO	-0.08%	NO
News	+2.78%	NO	+0.92%	NO
Photos	-6.85%	NO	-12.16%	NO
Media	+7.79%	NO	+11.13%	YES
Global	-2.89%	YES	-4.09%	YES
Help	+6.52%	NO	+5.76%	NO
SmartHome	-5.58%	YES	-4.32%	YES
QuestionAndAnswer	+3.10%	NO	+4.99%	YES
Search	-3.98%	NO	+3.78%	NO
Music	-0.45%	NO	+2.18%	YES
Notifications	+2.74%	NO	-2.49%	NO
OriginalContent	-3.66%	NO	-1.63%	NO
Recipes	-0.44%	NO	-0.39%	NO
Shopping	+5.36%	YES	-0.82%	NO
Sports	0%	NO	0%	NO
ToDoLists	-16.50%	YES	+1.08%	NO
Video	-2.73%	NO	-4%	YES
Weather	-3.89%	NO	+16.36%	YES
Overall	-0.07%	NO	+1.08%	YES

Table 8: Results for Tamil. Relative change in performance w.r.t baseline on the average of ten boot-strapped test data sets. '+' indicates degradation, '-' indicates improvement

Topic	% Change in IndicSOUNDEX	Is Significant	% Change in ISO-15919	Is Significant
Books	-14.06%	YES	-18.28%	YES
Calendar	-8.52%	YES	-11.93%	YES
MovieTimes	-7.91%	YES	-7.24%	NO
CallingAndMssaging	-12.44%	YES	-6.38%	YES
News	-15.50%	YES	-6.14%	YES
Media	-12.23%	YES	0%	NO
Global	-4.20%	YES	-4.41%	YES
Help	-20.84%	YES	-17.72%	YES
SmartHome	-7.29%	YES	+0.05%	YES
Search	+7.15%	YES	+3.08%	NO
Music	-8.03%	YES	-8.08%	YES
Notifications	-10.98%	YES	-6.81%	YES
OriginalContent	-9.92%	YES	-23.21%	YES
Shopping	-16.22%	YES	-13.44%	YES
Sports	+8.01%	NO	-30.10%	YES
ToDoLists	-2.14%	NO	+3.03%	YES
Video	-4.01%	YES	-14.65%	YES
Weather	-10.23%	YES	-10.91%	YES
Overall	-7.56%	YES	-6.23%	YES

Table 9: Results for Marathi. Relative change in performance w.r.t baseline on the average of ten bootstrapped test data sets. '+' indicates degradation, '-' indicates improvement

Topic	% Change in IndicSOUNDEX	Is Significant	% Change in ISO-15919	Is Significant
Books	-6.95%	YES	-11.81%	YES
Calendar	+9.28%	YES	-0.11%	YES
MovieTimes	-13.74%	YES	-11.03%	YES
CallingAndMessaging	+3.09%	YES	4.97%	YES
News	+16.76%	YES	+1.90%	YES
Media	-24.50%	YES	-12.84%	YES
Global	+0.13%	NO	-2.81%	YES
Help	-8.51%	YES	-0.76%	NO
SmartHome	-14.36%	YES	-5.04%	YES
Search	-0.63%	NO	-1.70%	YES
Music	-0.45%	NO	-4.66%	YES
Notifications	+2.49%	YES	+5.50%	YES
OriginalContent	-22.84%	YES	+8.10%	YES
Shopping	+2.97%	NO	+12.17%	YES
Sports	-38.48%	YES	-35.97%	YES
ToDoLists	+0.70%	NO	-0.23%	NO
Video	+5.25%	YES	+1.59%	NO
Weather	+12.29%	YES	+32.18%	YES
Overall	-2.29%	YES	-1.47%	YES

Table 10: Results for Telugu. Relative change in performance w.r.t baseline on the average of ten bootstrapped test data sets. '+' indicates degradation, '-' indicates improvement

Topic	% Change in IndicSOUNDEX	Is Significant	% Change in ISO-15919	Is Significant
Books	+2.42%	NO	+0.37%	NO
Calendar	+4.51%	YES	-10.33%	YES
MovieTimes	-13.57%	YES	-8.83%	YES
CallingAndMessaging	+5.41%	YES	+3.79%	YES
News	+0.97%	NO	+15.24%	YES
Media	-13.91%	YES	-0.61%	NO
Global	+2.93%	YES	+3.57%	NO
Help	+12.35%	YES	-0.45%	NO
SmartHome	-0.15%	NO	+0.31%	NO
Search	-7.41%	YES	+2.90%	YES
Music	+1.02%	NO	-4.55%	YES
Notifications	+1.33%	NO	-4.15%	NO
OriginalContent	-3.94%	NO	+2.10%	NO
Shopping	+0.55%	NO	+1.59%	NO
Sports	-4.43%	NO	-14.31%	NO
ToDoLists	+10.44%	YES	+10.05%	YES
Video	-0.72%	NO	-0.97%	NO
Weather	-25.98%	YES	-35.37%	YES
Overall	-0.21%	NO	-2.42%	YES

On Incorporating Structural Information to improve Dialogue Response Generation

Nikita Moghe[‡], **Priyesh Vijayan**[2], **Balaraman Ravindran**[3,4], and **Mitesh M. Khapra**[3,4]

[1]School of Informatics, University of Edinburgh
[2]School of Computer Science, McGill University and Mila
[3]Indian Institute of Technology Madras
[4]Robert Bosch Centre for Data Science and Artificial Intelligence (RBC-DSAI),
Indian Institute of Technology Madras
`nikita.moghe@ed.ac.uk priyesh.vijayan@mail.mcgill.ca`

Abstract

We consider the task of generating dialogue responses from background knowledge comprising of domain specific resources. Specifically, given a conversation around a movie, the task is to generate the next response based on background knowledge about the movie such as the plot, review, Reddit comments *etc.* This requires capturing structural, sequential, and semantic information from the conversation context and background resources. We propose a new architecture that uses the ability of BERT to capture deep contextualized representations in conjunction with explicit structure and sequence information. More specifically, we use (i) Graph Convolutional Networks (GCNs) to capture structural information, (ii) LSTMs to capture sequential information, and (iii) BERT for the deep contextualized representations that capture semantic information. We analyze the proposed architecture extensively. To this end, we propose a plug-and-play *Semantics-Sequences-Structures (SSS)* framework which allows us to effectively combine such linguistic information. Through a series of experiments, we make some interesting observations. First, we observe that the popular adaptation of the GCN model for NLP tasks where structural information (GCNs) was added on top of sequential information (LSTMs) performs poorly on our task. This leads us to explore interesting ways of combining semantic and structural information to improve performance. Second, we observe that while BERT already outperforms other deep contextualized representations such as ELMo, it still benefits from the additional structural information explicitly added using GCNs. This is a bit surprising given the recent claims that BERT already captures structural information. Lastly, the proposed *SSS* framework gives an improvement of 7.95% BLEU score over the baseline.

The work was done by Nikita and Priyesh at Indian Institue of Technology Madras.

1 Introduction

Neural conversation systems that treat dialogue response generation as a sequence generation task (Vinyals and Le, 2015) often produce generic and incoherent responses (Shao et al., 2017). The primary reason for this is that, unlike humans, such systems do not have any access to background knowledge about the topic of conversation. For example, while chatting about movies, we use our background knowledge about the movie in the form of plot details, reviews, and comments that we might have read. To enrich such neural conversation systems, some recent works (Moghe et al., 2018; Dinan et al., 2019; Zhou et al., 2018) incorporate external knowledge in the form of documents which are relevant to the current conversation. For example, Moghe et al. (2018) released a dataset containing conversations about movies where every alternate utterance is extracted from a background document about the movie. This background document contains plot details, reviews, and Reddit comments about the movie. The focus thus shifts from sequence generation to identifying relevant snippets from the background document and modifying them suitably to form an appropriate response given the current conversational context.

Intuitively, any model for this task should exploit semantic, structural and sequential information from the conversation context and the background document. For illustration, consider the chat shown in Figure 1 from the Holl-E movie conversations dataset (Moghe et al., 2018). In this example, Speaker 1 nudges Speaker 2 to talk about how James's wife was irritated because of his career. The right response to this conversation comes from the line beginning at *"His wife Mae ..."*. However, to generate this response, it is essential to understand that (i) *His* refers to James from the previous sentence; (ii) *quit boxing* is a contigu-

11

Source Doc: ... At this point James Braddock (Russel Crowe) was a light heavyweight boxer, who was forced to retired from the ring after breaking his hand in his last fight. **His wife Mae had prayed for years that he would quit boxing, before becoming permanently injured.** ...

Conversation:

Speaker 1(N): Yes very true, this is a real rags to riches story. Russell Crowe was excellent as usual.

Speaker 2(R): Russell Crowe owns the character of James Bradock, the unlikely hero who makes the most of his second chance. He's a good fighter turned hack.

Speaker 1(N): Totally! Oh by the way do you remember his wife ... how she wished he would stop

Speaker 2(P): His wife Mae had prayed for years that he would quit boxing, before becoming permanently injured.

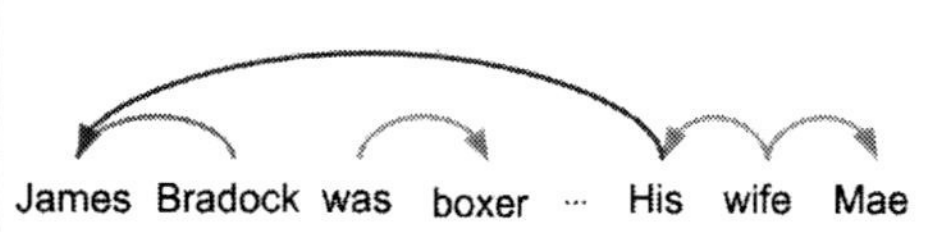

Figure 1: Sample conversation from the Holl-E Dataset. The text in bold in the first block is the background document which is used to generate the last utterance in this conversation. N, P, and R correspond to the type of background knowledge used: None, Plot, and Review as per the dataset definitions. For simplicity, we show only a few of the edges for the background knowledge at the bottom. The edge in blue corresponds to the co-reference edge, the edges in green are dependency edges and the edge in red is the entity edge.

ous phrase, and (iii) *quit* and *he would stop* mean the same. We need to exploit (i) **structural** information, such as, the co-reference edge between *His-James* (ii) the **sequential** information in *quit boxing* and (iii) the **semantic** similarity (or synonymy relation) between *quit* and *he would stop*.

To capture such multi-faceted information from the document and the conversation context we propose a new architecture that combines BERT with explicit sequence and structure information. We start with the deep contextualized word representations learnt by BERT which capture distributional semantics. We then enrich these representations with sequential information by allowing the words to interact with each other by passing them through a bidirectional LSTM as is the standard practice in many NLP tasks. Lastly, we add explicit structural information in the form of dependency graphs, co-reference graphs, and entity co-occurrence graphs. To allow interactions between words related through such structures, we use GCNs which essentially aggregate information from the neighborhood of a word in the graph.

Of course, combining BERT with LSTMs in itself is not new and has been tried in the original work (Devlin et al., 2019) for the task of Named Entity Recognition. Similarly, Bastings et al. (2017) combine LSTMs with GCNs for the task of machine translation. To the best of our knowledge, this is the first work that combines BERT with explicit structural information. We investigate several interesting questions in the context of dialogue response generation. For example,

1. Are BERT-based models best suited for this task?

2. Should BERT representations be enriched with sequential information first or structural information?

3. Are dependency graph structures more important for this task or entity co-occurrence graphs?

4. Given the recent claims that BERT captures syntactic information, does it help to explicitly enrich it with syntactic information using GCNs?

To systematically investigate such questions we propose a simple plug-and-play *Semantics-Sequences-Structures* (*SSS*) framework which allows us to combine different semantic representations (GloVe (Pennington et al., 2014), BERT(Devlin et al., 2018), ELMo (Peters et al., 2018a)) with different structural priors (dependency graphs, co-reference graphs, *etc.*). It also allows us to use different ways of combining structural and sequential information, *e.g.*, LSTM first followed by GCN or vice versa, or both in parallel. Using this framework we perform a series of experiments on the *Holl-E* dataset and make some interesting observations. First, we observe that the conventional adaptation of GCNs for NLP tasks, where contextualized embeddings obtained through LSTMs are fed as input to a GCN, exhibits poor performance. To overcome this, we propose some simple alternatives and show that they lead to better performance. Second, we observe that while BERT performs better than GloVe and ELMo, it still benefits from explicit structural information captured by GCNs. We find this interesting because some recent works (Tenney et al., 2019; Jawahar et al., 2019; Hewitt and Manning, 2019) suggest that BERT captures syntactic information, but our results suggest that there is still more information to be captured by adding explicit structural priors. Third, we observe that certain graph structures are more useful for this task than others. Lastly, our best model which uses a specific combination of semantic, sequential, and structural information improves over the baseline by 7.95% on the BLEU score.

2   Related work

There is an active interest in using external knowledge to improve the informativeness of responses for goal-oriented as well as chit-chat conversations (Lowe et al., 2015; Ghazvininejad et al., 2018; Moghe et al., 2018; Dinan et al., 2019). Even the teams participating in the annual Alexa Prize competition (Ram et al., 2017) have benefited by using several knowledge resources. This external knowledge can be in the form of knowledge graphs or unstructured texts such as documents.

Many NLP systems including conversation systems use RNNs as their basic building block which typically captures n-gram or sequential information. Adding structural information through tree-based structures (Tai et al., 2015) or graph-based structures (Marcheggiani and Titov, 2017) on top of this has shown improved results on several tasks. For example, GCNs have been used to improve neural machine translation (Marcheggiani et al., 2018) by exploiting the semantic structure of the source sentence. Similarly, GCNs have been used with dependency graphs to incorporate structural information for semantic role labelling (Marcheggiani and Titov, 2017), neural machine translation (Bastings et al., 2017) and entity relation information in question answering (De Cao et al., 2019) and temporal information for neural dating of documents (Vashishth et al., 2018).

There have been advances in learning deep contextualized word representations (Peters et al., 2018b; Devlin et al., 2019) with a hope that such representations will implicitly learn structural and relational information with the interaction between words at multiple layers (Jawahar et al., 2019; Pe-

ters et al., 2018c). These recent developments have led to many interesting questions about the best way of exploiting rich information from sentences and documents. We try to answer some of these questions in the context of background aware dialogue response generation.

3   Background

In this section, we provide a background on how GCNs have been leveraged in NLP to incorporate different linguistic structures.

The Syntactic-GCN proposed in (Marcheggiani and Titov, 2017) is a GCN (Kipf and Welling, 2017) variant which can model multiple edge types and edge directions. It can also dynamically determine the importance of an edge. They only work with one graph structure at a time with the most popular structure being the dependency graph of a sentence. For convenience, we refer to Syntactic-GCNs as GCNs from here on.

Let G denote a graph defined on a text sequence (sentence, passage or document) with nodes as words and edges representing a directed relation between words. Let $\mathcal{N}$ denote a dictionary of list of neighbors with $\mathcal{N}(v)$ referring to the neighbors of a specific node v, including itself (self-loop). Let $dir(u, v) \in \{in, out, self\}$ denote the direction of the edge, (u, v). Let $\mathcal{L}$ be the set of different edge types and let $L(u, v) \in \mathcal{L}$ denote the label of the edge, (u, v). The $(k + 1)$-hop representation of a node v is computed as

$$h_v^{(k+1)} = \sigma\Big(\sum_{u \in \mathcal{N}(v)} g_{(u,v)}^{(k)} (W_{dir(u,v)}^{(k)} h_u^{(k)} + b_{L(u,v)}^{(k)}) \Big) \tag{1}$$

where σ is the activation function, $g_{(u,v)} \in \mathbb{R}$ is the predicted importance of the edge (u, v) and $h_v \in \mathcal{R}^m$ is node, v's embedding. $W_{dir(u,v)} \in \{W_{in}, W_{out}, W_{self}\}$ depending on the direction $dir(u, v)$ and W_{in}, W_{self} and $W_{out} \in \mathcal{R}^{m*m}$. The importance of an edge $g_{(u,v)}$ is determined by an edge gating mechanism w.r.t. the node of interest, u as given below:

$$g_{(u,v)} = sigmoid\big(h_u . W_{dir(u,v)} + b_{L(u,v)}\big) \tag{2}$$

In summary, a GCN computes new representation of a node u by aggregating information from it's neighborhood $\mathcal{N}(v)$. When $k=0$, the aggregation happens only from immediate neighbors, i.e., 1 hop neighbors. As the value of k increases the aggregation implicitly happens from a larger neighborhood.

4 Proposed Model

Given a document D and a conversational context Q the task is to generate the response $\mathbf{y} = y_1, y_2, ..., y_m$. This can be modeled as the problem of finding a $\mathbf{y}$ that maximizes the probability $P(\mathbf{y}|D, Q)$ which can be further decomposed as

$$\mathbf{y} = \arg\max_{\mathbf{y}} \prod_{t=1}^{m} P(y_t|y_1, ..., y_{t-1}, Q, D)$$

As has become a standard practice in most NLG tasks, we model the above probability using a neural network comprising of an encoder, a decoder, an attention mechanism, and a copy mechanism. The copy mechanism essentially helps to directly copy words from the document D instead of predicting them from the vocabulary. Our main contribution is in improving the document encoder where we use a plug-and-play framework to combine semantic, structural, and sequential information from different sources. This enriched document encoder could be coupled with any existing model. In this work, we couple it with the popular Get To The Point (GTTP) model (See et al., 2017) as used by the authors of the *Holl-E* dataset. In other words, we use the same attention mechanism, decoder, and copy mechanism as GTTP but augment it with an enriched document encoder. Below, we first describe the document encoder and then very briefly describe the other components of the model. We also refer the reader to the supplementary material for more details.

4.1 Encoder

Our encoder contains a semantics layer, a sequential layer and a structural layer to compute a representation for the document words which is a sequence of words $w_1, w_2, ..., w_m$. We refer to this as a plug-and-play document encoder simply because it allows us to plug in different semantic representations, different graph structures, and different simple but effective mechanisms for combining structural and semantic information.

Semantics Layer: Similar to almost all NLP models, we capture semantic information using word embeddings. In particular, we utilize the ability of BERT to capture deep contextualized representations and later combine it with explicit structural information. This allows us to evaluate (i) whether BERT is better suited for this task as compared to other embeddings such as ELMo and GloVe and

(ii) whether BERT already captures syntactic information completely (as claimed by recent works) or can it benefit form additional syntactic information as described below.

Structure Layer: To capture structural information we propose multi-graph GCN, *M-GCN*, a simple extension of GCN to extract relevant multi-hop multi-relational dependencies from multiple structures/graphs efficiently. In particular, we generalize G to denote a labelled multi-graph, *i.e.*, a graph which can contain multiple (parallel) labelled edges between the same pair of nodes. Let $\mathcal{R}$ denote the set of different graphs (structures) considered and let $G = \{\mathcal{N}_1, \mathcal{N}_2 \ldots \mathcal{N}_{|\mathcal{R}|}\}$ be a set of dictionary of neighbors from the $|\mathcal{R}|$ graphs. We extend the Syntactic GCN defined in Eqn: 1 to multiple graphs by having $|\mathcal{R}|$ graph convolutions at each layer as given in Eqn: 3. Here, $g\_conv(\mathcal{N})$ is the graph convolution defined in Eqn: 1 with σ as the identity function. Further, we remove the individual node (or word) i from the neighbourhood list $\mathcal{N}(i)$ and model the node information separately using the parameter W_{self}.

$$h_i^{(k+1)} = ReLU\left((h_i^{(k)} W_{self}^{(k)} + \sum_{\mathcal{N} \in G} g\_conv(\mathcal{N})\right)$$

(3)

This formulation is advantageous over having $|\mathcal{R}|$ different GCNs as it can extract information from multi-hop pathways and can use information across different graphs with every GCN layer (hop). Note that h_i^0 is the embedding obtained for word v from the semantic layer. For ease of notation, we use the following functional form to represent the final representation computed by M-GCN after k-hops starting from the initial representation h_i^0, given G.

$$h_i = M\text{-}GCN(h_i^0, G, k)$$

Sequence Layer: The purpose of this layer is to capture sequential information. Once again, following standard practice, we pass the word representations computed by the previous layer through a bidirectional LSTM to compute a sequence contextualized representation for each word. As described in the next subsection, depending upon the manner in which we combine these layers, the previous layer could either be the structure layer or the semantics layer.

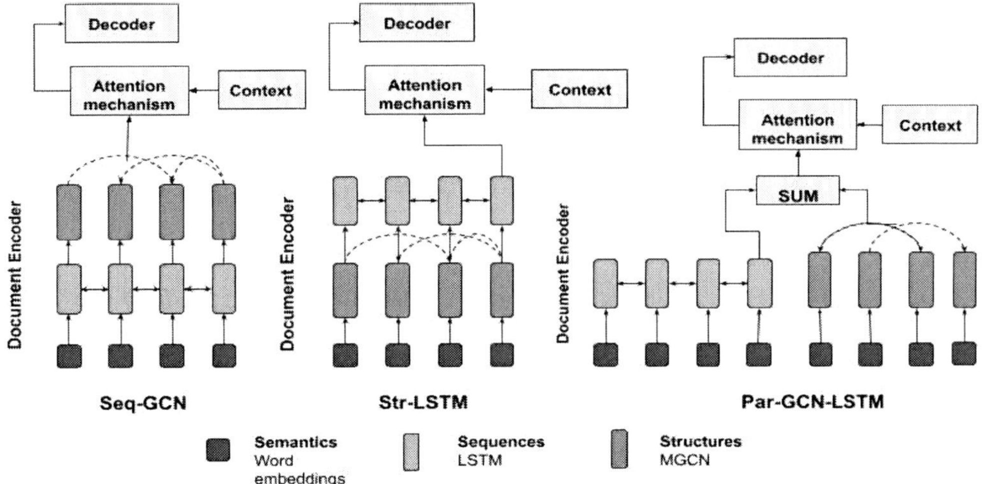

Figure 2: The *SSS* framework. The Word Embeddings include GloVe, ELMo, and BERT. *Seq-GCN* considers obtaining an LSTM representation first which this then passed through an M-GCN module. In *Str-LSTM*, we compute the M-GCN representation first which is then passed to an LSTM layer while *Par-GCN-LSTM* computes both LSTM and M-GCN representations independently which are then combined into a final representation.

4.2 Combining structural and sequential information

As mentioned earlier, for a given document D containing words $w_1, w_2, w_3, \ldots, w_m$, we first obtain word representations $x_1, x_2, x_3, \ldots, x_m$ using BERT (or ELMo or GloVe). At this point, we have three different choices for enriching the representations using structural and sequential information: (i) structure first followed by sequence (ii) sequence first followed by structure or (iii) structure and sequence in parallel. We depict these three choices pictorially in Figure 2 and describe them below with appropriate names for future reference. Please note that the choice of "Seq" denotes the sequential nature of LSTMs while "Str" denotes the structural nature of GCNs. Though we use a specific variant of GCN, described as M-GCN in the previous section, any other variant of GCN can be replaced in the "Str" layer.

4.2.1 Sequence contextualized GCN (*Seq-GCN*)

Seq-GCN is similar to the model proposed in (Bastings et al., 2017; Marcheggiani and Titov, 2017) where the word representations $x_1, x_2, x_3, \ldots, x_m$ are first fed through a BiLSTM to obtain sequence contextualized representations as shown below.

$$h_i^{seq} = BiLSTM(h_{i-1}^{seq}, x_i)$$

These representations $h_1, h_2, h_3, \ldots, h_m$ are

then fed to the M-GCN along with the graph G to compute a k-hop aggregated representation as shown below:

$$h_i^{str} = M\text{-}GCN(h_i^{seq}, G, k)$$

This final representation $h_i^{final} = h_i^{str}$ for the i-th word thus combines semantics, sequential and structural information in that order. This is a popular way of combining GCNs with LSTMs but our experiments suggest that this does not work well for our task. We thus explore two other variants as explained below.

4.2.2 Structure contextualized LSTM (*Str-LSTM*)

Here, we first feed the word representations $x_1, x_2, x_3, \ldots, x_m$ to M-GCN to obtain structure aware representations as shown below.

$$h_i^{str} = M\text{-}GCN(x_i, G, k)$$

These structure aware representations are then passed through a BiLSTM to capture sequence information as shown below:

$$h_i^{seq} = BiLSTM(h_{i-1}^{seq}, h_i^{str})$$

This final representation $h_i^{final} = h_i^{seq}$ for the i-th word thus combines semantics, structural and sequential information in that order.

4.2.3 Parallel GCN-LSTM (*Par-GCN-LSTM*)

Here, both M-GCN and BiLSTMs are fed with word embeddings x_i as input to aggregate structural and sequential information independently as shown below:

$$h_i^{str} = M\text{-}GCN(x_i, G, k)$$
$$h_i^{seq} = BiLSTM(h_{i-1}^{seq}, x_i)$$

The final representation, h_i^{final}, for each word is computed as $h_i^{final} = h_i^{str} + h_i^{seq}$ and combines structural and sequential information in parallel as opposed to a serial combination in the previous two variants.

4.3 Decoder, Attention, and Copy Mechanism

Once the final representation for each word is computed, an attention weighted aggregation, c_t, of these representations is fed to the decoder at each time step t. The decoder itself is a LSTM which computes a new state vector s_t at every timestep t as

$$s_t = LSTM(s_{t-1}, c_t)$$

The decoder then uses this s_t to compute a distribution over the vocabulary where the probability of the i-th word in the vocabulary is given by $p_i = softmax(V s_t + W c_t + b)_i$. In addition, the decoder also has a copy mechanism wherein, at every timestep t, it could either choose the word with the highest probability p_i or copy that word from the input which was assigned the highest attention weight at timestep t. Such copying mechanism is useful in tasks such as ours where many words in the output are copied from the document D. We refer the reader to the GTTP paper for more details of the standard copy mechanism.

5 Experimental setup

In this section, we briefly describe the dataset and task setup followed by the pre-processing steps we carried to obtain different linguistic graph structures on this dataset. We then describe the different baseline models. Our code is available at: `https://github.com/nikitacs16/horovod_gcn_pointer_generator`

5.1 Dataset description

We evaluate our models using Holl-E, an English language movie conversation dataset (Moghe et al., 2018) which contains $\sim$ 9k movie chats and $\sim$ 90k utterances. Every chat in this dataset is associated with a specific background knowledge resource from among the plot of the movie, the review of the movie, comments about the movie, and occasionally a fact table. Every even utterance in the chat is generated by copying and or modifying sentences from this unstructured background knowledge. The task here is to generate/retrieve a response using conversation history and appropriate background resources. Here, we focus only on the *oracle* setup where the correct resource from which the response was created is provided explicitly. We use the same train, test, and validation splits as provided by the authors of the paper.

5.2 Construction of linguistic graphs

We consider leveraging three different graph-based structures for this task. Specifically, we evaluate the popular syntactic word dependency graph (*Dep-G*), entity co-reference graph (*Coref-G*) and entity co-occurrence graph (*Ent-G*). Unlike the word dependency graph, the two entity-level graphs can capture dependencies that may span across sentences in a document. We use the dependency parser provided by SpaCy (`https://spacy.io/`) to obtain the dependency graph (*Dep-G*) for every sentence. For the construction of the co-reference graph (*Coref-G*), we use the NeuralCoref model (`https://github.com/huggingface/neuralcoref`) integrated with SpaCy. For the construction of the entity graph (*Ent-G*), we first perform named-entity recognition using SpaCy and connect all the entities that lie in a window of $k = 20$.

5.3 Baselines

We categorize our baseline methods as follows:
Without Background knowledge: We consider the simple Sequence-to-Sequence (S2S) (Vinyals and Le, 2015) architecture that conditions the response generation only on the *previous* utterance and completely ignores the other utterances as well as the background document. We also consider HRED (Serban et al., 2016), a hierarchical variant of the S2S architecture which conditions response generation on the entire conversation history in addition to the last utterance. Of course, we do not expect these models to perform well as they completely ignore the background knowledge but we include them for the sake of completeness.
With Background Knowledge: To the S2S architecture we add an LSTM encoder to encode the

document. The output is now conditioned on this representation in addition to the previous utterance. We refer to this architecture as S2S-D. Next, we use GTTP (See et al., 2017) which is a variant of the S2S-D architecture with a copy-or-generate decoder; at every time-step, the decoder decides to copy from the background knowledge or generate from the fixed vocabulary. We also report the performance of the BiRNN + GCN architecture that uses the dependency graph only as discussed in (Marcheggiani and Titov, 2017). Finally, we note that in our task many words in the output need to be copied sequentially from the input background document which makes it very similar to the task of span prediction as used in Question Answering. We thus also evaluate BiDAF (Seo et al., 2017), a popular question-answering architecture, that extracts a span from the background knowledge as a response using complex attention mechanisms. For a fair comparison, we evaluate the spans retrieved by the model against the ground truth responses.

We use BLEU-4 and ROUGE (1/2/L) as the evaluation metrics as suggested in the dataset paper. Using automatic metrics is more reliable in this setting than the open domain conversational setting as the variability in responses is limited to the information in the background document. We provide implementation details in Appendix A.

6   Results and Discussion

In Table 1, we compare our architecture against the baselines as discussed above. *SSS*(BERT) is our proposed architecture in terms of the *SSS* framework. We report best results within *SSS* chosen across 108 configurations comprising of four different graph combinations, three different contextual and structural infusion methods, three M-GCN layers, and, three embeddings. The best model was chosen based on performance of the validation set. From Table 1, it is clear that our improvements in incorporating structural and sequential information with BERT in the *SSS* encoder framework significantly outperforms all other models.

6.1   Qualitative Evaluation

We conducted human evaluation for the *SSS* models from Table 1 against the generated responses of GTTP. We presented 100 randomly sampled outputs to three different annotators. The annotators were asked to pick from four options: A, B, both, and none. The annotators were told these were con-

Model	BLEU	ROUGE		
		1	2	L
S2S	4.63	26.91	9.34	21.58
HRED	5.23	24.55	7.61	18.87
S2S-D	11.71	26.36	13.36	21.96
GTTP	13.97	36.17	24.84	31.07
BiRNN+GCN	14.70	36.24	24.60	31.29
BiDAF	16.79	26.73	18.82	23.58
SSS(GloVe)	18.96	38.61	26.92	33.77
SSS(ELMo)	19.32	39.65	27.37	34.86
SSS(BERT)	**22.78**	**40.09**	**27.83**	**35.20**

Table 1: Results of automatic evaluation. The architectures within the *SSS* framework outperform the baseline methods with our proposed architecture *SSS*(BERT) performing the best.

versations between friends. Tallying the majority vote, we obtain win/loss/both/none for *SSS*(BERT) as 29/25/29/17, *SSS*(GloVe) as 24/17/47/12 and *SSS*(ELMo) as 22/23/41/14. This suggests qualitative improvement using the *SSS* framework. We also provide some generated examples in Appendix B1. We found that the SSS framework had less confusion in generating the opening responses than the GTTP baseline. These "conversation starters" have a unique template for every opening scenario and thus have different syntactic structures respectively. We hypothesize that the presence of dependency graphs over these respective sentences helps to alleviate the confusion as seen in Example 1. The second example illustrates why incorporating structural information is important for this task. We also observed that the *SSS* encoder framework does not improve on the aspects of human creativity such as diversity, initiating a context-switch, and commonsense reasoning as seen in Example 3.

6.2   Ablation studies on the *SSS* framework

We report the component-wise results for the *SSS* framework in Table 2. The *Sem* models condition the response generation directly on the word embeddings. As expected, we observe that ELMo and BERT perform much better than GloVe embeddings.

The *Sem+Seq* models condition the decoder on the representation obtained after passing the word embeddings through the LSTM layer. These models outperform their respective *Sem* models. The gain with ELMo is not significant because the underlying architecture already has two BiLSTM layers which are already being fine-tuned for the task.

Emb	Paradigm	BLEU	ROUGE		
			1	2	L
GloVe	Sem	4.4	29.72	11.72	22.99
	Sem+Seq	14.83	36.17	24.84	31.07
	SSS	18.96	38.61	26.92	33.77
ELMo	Sem	14.36	32.04	18.75	26.71
	Sem+Seq	14.61	35.54	24.58	30.71
	SSS	19.32	39.65	27.37	34.86
BERT	Sem	11.26	33.86	16.73	26.44
	Sem+Seq	18.49	37.85	25.32	32.58
	SSS	22.78	40.09	27.83	35.2

Table 2: Performance of components within the *SSS* framework. BERT based models outperform both ELMo and GloVe based architectures in the respective paradigms. Notably, adding all the three levels of information: semantic, sequential, and structural is useful.

Hence the addition of one more LSTM layer may not contribute to learning any new sequential word information. It is clear from Table 2 that the *SSS* models, that use structure information as well, obtain a significant boost in performance, validating the need for incorporating all three types of information in the architecture.

6.3 Combining structural and sequential information

The response generation task of our dataset is a span based generation task where phrases of text are expected to be copied or generated as they are. The sequential information is thus crucial to reproduce these long phrases from background knowledge. This is strongly reflected in Table 3 where *Str-LSTM* which has the LSTM layer on top of GCN layers performs the best across the hybrid architectures discussed in Figure 2. The *Str-LSTM* model can better capture sequential information with structurally and syntactically rich representations obtained through the initial GCN layer. The *Par-GCN-LSTM* model performs second best. However, in the parallel model, the LSTM cannot leverage the structural information directly and relies only on the word embeddings. *Seq-GCN* model performs the worst among all the three as the GCN layer at the top is likely to modify the sequence information from the LSTMs.

6.4 Understanding the effect of structural priors

While a combination of intra-sentence and inter-sentence graphs is helpful across all the models, the best performing model with BERT embeddings relies only on the dependency graph. In the case of GloVe based experiments, the entity and co-reference relations were not independently useful with the *Str-LSTM* and *Par-GCN-LSTM* models, but when used together gave a significant performance boost, especially for *Str-LSTM*. However, most of the BERT based and ELMo based models achieved competitive performance with the individual entity and co-reference graphs. There is no clear trend across the models. Hence, probing these embedding models is essential to identify which structural information is captured implicitly by the embeddings and which structural information needs to be added explicitly. For the quantitative results, please refer to Appendix B2.

6.5 Structural information in deep contextualised representations

Earlier work has suggested that deep contextualized representations capture syntax and co-reference relations (Peters et al., 2018c; Jawahar et al., 2019; Tenney et al., 2019; Hewitt and Manning, 2019). We revisit Table 2 and consider the *Sem+Seq* models with ELMo and BERT embeddings as two architectures that *implicitly* capture structural information. We observe that the *SSS* model using the simpler GloVe embedding outperforms the ELMo *Sem+Seq* model and performs slightly better than the BERT *Sem+Seq* model.

Given that the *SSS* models outperform the corresponding *Sem+Seq* model, the extent to which the deep contextualized word representations learn the syntax and other linguistic properties implicitly are questionable. Also, this calls for better loss functions for learning deep contextualized representations that can incorporate structural information explicitly.

More importantly, all the configurations of *SSS* (GloVe) have a lesser memory footprint in comparison to both ELMo and BERT based models. Validation and training of GloVe models require one-half, sometimes even one-fourth of computing resources. Thus, the simple addition of structural information through the GCN layer to the established Sequence-to-Sequence framework that can perform comparably to stand-alone expensive models is an important step towards Green AI(Schwartz et al., 2019).

Emb	Seq-GCN				Str-LSTM				Par-GCN-LSTM			
	BLEU	ROUGE			BLEU	ROUGE			BLEU	ROUGE		
		1	2	L		1	2	L		1	2	L
GloVe	15.61	36.6	24.54	31.68	18.96	38.61	26.92	33.77	17.1	37.04	25.70	32.2
ELMo	18.44	37.92	26.62	33.05	19.32	39.65	27.37	34.86	16.35	37.28	25.67	32.12
BERT	20.43	40.04	26.94	34.85	22.78	40.09	27.83	35.20	21.32	39.9	27.60	34.87

Table 3: Performance of different hybrid architectures to combine structural information with sequence information. We observe that using structural information followed by sequential information, Str-LSTM, provides the best results.

7 Conclusion and Future Work

We demonstrated the usefulness of incorporating structural information for the task of background aware dialogue response generation. We infused the structural information explicitly in the standard semantic+sequential model and observed a performance boost. We studied different structural linguistic priors and different ways to combine sequential and structural information. We also observe that explicit incorporation of structural information helps the richer deep contextualized representation based architectures. The framework provided in this work is generic and can be applied to other background aware dialogue datasets and several tasks such as summarization and question answering. We believe that the analysis presented in this work would serve as a blueprint for analyzing future work on GCNs ensuring that the gains reported are robust and evaluated across different configurations.

Acknowledgements

We would like to thank the anonymous reviewers for their useful comments and suggestions. We would like to thank the Department of Computer Science and Engineering, and Robert Bosch Center for Data Sciences and Artificial Intelligence, IIT Madras (RBC-DSAI) for providing us with adequate resources. Lastly, we extend our gratitude to the volunteers who participated in the human evaluation experiments.

References

Joost Bastings, Ivan Titov, Wilker Aziz, Diego Marcheggiani, and Khalil Sima'an. 2017. Graph convolutional encoders for syntax-aware neural machine translation. In *Proceedings of the 2017 Conference on Empirical Methods in Natural Language Processing*, pages 1957–1967, Copenhagen, Denmark. Association for Computational Linguistics.

Nicola De Cao, Wilker Aziz, and Ivan Titov. 2019. Question answering by reasoning across documents with graph convolutional networks. In *Proceedings of the 2019 Conference of the North American Chapter of the Association for Computational Linguistics: Human Language Technologies, Volume 1 (Long and Short Papers)*, pages 2306–2317, Minneapolis, Minnesota. Association for Computational Linguistics.

Jacob Devlin, Ming-Wei Chang, Kenton Lee, and Kristina Toutanova. 2018. BERT: pre-training of deep bidirectional transformers for language understanding. *CoRR*, abs/1810.04805.

Jacob Devlin, Ming-Wei Chang, Kenton Lee, and Kristina Toutanova. 2019. BERT: Pre-training of deep bidirectional transformers for language understanding. In *Proceedings of the 2019 Conference of the North American Chapter of the Association for Computational Linguistics: Human Language Technologies, Volume 1 (Long and Short Papers)*, pages 4171–4186, Minneapolis, Minnesota. Association for Computational Linguistics.

Emily Dinan, Stephen Roller, Kurt Shuster, Angela Fan, Michael Auli, and Jason Weston. 2019. Wizard of wikipedia: Knowledge-powered conversational agents. *International Conference on Learning Representations*.

Marjan Ghazvininejad, Chris Brockett, Ming-Wei Chang, Bill Dolan, Jianfeng Gao, Wen-tau Yih, and Michel Galley. 2018. A knowledge-grounded neural conversation model. In *Proceedings of the Thirty-Second AAAI Conference on Artificial Intelligence, (AAAI-18), the 30th innovative Applications of Artificial Intelligence (IAAI-18), and the 8th AAAI Symposium on Educational Advances in Artificial Intelligence (EAAI-18), New Orleans, Louisiana, USA, February 2-7, 2018*, pages 5110–5117.

John Hewitt and Christopher D. Manning. 2019. A structural probe for finding syntax in word representations. In *Proceedings of the 2019 Conference of the North American Chapter of the Association for Computational Linguistics: Human Language Technologies, Volume 1 (Long and Short Papers)*, pages 4129–4138, Minneapolis, Minnesota. Association for Computational Linguistics.

Ganesh Jawahar, Benoît Sagot, and Djamé Seddah. 2019. What does BERT learn about the structure of language? In *Proceedings of the 57th Annual Meeting of the Association for Computational Linguistics*, pages 3651–3657, Florence, Italy. Association for Computational Linguistics.

Thomas N. Kipf and Max Welling. 2017. Semi-supervised classification with graph convolutional networks. In *5th International Conference on Learning Representations, ICLR 2017, Toulon, France, April 24-26, 2017, Conference Track Proceedings*.

Ryan Lowe, Nissan Pow, Iulian Serban, Laurent Charlin, and Joelle Pineau. 2015. Incorporating unstructured textual knowledge sources into neural dialogue systems. In *Neural Information Processing Systems Workshop on Machine Learning for Spoken Language Understanding*.

Diego Marcheggiani, Joost Bastings, and Ivan Titov. 2018. Exploiting semantics in neural machine translation with graph convolutional networks. In *Proceedings of the 2018 Conference of the North American Chapter of the Association for Computational Linguistics: Human Language Technologies, Volume 2 (Short Papers)*, pages 486–492, New Orleans, Louisiana. Association for Computational Linguistics.

Diego Marcheggiani and Ivan Titov. 2017. Encoding sentences with graph convolutional networks for semantic role labeling. In *Proceedings of the 2017 Conference on Empirical Methods in Natural Language Processing*, pages 1506–1515, Copenhagen, Denmark. Association for Computational Linguistics.

Nikita Moghe, Siddhartha Arora, Suman Banerjee, and Mitesh M. Khapra. 2018. Towards exploiting background knowledge for building conversation systems. In *Proceedings of the 2018 Conference on Empirical Methods in Natural Language Processing*, pages 2322–2332, Brussels, Belgium. Association for Computational Linguistics.

Jeffrey Pennington, Richard Socher, and Christopher D. Manning. 2014. Glove: Global vectors for word representation. In *Proceedings of the 2014 Conference on Empirical Methods in Natural Language Processing, EMNLP 2014, October 25-29, 2014, Doha, Qatar, A meeting of SIGDAT, a Special Interest Group of the ACL*, pages 1532–1543.

Matthew Peters, Mark Neumann, Mohit Iyyer, Matt Gardner, Christopher Clark, Kenton Lee, and Luke Zettlemoyer. 2018a. Deep contextualized word representations. In *Proceedings of the 2018 Conference of the North American Chapter of the Association for Computational Linguistics: Human Language Technologies, Volume 1 (Long Papers)*, pages 2227–2237. Association for Computational Linguistics.

Matthew Peters, Mark Neumann, Mohit Iyyer, Matt Gardner, Christopher Clark, Kenton Lee, and Luke Zettlemoyer. 2018b. Deep contextualized word representations. In *Proceedings of the 2018 Conference of the North American Chapter of the Association for Computational Linguistics: Human Language Technologies, Volume 1 (Long Papers)*, pages 2227–2237, New Orleans, Louisiana. Association for Computational Linguistics.

Matthew Peters, Mark Neumann, Luke Zettlemoyer, and Wen-tau Yih. 2018c. Dissecting contextual word embeddings: Architecture and representation. In *Proceedings of the 2018 Conference on Empirical Methods in Natural Language Processing*, pages 1499–1509, Brussels, Belgium. Association for Computational Linguistics.

Matthew E. Peters, Sebastian Ruder, and Noah A. Smith. 2019. To tune or not to tune? adapting pre-trained representations to diverse tasks. In *Proceedings of the 4th Workshop on Representation Learning for NLP (RepL4NLP-2019)*, pages 7–14, Florence, Italy. Association for Computational Linguistics.

Ashwin Ram, Rohit Prasad, Chandra Khatri, Anu Venkatesh, Raefer Gabriel, Qing Liu, Jeff Nunn, Behnam Hedayatnia, Ming Cheng, Ashish Nagar, Eric King, Kate Bland, Amanda Wartick, Yi Pan, Han Song, Sk Jayadevan, Gene Hwang, and Art Pettigrue. 2017. Conversational AI: the science behind the alexa prize. *Alexa Prize Proceedings*.

Roy Schwartz, Jesse Dodge, Noah A Smith, and Oren Etzioni. 2019. Green AI.

Abigail See, Peter J. Liu, and Christopher D. Manning. 2017. Get to the point: Summarization with pointer-generator networks. In *Proceedings of the 55th Annual Meeting of the Association for Computational Linguistics (Volume 1: Long Papers)*, pages 1073–1083, Vancouver, Canada. Association for Computational Linguistics.

Min Joon Seo, Aniruddha Kembhavi, Ali Farhadi, and Hannaneh Hajishirzi. 2017. Bidirectional attention flow for machine comprehension. In *5th International Conference on Learning Representations, ICLR 2017, Toulon, France, April 24-26, 2017, Conference Track Proceedings*.

Iulian Vlad Serban, Alessandro Sordoni, Yoshua Bengio, Aaron C. Courville, and Joelle Pineau. 2016. Building end-to-end dialogue systems using generative hierarchical neural network models. In *Proceedings of the Thirtieth AAAI Conference on Artificial Intelligence, February 12-17, 2016, Phoenix, Arizona, USA.*, pages 3776–3784.

Yuanlong Shao, Stephan Gouws, Denny Britz, Anna Goldie, Brian Strope, and Ray Kurzweil. 2017. Generating high-quality and informative conversation responses with sequence-to-sequence models. In *Proceedings of the 2017 Conference on Empirical Methods in Natural Language Processing*, pages 2210–2219, Copenhagen, Denmark. Association for Computational Linguistics.

Kai Sheng Tai, Richard Socher, and Christopher D. Manning. 2015. Improved semantic representations from tree-structured long short-term memory networks. In *Proceedings of the 53rd Annual Meeting of the Association for Computational Linguistics and the 7th International Joint Conference on Natural Language Processing (Volume 1: Long Papers)*, pages 1556–1566, Beijing, China. Association for Computational Linguistics.

Ian Tenney, Dipanjan Das, and Ellie Pavlick. 2019. BERT rediscovers the classical NLP pipeline. In *Proceedings of the 57th Annual Meeting of the Association for Computational Linguistics*, pages 4593–4601, Florence, Italy. Association for Computational Linguistics.

Shikhar Vashishth, Shib Sankar Dasgupta, Swayambhu Nath Ray, and Partha Talukdar. 2018. Dating documents using graph convolution networks. In *Proceedings of the 56th Annual Meeting of the Association for Computational Linguistics (Volume 1: Long Papers)*, pages 1605–1615, Melbourne, Australia. Association for Computational Linguistics.

Oriol Vinyals and Quoc V. Le. 2015. A neural conversational model. In *ICML Deep Learning Workshop*.

Kangyan Zhou, Shrimai Prabhumoye, and Alan W Black. 2018. A dataset for document grounded conversations. In *Proceedings of the 2018 Conference on Empirical Methods in Natural Language Processing*, pages 708–713, Brussels, Belgium. Association for Computational Linguistics.

A Implementation Details

A.1 Base Model

The authors of Moghe et al. (2018) adapted the architecture of Get to the Point (See et al., 2017) for background aware dialogue response generation task. In the summarization task, the input is a *document* and the output is a *summary* whereas in our case the input is a *{resource/document, context}* pair and the output is a *response*. Note that the context includes the previous two utterances (dialog history) and the current utterance. Since, in both the tasks, the output is a sequence (*summary* v/s *response*) we don't need to change the decoder (*i.e.*, we can use the decoder from the original model as it is). However, we need to change the input fed to the decoder. We use an RNN to compute a representation of the conversation history. Specifically, we consider the previous k utterances as a single sequence of words and feed these to an RNN. Let M be the total length of the context (*i.e.*, all the k utterances taken together) then the RNN computes representations $h_1^d, h_2^d, ..., h_M^d$ for all the words in

the context. The final representation of the context is then the attention weighted sum of these word representations:

$$
\begin{aligned}
f_i^t &= v^T tanh(W_c h_i^d + V s_t + b_d) \\
m^t &= softmax(f^t) \\
d_t &= \sum_i m_i^t h_i^d
\end{aligned}
\tag{4}
$$

Similar to the original model, we use an RNN to compute the representation of the document. Let N be the length of the document then the RNN computes representations $h_1^r, h_2^r, ..., h_N^r$ for all the words in the resource (we use the superscript r to indicate resource). We then compute the query aware resource representation as follows.

$$
\begin{aligned}
e_i^t &= v^T tanh(W_r h_i^r + U s_t + V d_t + b_r) \\
a^t &= softmax(e^t) \\
c_t &= \sum_i a_i^t h_i^r
\end{aligned}
\tag{5}
$$

where c_t is the attended context representation. Thus, at every decoder time-step, the attention on the document words is also based on the currently attended context representation.

The decoder then uses r_t (document representation) and s_t (decoder's internal state) to compute a probability distribution over the vocabulary P_{vocab}. In addition, the model also computes p_{gen} which indicates that there is a probability p_{gen} that the next word will be *generated* and a probability $(1 - p_{gen})$ that the next word will be *copied*. We use the following modified equation to compute p_{gen}

$$
p_{gen} = \sigma(w_r^T r_t + w_s^T s_t + w_x^T x_t + b_g) \tag{6}
$$

where x_t is the previous word predicted by the decoder and fed as input to the decoder at the current time step. Similarly, s_t is the current state of the decoder computed using this input x_t. The final probability of a word w is then computed using a combination of two distributions, *viz.*, (P_{vocab}) as described above and the attention weights assigned to the document words as shown below

$$
P(w) = p_{gen} P_{vocab}(w) + (1 - p_{gen}) \sum_{i:w_i = w} a_i^t \tag{7}
$$

where a_i^t are the attention weights assigned to every word in the document as computed in Equation 5. Thus, effectively, the model could learn to copy a word i if p_{gen} is low and a_i^t is high. This is the baseline with respect to the LSTM architecture (Sem + Seq). For, GCN based encoders, the h_i^r is the final outcome after the desired GCN/LSTM configuration.

A.2 Hyperparameters

We selected the hyper-parameters using the validation set. We used Adam optimizer with a learning rate of 0.0004 and a batch size of 64. We used GloVe embeddings of size 100. For the RNN-based encoders and decoders, we used LSTMs with a hidden state of size 256. We used gradient clipping with a maximum gradient norm of 2. We used a hidden state of size 512 for *Seq-GCN* and 128 for the remaining GCN-based encoders. We ran all the experiments for 15 epochs and we used the checkpoint with the least validation loss for testing. For models using ELMo embeddings, a learning rate of 0.004 was most effective. For the BERT-based models, a learning rate of 0.0004 was suitable. Rest of the hyper-parameters and other setup details remain the same for experiments with BERT and ELMo. Our work follows a task specific architecture as described in the previous section. Following the definitions in (Peters et al., 2019), we use the "feature extraction" setup for both ELMo and BERT based models.

B   Extended Results

B.1   Qualitative examples

We illustrate different scenarios from the dataset to identify the strengths and weaknesses of our models under the *SSS* framework in Table 4. We compare the outputs from the best performing model on the three different embeddings and use GTTP as our baseline. The best performing combination of sequential and structural information for all the three models in the *SSS* framework is *Str-LSTM*. The best performing *SSS*(GloVe) and *SSS*(ELMo) architectures use all the three graphs while *SSS*(BERT) uses only the dependency graph.

We find that the *SSS* framework improves over the baseline for the cases of opening statements (see Example 1). The baseline had confusion in picking opening statements and often mixed the responses for "Which is your favorite character?", "Which is your favorite scene" and "What do you think about the movie?". The responses to these questions have different syntactic structures - "My favorite character is XYZ", "I liked the one in which XYZ", and " I think this movie

is XYZ" where XYZ was the respective crowd-sourced phrase. The presence of dependency graphs over the respective sentences may help to alleviate the confusion.

Now consider the example under *Hannibal* in Table 4. We find that the presence of a co-reference graph between "Anthony Hopkins" in the first sentence and "he" in the second sentence can help in continuing the conversation on the actor "Anthony Hopkins". Moreover, connecting tokens in "Anthony Hopkins" to refer to "he" in the second sentence is possible because of the explicit entity-entity connection between the two tokens. However, this is applicable only to *SSS*(GloVe) and *SSS*(ELMo) as their best performing versions use these graphs along with the dependency graph while the best performing *SSS*(BERT) only uses dependency graph and may have learnt the inter-sentence relations implicitly.

There is a limited diversity of responses generated by the *SSS* framework as it often resorts to the patterns seen during training while it is not copying from the background knowledge. We also identify that *SSS* framework cannot handle the cases where Speaker2 initiates a context switch, *i,e;* when Speaker2 introduces a topic that has not been discussed in the conversation so far. In the chat on *The Road Warrior* in Table 4, we find that *Mad Max: Fury Road* has been used to initiate a discussion that compares the themes of both the movies. All the models produce irrelevant responses.

B.2   Quantitative results

We explore the effect of using different graphs in Table 5.

Movie	Rocky V (Example 1)	Hannibal (Example 2)	The Road Warrior (Example 3)
Resource	Rocky V, terribly under-rated. I liked the one in which Rocky .... . My favorite character was Adrian because she was ...I think it was enjoyable, though slightly less than th.	Anthony Hopkins gave .... However, the material he was given to work .... almost seemed like an excuse to present us	Box Office: $ 9,003,011 Similar Movies: Lethal Weapon, Mad Max: Fury Road ...
Chat	Speaker 1: Which is your favourite character in this?	Speaker 1: What is your opinion about the movie? Speaker 2: I think it was a fair sequel. Speaker 1: Anthony Hopkins gave an impeccable performance.	Speaker 1: Which is your favourite character in this? Speaker 2: My favorite character was Dog Speaker 1: I liked the feral kid even after he's found in the car and Max evicts him without ceremony he doesn't give up.
Ground Truth	my favorite character was adrian because she was strong and did her best to keep her family together through tough times .	however , the material he was given to work with was not as good as silence of the lambs .	Have you seen the new Mad Max: Fury Road?
Baseline	i liked the one in which rocky and gunn fight in the street .	in fairness , perhaps there was no way it could be .	lethal weapon .
SSS(GloVe)	my favorite character was adrian because she was strong and did her best to keep her together through tough times .	however , the material he was given to work with was not as good as silence of the lambs .	it made $ 9,003,011
SSS(ELMo)	my favorite character was adrian because she was strong and did her best to keep her family together through tough times .	the material he was given to work with was not as good as silence of the lambs .	[UNK] only one man can make the difference in the future .
SSS(BERT)	my favorite character was adrian because she was strong and did her best to keep her family together through tough times .	the material he was given to work with was not as good as silence of the lambs .	yes .[UNK] only one man can make the difference in the future .

Table 4: Sample outputs from the *SSS* framework compared with baseline and ground truth responses.

Graph	GloVe				ELMo				BERT			
	BLEU	ROUGE			BLEU	ROUGE			BLEU	ROUGE		
		1	2	L		1	2	L		1	2	L
Dep	16.79	37.77	25.89	32.88	17.00	37.56	26.14	32.77	22.78	40.09	27.83	35.2
Dep+Ent	14.44	35.14	24.61	30.43	18.34	39.55	28.00	34.76	19.33	39.37	27.52	34.33
Dep+Coref	16.58	37.60	25.72	32.63	18.56	40.08	28.42	35.06	20.99	40.10	28.66	35.11
Dep+Ent +Coref	18.96	38.61	26.92	33.77	19.32	39.65	27.37	34.86	20.37	39.11	27.2	34.19

Table 5: Comparing performance of different structural priors across different semantic information on the *Str-LSTM* architecture.

CopyBERT: A Unified Approach to Question Generation with Self-Attention

Stalin Varanasi **Saadullah Amin** **Günter Neumann**

German Research Center for Artificial Intelligence (DFKI)
Multilinguality and Language Technology Lab
{stalin.varanasi,saadullah.amin,guenter.neumann}@dfki.de

Abstract

Contextualized word embeddings provide better initialization for neural networks that deal with various natural language understanding (NLU) tasks including question answering (QA) and more recently, question generation (QG). Apart from providing meaningful word representations, pre-trained transformer models, such as BERT also provide self-attentions which encode syntactic information that can be probed for dependency parsing and POS-tagging. In this paper, we show that the information from self-attentions of BERT are useful for language modeling of questions conditioned on paragraph and answer phrases. To control the attention span, we use semi-diagonal mask and utilize a shared model for encoding and decoding, unlike sequence-to-sequence. We further employ copy mechanism over self-attentions to achieve state-of-the-art results for question generation on SQuAD dataset.

1 Introduction

Automatic question generation (QG) is the task of generating meaningful questions from text. With more question answering (QA) datasets like SQuAD (Rajpurkar et al., 2016) that have been released recently (Trischler et al., 2016; Choi et al., 2018; Reddy et al., 2019; Yang et al., 2018), there has been an increased interest in QG, as these datasets can not only be used for creating QA models but also for QG models.

QG, similar to QA, gives an indication of machine's ability to comprehend natural language text. Both QA and QG are used by conversational agents. A QG system can be used in the creation of artificial question answering datasets which in-turn helps QA (Duan et al., 2017). It specifically can be used in conversational agents for starting a conversation or draw attention to specific information

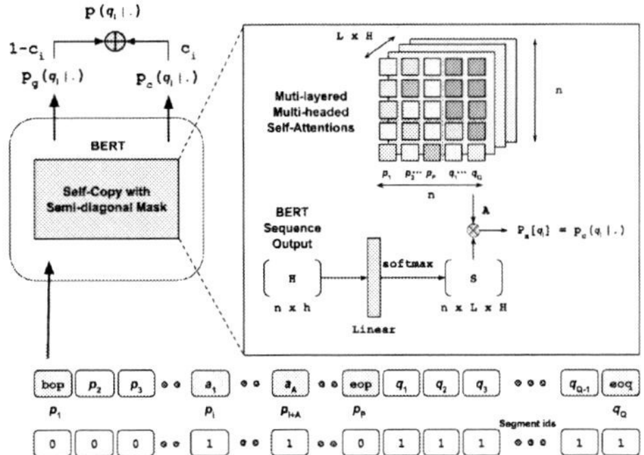

Figure 1: CopyBERT architecture for conditional question generation: Given a sequence of length n, with question tokens $\{q_i\}_{i=1}^{Q}$, paragraph tokens $\{p_i\}_{i=1}^{P}$ with answer phrase $\{a_i\}_{i=1}^{A}$ and semi-diagonal mask $\mathbf{M}$ (§3.2), the model explicitly uses H multi-headed self-attention matrices from L layers of transformers to create $\mathbf{A} \in \mathbb{R}^{n \times n \times L \times H}$. This matrix along with $\mathbf{S} \in \mathbb{R}^{n \times L \times H}$, obtained from the BERT sequence output $\mathbf{H} \in \mathbb{R}^{n \times h}$, is used to learn copy probability $p_c(q_i|.)$ (§3.3.2). Finally, a weighted combination $p(q_i|.)$ is obtained with simple generation probability $p_g(q_i|.)$ (§3.4).

(Mostafazadeh et al., 2016). Yao et al. (2012) and Nouri et al. (2011) use QG to create and augment conversational characters. In a similar approach, Kuyten et al. (2012) creates a virtual instructor to explain clinical documents. In this paper, we propose a QG model with following contributions:

- We introduce copy mechanism for BERT-based models with a unified encoder-decoder framework for question generation. We further extend this copy mechanism using self-attentions.

- Without losing performance, we improve the speed of training BERT-based language models by choosing predictions on output embeddings that are offset by one position.

Proceedings of the 2nd Workshop on Natural Language Processing for Conversational AI, pages 25–31
July 9, 2020. ©2020 Association for Computational Linguistics

2   Related Work

Most of the QG models that use neural networks rely on a sequence-to-sequence architecture where a paragraph and an answer is encoded appropriately before decoding the question. Sun et al. (2018) uses an *answer-position* aware attention to enrich the encoded input representation. Recently, Liu et al. (2019) showed that learning to predict clue words based on answer words helps in creating a better QG system. With similar motivation, gated self-networks were used by Zhao et al. (2018) to fuse appropriate information from paragraph before generating question. More recently, self-attentions of a transformer has been shown to perform answer agnostic question generation (Scialom et al., 2019).

The pre-training task of masked language modeling for BERT (Devlin et al., 2019) and other such models (Joshi et al., 2019) make them suitable for natural language generation tasks. Wang and Cho (2019) argues that BERT can be used as a generative model. However, only few attempts have been made so far to make use of these pre-trained models for conditional language modeling. Dong et al. (2019) and Chan and Fan (2019) use a single BERT model for both encoding and decoding and achieve state-of-the-art results in QG. However, both of them use the [MASK] token as the input for predicting the word in place, which makes the training slower as it warranties recurrent generation (Chan and Fan, 2019) or generation with random masking (Dong et al., 2019). Both models only consider the output representations of BERT to do language modeling.

However, Jawahar et al. (2019) and Tenney et al. (2019) show that BERT learns different linguistic features at different layers. Also, Hewitt and Manning (2019) successfully probed for dependency trees from self-attention matrices of BERT. With this, we hypothesize that BERT can implicitly encode the different aspects of input for QG (Sun et al., 2018; Zhao et al., 2018) within the self-attentions across layers. As self-attention can learn soft-alignments, it can be used explicitly for copy mechanism (§3.3.2), and can yield better results (§4.3) than a model that only implicitly use self-attentions for QG (§3.3.1). Similar to Dong et al. (2019), we also employ a shared architecture for unified encoding-decoding but make an *explicit* use of self-attentions across layers, leading to similar or better results at a fraction of their training cost.

3   Model

In sequence-to-sequence learning framework, a separate encoder and a decoder model is used. Such an application to BERT will lead to high computational complexity. To alleviate this, we use a shared model for encoding and decoding (Dong et al., 2019). This not only leads to a reduced number of parameters but also allows for cross attentions between source and target words in each layer of the transformer model. While such an architecture can be used in any conditional natural language generation task, here we apply it for QG.

3.1   Question Generation

For a sequence of paragraph tokens $P = [p_1, p_2, ..., p_P]$, start and end positions of an answer phrase $s_a = (a_s, a_e)$ in the paragraph and question tokens $Q = [q_1, q_2, ..., q_Q]$ with $p_1 = \texttt{bop}$, $p_P = \texttt{eop}$ and $q_Q = \texttt{eoq}$ representing *begin of paragraph*, *end of paragraph* and *end of question* respectively, the task of question generation is to maximize the likelihood of Q given P and s_a. To this end, with m such training examples, we maximize the following objective:

$$\max_{\Theta} \sum_{j=1}^{m} \sum_{i=1}^{n} \log p(q_i^{(j)} | q_{<i}^{(j)}, P^{(j)}, s_a^{(j)})$$

where $q_{<i}$ represents previous question tokens $[q_1, q_2, ..., q_{i-1}]$. A fixed length n sequence is created by concatenating P and Q with pad tokens into $S = [P; Q]$. Similar to Devlin et al. (2019), each input token is accompanied by a segment id to differentiate between the parts of the text. The answer tokens in the paragraph and the question tokens are given segment ids 1 and the rest 0, as illustrated in Figure 1. We pass these as inputs to a pre-trained BERT-based model.

3.2   Semi-diagonal Masking

To control the information flow, we employ a semi-diagonal mask. A simple diagonal mask on the self-attentions of the transformer decoder ensures that each word only attends to the words that are seen thus far (Vaswani et al., 2017). Self-attentions of the encoder do not require such masking because the input words should inform each other while encoding. Since we use a unified encoder-decoder architecture, we ensure our masking is such that each word in the paragraph attends to all other words in the paragraph but not to any of the words in the question and each word in the question only attends to previous words in the question in addition to all the words in the paragraph. This results in a semi-diagonal mask which is also proposed by Dong et al. (2019) and shown in Figure 1.

Formally, from S in §3.1, we have $I_p = [1, 2, ..., P]$ as the sequence of paragraph indices and $I_q = [P+1, P+2, .., P+Q]$ as the sequence of question indices with $n = P + Q$ (ignoring the pad tokens). The semi-diagonal mask $\mathbf{M} \in \mathbb{R}^{n \times n}$ is defined as:

$$\mathbf{M}_{i,j} = \begin{cases} -\infty & \begin{aligned} & (i \in I_p \wedge j \in I_q) \vee \\ & (i \in I_q \wedge j > i) \end{aligned} \\ 1, & \text{else} \end{cases}$$

3.3 Copy Mechanism

Pre-trained transformer models not only yield better contextual word embeddings but also give informative self-attentions (Hewitt and Manning, 2019; Reif et al., 2019). We explicitly make use of these pre-trained self-attentions into our QG models. This also matches with our motivation to use the copy mechanism (Gu et al., 2016) for BERT, as the self-attentions can be used to obtain attention probabilities over input paragraph text which are necessary for copy-mechanism.

For the input sequence S with the semi-diagonal mask $\mathbf{M} \in \mathbb{R}^{n \times n}$ and segment ids D, we first encode with $\text{BERT}(S, \mathbf{M}, D)$ to obtain hidden representations of the sequence $\mathbf{H} = \{\mathbf{h}_i\}_{i=1}^{n} \in \mathbb{R}^{n \times h}$. We then define copy probability $p_c(y_i|.) := p_c(y_i|q_{<i}, P, s_a)$ as:

$$p_c(y_i|.) = \begin{cases} \sum_{k=1:y_i=t_k}^{P+i-1} p_a(k|y_i), & t_k \in Y \\ 0, & \text{else} \end{cases}$$

where $p_a(k|y_i) \in \mathbb{R}$ is the attention probability of copying token $t_k \in Y = \{P\} \cup \{y_j\}_{j=1}^{i-1}$ (set of all the paragraph tokens and question predictions thus far) from input position k to question position i. The distribution $p_a \in \mathbb{R}^n$ is set to zero for tokens not appearing in Y, whereas we add the corresponding attention probabilities for tokens occurring multiple times. We summarize these per position probabilities compactly in a matrix $\mathbf{P}_a \in \mathbb{R}^{n \times n}$. Now, we define several methods to obtain $\mathbf{P}_a$ with different copy mechanisms.

3.3.1 Normal Copy

First, we employ a simpler way to obtain attention probabilities, called *normal copy*:

$$\mathbf{P}_a = \text{softmax}(\mathbf{H}\mathbf{W}_n\mathbf{H}^T) \in \mathbb{R}^{n \times n}$$

where $\mathbf{W}_n \in \mathbb{R}^{h \times h}$ is a parameter matrix.

3.3.2 Self-Copy

In a transformer architecture (Vaswani et al., 2017), if there are L layers and H attention heads at each layer, there will be $M = L \times H$ self-attention matrices of size $n \times n$. For example, in BERT-Large model (Devlin et al., 2019), there would be $24 \times 16 = 384$ such matrices. Each of these self-attention matrices carry unique information. In this method for copy mechanism, called *self-copy*, we obtain $\mathbf{P}_a$ as a weighted average of all these self-attentions[1].

We obtain at each time step, a probability score for each of the M self-attention matrices in $\mathcal{A} \in n \times n \times M$ signifying their corresponding importance. Given a parameter matrix $\mathbf{W}_a \in \mathbb{R}^{h \times M}$, we obtain:

$$\mathbf{S} = \text{softmax}(\mathbf{H}\mathbf{W}_a) \in \mathbb{R}^{n \times M}$$
$$\widetilde{\mathbf{P}}_a = [\mathcal{S}_1\mathcal{A}_1^T; ...; \mathcal{S}_n\mathcal{A}_n^T] \in \mathbb{R}^{n \times 1 \times n}$$

where $\mathcal{S} \in \mathbb{R}^{n \times 1 \times M}$ is a 3D tensor with added dimension 2 to $\mathbf{S}$, $\mathcal{A}^T \in \mathbb{R}^{n \times M \times n}$ is the transposed tensor of 3D self-attention matrices $\mathcal{A}$. $\mathcal{S}_i \in \mathbb{R}^{1 \times M}$ and $\mathcal{A}_i^T \in \mathbb{R}^{M \times n}$ are the i-th slices of the tensors $\mathcal{S}$ and $\mathcal{A}^T$. The final attention probabilities $\mathbf{P}_a$ are obtained by removing the dimension 2 from $\widetilde{\mathbf{P}}_a$. Thus, the final attention probabilities are obtained as a weighted average over all self-attention matrices.

3.3.3 Two-Hop Self-Copy

A self-attention matrix as mentioned above can be considered as an adjacency matrix of a graph whose nodes are words. The probability scores represent soft edge between two words. A self-attention matrix, thus, can be considered as 1-hop attention. We would like to explore 2-hop attentions, i.e, we look for neighbouring nodes of neighbouring nodes. Note that if $\mathbf{P}_a$ is an adjacency matrix, the nodes that are connected in two hops are given by $\mathbf{P}_a^2$. Both 1-hop attentions and 2-hop attentions can be useful for copying mechanism. Let $\mathbf{P}_{\text{1-hop}} = \mathbf{P}_a$ and $\mathbf{P}_{\text{2-hop}} = \mathbf{P}'^2_a$ where $\mathbf{P}'_a$ and $\mathbf{P}_a$ are defined as mentioned in §3.3.2 with different parameters, then we define *two-hop self-copy* as follows:

$$\mathbf{P}_a(q_i) = h_i\mathbf{P}_{\text{1-hop}}(q_i) + (1 - h_i)\mathbf{P}_{\text{2-hop}}(q_i)$$

where $h_i = \sigma(\mathbf{h}_{q_i}^T\mathbf{W}_h)$ and $\mathbf{W}_h \in \mathbb{R}^h$ is a parameter matrix.

---

[1] The semi-diagonal mask is applied to all such self-attention matrices.

3.4 Copy-Generate Probability

Once the copy probability p_c is obtained, the combined probability is obtained as weighted combination with the generation probability p_g:

$$p(q_i|.) = (1 - c_i)p_g(q_i|.) + c_i p_c(q_i|.)$$

where c_i is the likelihood to generate a token from the vocabulary or copy a token from the source and predicted tokens at position i:

$$c_i = \sigma(\mathbf{h}_{q_{i-1}}^T \mathbf{w})$$

with $\mathbf{h}_{q_{i-1}} \in \mathbb{R}^{h \times 1}$ as the hidden representation for the question token at position $i - 1$, $\mathbf{w} \in \mathbb{R}^{h \times 1}$ is a parameter vector and σ is sigmoid non-linearity. The generation probability is given by:

$$p_g(q_i|.) = \text{softmax}(\mathbf{h}_{q_{i-1}}^T \mathbf{V})$$

where $\mathbf{V} \in \mathbb{R}^{h \times |V|}$ is a parameter matrix over input vocabulary of size $|V|$.

4 Experiments

We apply the different variations of CopyBERT model as mentioned in the previous section on SQuAD v1.1 (Rajpurkar et al., 2016). For our experiments[2], we follow the training, validation and test split as used in Du et al. (2017).

4.1 Training Setup

For training, we used a batch size of 6, learning rate of $3e^{-5}$ with early stopping. The loss reaches its minimum between 2 to 3 epochs. We also trained with a batch size of 24 using gradient accumulation and found it gave similar results after the same number of optimization steps. We fixed the maximum sequence length as 384 and chose the part (document stride) of the paragraph that contained the answer phrase in case of exceeded sequence length. We decoded using beam search with a beam width of 5 and stopping at the generated token `eoq`. In our experiments we used `[CLS]` as `bop` token, `[MASK]` as `eop` token and `[SEP]` as `eoq` token.

4.2 Evaluation Metrics and Models

For evaluating our models, we report standard metrics of BLEU4, METEOR and ROUGE-L. As baselines, we take two of the non-BERT state-of-the-art models (Du and Cardie, 2018; Zhang and Bansal,

Model	BLEU4	METEOR	ROUGE-L
CorefNQG (Du and Cardie, 2018)	15.16	19.12	-
SemdriftQG (Zhang and Bansal, 2019)	18.37	22.65	6.68
Recurrent-BERT (Chan and Fan, 2019)	20.33	23.88	48.23
UniLM (Dong et al., 2019)	22.12	**25.06**	51.07
BERT + No Copy	19.37	22.49	49.12
BERT + Normal Copy	20.30	23.03	49.35
BERT + Self-Copy	21.17	23.48	49.91
BERT + Two-Hop Self-Copy	20.90	23.37	49.89
SpanBERT + Self-Copy	**22.71**	24.48	**51.60**

Table 1: Question generation results on SQuAD test split from Du et al. (2017). BERT refers to BERT-Large(cased) model (Devlin et al., 2019)

2019) and the two BERT-based QG models (Dong et al., 2019; Chan and Fan, 2019). We experimented with 4 settings: one without using any copy mechanism (No Copy), one using normal copy (Normal Copy; §3.3.1), one using self-copy (Self-Copy; §3.3.2) and finally with two-hop self-copy (Two-Hop Self-Copy; §3.3.3).

4.3 Results

Table 1 shows our results [3]. First, we note that the baseline performance of BERT-Large (cased) model with No Copy (19.37 BLEU4) is comparable with the results reported by Chan and Fan (2019) (20.33 BLEU4). We see a clear increase in performance when Normal Copy is used (20.30 BLEU4). Further, we see considerable gain in BLEU4 by using Self-Copy ($+1.8$ over No Copy and $+0.87$ over Normal Copy), supporting the hypothesis of using multi-layered, multi-headed self-attentions for copy mechanism. UniLM, which is a pre-trained model from BERT-Large checkpoint with three sequence generation pre-training tasks (Dong et al., 2019) and further fine-tuned on SQuAD dataset for 10 epochs achieves 22.12 BLUE4 score. We achieve comparable performance by only using self-copy mechanism. Figure 2 shows attention patterns of self-copy in question generation.

To further validate the self-copy mechanism, we also experimented by initializing with a variant of BERT[4] called SpanBERT (Joshi et al., 2019), which is pre-trained to predict longer masked spans to encourage better entity masking and has already shown to improve QA results when compared to BERT (Joshi et al., 2019). Although, Two-Hop Self-Copy did not improve upon the Self-Copy,

---

[2]The code is available at https://github.com/StalVars/CopyBERT

[3]We used the evaluation script from https://github.com/microsoft/unilm/tree/master/unilm-v1

[4]Note that Self-Copy mechanism can be applied with any BERT-like pre-trained model

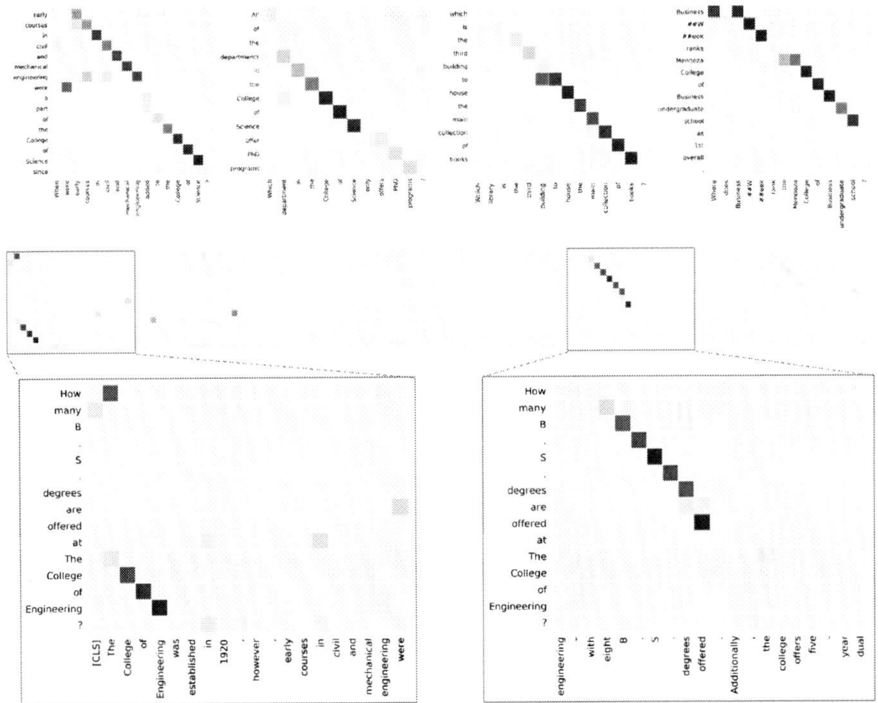

Figure 2: CopyBERT attention visualizations of copy probability on SQuAD examples. *Top*: Attention focused paragraph tokens on y-axis and generated question tokens on x-axis, where we see that the learnt copy probabilities consistently extract words from the paragraph context. *Bottom*: Long-span attention pattern over the paragraph words (x-axis), where the copy probability looks for question words (y-axis) even when most of the question words are present in the local context around the answer phrase.

these attentions can serve as explainability of QG, a good intuition behind copying different words, which we plan to explore in our future work.

4.4 Training Speed

CopyBERT trains significantly faster than UniLM. For UniLM, to fine-tune further on QG task it takes around 10 epochs to obtain its best performance. This is because the model uses input token [MASK] to predict a target question word and as a result can only train with some percentage of randomly chosen words to ensure that the probability is conditioned on previous question words. CopyBERT, in contrast, takes only 2 to 3 epochs to achieve its best performance. It took CopyBERT around 14 hours on a single GPU with 12GB main memory to train for 3 epochs, whereas UniLM took around 45 hours on the same hardware to train for 10 epochs to achieve similar results as reported in Dong et al. (2019). We expect Recurrent-BERT (Chan and Fan, 2019) to take even longer time to train due to its sequential nature.

5 Conclusion

We showed that having a unified encoder-decoder transformer model initialized with contextualized word embeddings and further extended with copy mechanism can already give state-of-the-art, without additional pre-training on generation tasks (Dong et al., 2019). We also sped up the training of QG models that use BERT by choosing predictions on output embeddings that are offset by one position (§3.3). This work shows the significance of explicitly using self-attentions of BERT like models. These models can further be used in other tasks such as abstractive summarization and machine translation to see qualitative improvements.

Acknowledgements

The authors would like to thank the anonymous reviewers for helpful feedback. The work was partially funded by the German Federal Ministry of Education and Research (BMBF) through the project DEEPLEE (01IW17001).

References

Ying-Hong Chan and Yao-Chung Fan. 2019. A recurrent BERT-based model for question generation. In *Proceedings of the 2nd Workshop on Machine Reading for Question Answering*, pages 154–162, Hong Kong, China. Association for Computational Linguistics.

Eunsol Choi, He He, Mohit Iyyer, Mark Yatskar, Wentau Yih, Yejin Choi, Percy Liang, and Luke Zettlemoyer. 2018. Quac: Question answering in context. In *Proceedings of the 2018 Conference on Empirical Methods in Natural Language Processing*, pages 2174–2184.

Jacob Devlin, Ming-Wei Chang, Kenton Lee, and Kristina Toutanova. 2019. Bert: Pre-training of deep bidirectional transformers for language understanding. In *Proceedings of the 2019 Conference of the North American Chapter of the Association for Computational Linguistics: Human Language Technologies, Volume 1 (Long and Short Papers)*, pages 4171–4186.

Li Dong, Nan Yang, Wenhui Wang, Furu Wei, Xiaodong Liu, Yu Wang, Jianfeng Gao, Ming Zhou, and Hsiao-Wuen Hon. 2019. Unified language model pre-training for natural language understanding and generation. In *Advances in Neural Information Processing Systems*, pages 13042–13054.

Xinya Du and Claire Cardie. 2018. Harvesting paragraph-level question-answer pairs from wikipedia. In *Proceedings of the 56th Annual Meeting of the Association for Computational Linguistics (Volume 1: Long Papers)*, pages 1907–1917.

Xinya Du, Junru Shao, and Claire Cardie. 2017. Learning to ask: Neural question generation for reading comprehension. In *Proceedings of the 55th Annual Meeting of the Association for Computational Linguistics (Volume 1: Long Papers)*, pages 1342–1352.

Nan Duan, Duyu Tang, Peng Chen, and Ming Zhou. 2017. Question generation for question answering. In *Proceedings of the 2017 Conference on Empirical Methods in Natural Language Processing*, pages 866–874.

Jiatao Gu, Zhengdong Lu, Hang Li, and Victor OK Li. 2016. Incorporating copying mechanism in sequence-to-sequence learning. In *Proceedings of the 54th Annual Meeting of the Association for Computational Linguistics (Volume 1: Long Papers)*, pages 1631–1640.

John Hewitt and Christopher D Manning. 2019. A structural probe for finding syntax in word representations. In *Proceedings of the 2019 Conference of the North American Chapter of the Association for Computational Linguistics: Human Language Technologies, Volume 1 (Long and Short Papers)*, pages 4129–4138.

Ganesh Jawahar, Benoît Sagot, and Djamé Seddah. 2019. What does BERT learn about the structure of language? In *Proceedings of the 57th Annual Meeting of the Association for Computational Linguistics*, pages 3651–3657, Florence, Italy. Association for Computational Linguistics.

Mandar Joshi, Danqi Chen, Yinhan Liu, Daniel S Weld, Luke Zettlemoyer, and Omer Levy. 2019. Spanbert: Improving pre-training by representing and predicting spans. *arXiv preprint arXiv:1907.10529*.

Pascal Kuyten, Timothy Bickmore, Svetlana Stoyanchev, Paul Piwek, Helmut Prendinger, and Mitsuru Ishizuka. 2012. Fully automated generation of question-answer pairs for scripted virtual instruction. In *International Conference on Intelligent Virtual Agents*, pages 1–14. Springer.

Bang Liu, Mingjun Zhao, Di Niu, Kunfeng Lai, Yancheng He, Haojie Wei, and Yu Xu. 2019. Learning to generate questions by learning what not to generate. *arXiv preprint arXiv:1902.10418*.

Nasrin Mostafazadeh, Ishan Misra, Jacob Devlin, Margaret Mitchell, Xiaodong He, and Lucy Vanderwende. 2016. Generating natural questions about an image. In *Proceedings of the 54th Annual Meeting of the Association for Computational Linguistics (Volume 1: Long Papers)*, pages 1802–1813.

Elnaz Nouri, Ron Artstein, Anton Leuski, and David Traum. 2011. Augmenting conversational characters with generated question-answer pairs. In *2011 AAAI Fall Symposium Series*.

Pranav Rajpurkar, Jian Zhang, Konstantin Lopyrev, and Percy Liang. 2016. Squad: 100,000+ questions for machine comprehension of text. In *Proceedings of the 2016 Conference on Empirical Methods in Natural Language Processing*, pages 2383–2392.

Siva Reddy, Danqi Chen, and Christopher D Manning. 2019. Coqa: A conversational question answering challenge. *Transactions of the Association for Computational Linguistics*, 7:249–266.

Emily Reif, Ann Yuan, Martin Wattenberg, Fernanda B Viegas, Andy Coenen, Adam Pearce, and Been Kim. 2019. Visualizing and measuring the geometry of bert. In *Advances in Neural Information Processing Systems*, pages 8592–8600.

Thomas Scialom, Benjamin Piwowarski, and Jacopo Staiano. 2019. Self-attention architectures for answer-agnostic neural question generation. In *Proceedings of the 57th Annual Meeting of the Association for Computational Linguistics*, pages 6027–6032, Florence, Italy. Association for Computational Linguistics.

Xingwu Sun, Jing Liu, Yajuan Lyu, Wei He, Yanjun Ma, and Shi Wang. 2018. Answer-focused and position-aware neural question generation. In *Proceedings of the 2018 Conference on Empirical Methods in Natural Language Processing*, pages 3930–3939.

Ian Tenney, Dipanjan Das, and Ellie Pavlick. 2019. BERT rediscovers the classical NLP pipeline. In *Proceedings of the 57th Annual Meeting of the Association for Computational Linguistics*, pages 4593–4601, Florence, Italy. Association for Computational Linguistics.

Adam Trischler, Tong Wang, Xingdi Yuan, Justin Harris, Alessandro Sordoni, Philip Bachman, and Kaheer Suleman. 2016. Newsqa: A machine comprehension dataset. corr abs/1611.09830.

Ashish Vaswani, Noam Shazeer, Niki Parmar, Jakob Uszkoreit, Llion Jones, Aidan N Gomez, Łukasz Kaiser, and Illia Polosukhin. 2017. Attention is all you need. In *Advances in neural information processing systems*, pages 5998–6008.

Alex Wang and Kyunghyun Cho. 2019. Bert has a mouth, and it must speak: Bert as a markov random field language model. In *Proceedings of the Workshop on Methods for Optimizing and Evaluating Neural Language Generation*, pages 30–36.

Zhilin Yang, Peng Qi, Saizheng Zhang, Yoshua Bengio, William Cohen, Ruslan Salakhutdinov, and Christopher D Manning. 2018. Hotpotqa: A dataset for diverse, explainable multi-hop question answering. In *Proceedings of the 2018 Conference on Empirical Methods in Natural Language Processing*, pages 2369–2380.

Xuchen Yao, Emma Tosch, Grace Chen, Elnaz Nouri, Ron Artstein, Anton Leuski, Kenji Sagae, and David Traum. 2012. Creating conversational characters using question generation tools. *Dialogue & Discourse*, 3(2):125–146.

Shiyue Zhang and Mohit Bansal. 2019. Addressing semantic drift in question generation for semi-supervised question answering. *arXiv preprint arXiv:1909.06356*.

Yao Zhao, Xiaochuan Ni, Yuanyuan Ding, and Qifa Ke. 2018. Paragraph-level neural question generation with maxout pointer and gated self-attention networks. In *Proceedings of the 2018 Conference on Empirical Methods in Natural Language Processing*, pages 3901–3910.

How to Tame Your Data:
Data Augmentation for Dialog State Tracking

Adam Summerville   **Jordan Hashemi**   **James Ryan**   **William Ferguson**

California State Polytechnic University, Pomona   Raytheon BBN Technologies

`asummerville@cpp.edu`   `jordan.hashemin@rtx.com`
`james.o.ryan@rtx.com`
`bill.ferguson@rtx.com`

Abstract

Dialog State Tracking (DST) is a problem space in which the effective vocabulary is practically limitless. For example, the domain of possible movie titles or restaurant names is bound only by the limits of language. As such, DST systems often encounter out-of-vocabulary words at inference time that were never encountered during training. To combat this issue, we present a targeted data augmentation process, by which a practitioner observes the types of errors made on held-out evaluation data, and then modifies the training data with additional corpora to increase the vocabulary size at training time. Using this with a RoBERTa-based Transformer architecture, we achieve state-of-the-art results in comparison to systems that only mask trouble slots with special tokens. Additionally, we present a data-representation scheme for seamlessly retargeting DST architectures to new domains.

1   Introduction

Dialog State Tracking (DST) is a common problem for modern task-oriented dialog systems that need to be capable of tracking user requests. Commonly, there is an ontology that defines slots that must be filled according to a user's utterances – e.g., a `restaurant` slot that is filled in with a restaurant name given by the user. A key problem for DSTs is that the values that fill a slot at inference may have never been encountered at training time (consider that the set of all possible restaurant names is bound only by the limits of language).

In this work, we address the problems of training on a domain with effectively limitless possible vocabulary, and aim to create a DST system capable of scaling to unseen vocabulary at inference. We do this by first utilizing a language model (LM) based Transformer that is capable of handling any possible input and output in a textual manner, letting the same exact architecture scale to new intents,

slots, and slot values, with no modifications needed. Additionally, we present a practical *data augmentation* procedure for analyzing and addressing issues in the development of a DST system, leading to state-of-the-art performance.

2   Related Work

Work in DST has taken a number of different approaches. The annual DST Challenge (DSTC) has undergone eight iterations (although from the sixth competition on, it has been the more broad Dialog *System Technology* Challenge) (Williams et al., 2013; Henderson et al., 2014a,b). The M2M:Simulated Dialogue (Shah et al., 2018) dataset for dialog state tracking has been addressed by a number of different approaches. Rastogi et al. (2017) used a bi-directional GRU (Chung et al., 2014) along with an oracle delexicalizer to generate a candidate list for slot filling. Rastogi et al. (2018) later used a bi-directional LSTM (Hochreiter and Schmidhuber, 1997) without the oracle delexicalization to generate candidate lists for slot filling. Liu et al. (2018) use two bi-directional LSTMs – one at the utterance level, the other at the dialog level – to perform the dialog state tracking. However, this work is only tested on the simulated dataset Sim-GEN, meaning there is no comparison with the more challenging human crafted utterances contained in Sim-R and Sim-M.

The closest approach to the one detailed in this paper is that of Chao and Lane (2019). They used a system based off of BERT (Devlin et al., 2019), but removed the language-model head and instead used two specialized heads: one that does per-slot utterance level classification to determine whether a given slot is active in the utterance or is the special `dontcare` token, and another per-slot head that predicts whether a token represents the beginning or end of the span for that type of slot. Our

Proceedings of the 2nd Workshop on Natural Language Processing for Conversational AI, pages 32–37
July 9, 2020. ©2020 Association for Computational Linguistics

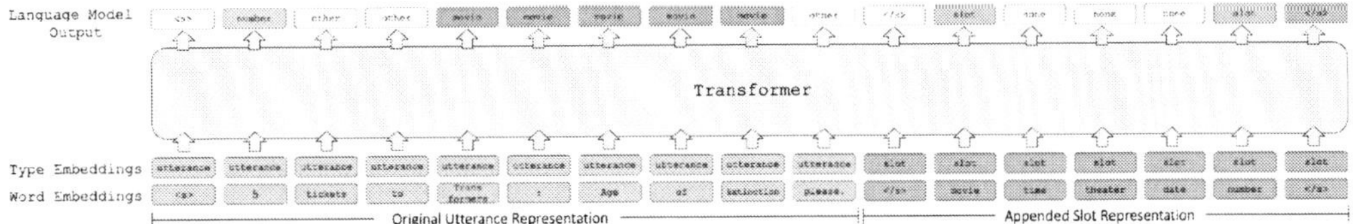

Figure 1: A depiction of the language model based Transformer architecture used in this work. For each token in the user utterance (light blue), the model predicts what slot it belongs to (green or purple), if any, else `other` (white). A token for each of the slots is concatenated to the end of the user utterance (orange) and the model predicts whether that slot is active in the utterance (pink), not active (white), or should be set to the special `dontcare` token (not in this example).

model differs in that we do not need to alter the architecture of the model with specialized heads, and instead fine-tune the existing language model head. In their experimentation, they adjusted the level of slot-specific dropout using targeted feature dropout, first used by Xu and Sarikaya (2014), where slots are replaced with a special `[UNK]` token. Our approach also differs in that instead of simply dropping out slots, we use the more nuanced method of targeted data augmentation.

Finally, data augmentation has been widely used for improving the robustness of dialog systems. Hou et al. (2018) used a LSTM-based sequence-to-sequence network to map from generic utterances (e.g., "show me the `<distance> <poitype>`") to a variety of different utterances (e.g., "where is the `<distance> <poitype>`" and "can you find the `<distance> <poitype>` to me"). This approach requires delexicalization and only alters grammatical structure, which is quite different from our approach which leaves grammatical structure alone, instead altering the non-delexicalized slot values. Quan and Xiong (2019) perform data augmentation via four different approaches: (1) replace words (excluding proper nouns, qualifiers, personal pronouns, and modal verbs) with their synonyms, (2) remove all stop words, (3) use existing neural machine-translation technology to translate from the source language to another and back again (similar to that of Hou et al. (2018), except they do not train their own seq2seq network), and (4) use an existing paraphraser to paraphrase the utterance.

3 Method

Our goal in this work is to to create a robust, readily extensible Dialog State Tracking system that requires minimal to no alteration of network architecture if the schema and/or domain of the dialog task changes. For instance, imagine a system that is being developed for the restaurant domain under a schema in which a set of slots are specified: cuisine, price, location. Now imagine that later it becomes necessary to add a new slot: kid-friendliness. Instead of changing the architecture and retraining from scratch, we would prefer to be able to fine-tune the existing model with the new slot now present. Additionally, we incorporate targeted data augmentation to combat over-fitting when a domain has limited vocabulary.

3.1 Language Model Based Transformer

To produce such a versatile DST system, we reformulate our data such that the problem is fully encoded textually, with no reliance on specialized output heads. Specifically, we carry out:

1. Utterance-level slot activation. Is the slot active in the current utterance? If it is, does the slot map to the special `dontcare` token? That is, for each slot we predict one of `slot`, `none`, or `dontcare`.

2. Token-level slot filling. For each token in the input, is it used in a slot or is it `other`?

To achieve (1), we modify the input utterance with an additional sequence. The additional sequence contains all of the slots present in the dialog schema. For instance, the sentence "5 tickets to *Transformers: Age of Extinction* please." is concatenated with "movie time theater date number". Adding a new slot(s) is handled by simply concatenating to the list – e.g., if the above movie domain was extended to add restaurants "cuisine restaurant location" could be concatenated to the list of slots.

For (2), at the output level a slot is predicted for every token in the original utterance and a slot intent is predicted for every schema token that is concatenated to that utterance: "5[number] tickets to *Transformers:*[movie] *Age*[movie] *of*[movie] *Extinction*[movie] please. <s>movie[slot] time[none] theater[none] date[none] number[slot]' See Figure 1 for a more detailed illustration. Despite the two objectives, the loss is simply the Categorical Cross-Entropy loss over the entire (combined) sequence.

The model aims to track the *joint goal* at each turn in the dialog, represented as all the slot values accumulated to that point. Rather than estimating the entire joint goal each turn, we predict changes to it – additions of slots, modifications to slot values – and maintain the joint goal by applying these changes.

4 Data Augmentation

There are a number of common issues in the datasets for these dialog tasks, including:

1. Small datasets. It is tedious and time-consuming to annotate, gather, or hand-modify believable dialogs.

2. Open classes. Given the open-ended nature of many of these tasks, training data cannot provide coverage of open classes (e.g., restaurant names or movie titles).

To counteract these issues, researchers have proposed a number of different data augmentation schemes (see Section 2). At the outset of our study, we tried the 10% slot-specific dropout used by Chao and Lane (2019), but our model still overfit to the training set. To combat this, we devised the following procedure:

1. **Determine problem slots.** Examine the incorrect predictions on the held-out evaluation set to determine whether there is a certain slot or intent that is not being predicted well.

2. **Augment for problem slots.** Find a corpus of values for that slot, and randomly insert a value from that corpus at training time.

In our work, we were using the Sim-R and Sim-M datasets (Shah et al., 2018), which are concerned with restaurant reservations and movie tickets respectively. We noticed that our system was nearly perfectly able to handle requests related to time, date, and number of people – slots whose values come from small structured sets – but was having difficulty with movie titles, restaurant names, and locations, even with the targeted 10% dropout.

We found corpora for movie names (42,306 movie titles found on Wikipedia as of 2013 (Bamman et al., 2013)), restaurant names (1445 humorous restaurant names (Samuel et al., 2016)), and locations (2067 US settlement names from 1880 to 2010 (Samuel et al., 2016)) which we then used to randomly replace the respective slots at training time at a rate of 50%.

We note that our replacement has two major effects. (1) By randomly replacing with real values instead of simply masking, the model is capable of learning a wider variety of slot values and value structures, instead of simply relying on syntactic information surrounding the names. (2) By randomly replacing values, the dialog becomes more difficult to follow – akin to a user who is prone to changing their mind – and this forces the system to learn to track a user's (fickle) goals better.

5 Experiments

As previously mentioned, we used the Sim-R and Sim-M datasets (Shah et al., 2018). This is because we found them to be of high quality (but with room for improvement), and there was a recent state-of-the-art approach that used a similar Transformer-based architecture to compare against (Chao and Lane, 2019). To assess the performance of the models, we use *joint goal accuracy* (Henderson et al., 2014a), the standard metric for assessing DST systems. At each turn of dialog, the ground truth must be perfectly matched.

For this specific work, we fine-tuned the RoBERTa masked language model of Liu et al. (2019); specifically, we used the Huggingface Transformers library (Wolf et al., 2019). All models were trained with the ADAM optimizer with an initial learning rate of $5e-5$, epsilon of $1e-8$, a linear learning rate schedule over 20 epochs, and an attention mask rate of 15%.

We compare three approaches in the experiment. (1) **RoBERTa-LM**, the RoBERTa LM architecture with 10% slot-specific dropout; (2) **RoBERTa-Separate**, the RoBERTa LM architecture with 50% slot-specific replacement, with separate models trained on the Sim-M and Sim-R datasets; and (3) **RoBERTa-Combined**, the RoBERTa LM architecture with 50% slot-specific replacement, with a single model trained on the combined Sim-M and

DST Model	Sim-M	Sim-R	Sim-M + Sim-R
DST+Oracle	96.8%	94.4%	95.2%
DST+LU	50.4%	87.1%	76.7%
BERT-DST	80.1%	89.6%	86.9%
RoBERTa-LM	71.1%	84.5%	80.8%
RoBERTa-Separate	84.2% *	92.5% *	90.2% *
RoBERTa-Combined	86.5% *	93.1% *	**91.2%** *

Table 1: Comparison of our approaches with prior work. * indicates that the approach is statistically significantly better than BERT-DST (Fisher's exact test with $p < 0.01$).

Sim-R datasets.

5.1 Baselines

To assess our model, we compare against three previous systems. The first work by Rastogi et al. (2017) uses a bi-directional GRU along with an oracle delexicalizer to generate a candidate list for slot filling (**DST+Oracle**). The follow-on work of Rastogi et al. (2018) uses a bi-directional LSTM to build a set of candidates without delexicalization (**DST+LU**). Finally, the most recent approach, by Chao and Lane (2019), builds off of the BERT Transformer architecture which achieved state-of-the-art results (**BERT-DST**).

5.2 Evaluation Results

A summary of the results can be seen in Table 1. We draw attention to the following results. **(1)** The language model based version of RoBERTa without data augmentation performs relatively poorly: it beats the non-Transformer based DST+LU at Sim-M but is worse at Sim-R, and is worse at both than BERT-DST. We did not perform a comprehensive hyperparameter search, so we are unable to discern if it is a critical failing of the model, or whether it was a result of our chosen hyperparameters. **(2)** The RoBERTa language model with data augmentation performed much better than the previous state-of-the-art – with 4.1% and 3.1% point gains respectively on Sim-M and Sim-R. **(3)** Finally, we note that the language model that was trained jointly on both the movie and restaurant data is significantly better than the models trained separately. In part, we believe that this is because the datasets have a lot of overlap – e.g., requesting dates, times, etc. We also believe that due to the relatively small sizes of the datasets, the increase in the size helps combat overfitting in the model – the Sim-M is a smaller dataset than Sim-R (1364 turns vs. 3416) and commensurately, while

there is a small gain in Sim-R performance, Sim-M performance is drastically improved (significant at $p < 0.00001$ with Fisher's exact test).

5.3 Discussion

We note that while we have achieved state-of-the-art performance on the Sim-M and Sim-R datasets, there is certainly a possibility that a better choice of augmenting corpora could help the generality of the final model. For instance, the corpus of restaurant names was focused mostly on humorous names, such as "A Brisket a Tasket" and "Et Tu New Brew." It will take further experimentation to determine if these names are more of a help (the model must be capable of handling a variety of names) or a hindrance (these names are not representative of most restaurant names).

Furthermore, we note the US-centric bias found in the training and evaluation datasets for the location names, and the corresponding bias in our chosen corpus. Similarly, it is an open question as to whether a wider – less US-focused – corpus of location names would help. Certainly, for a system deployed in the world, a wider corpus would likely be of use, but for the purpose of achieving state-of-the-art test accuracy, it is unknown.

6 Conclusions and Future Work

In this paper, we make two contributions. First, we introduce a process for a) examining the source of errors in Dialog State Tracking on held-out evaluation data, and b) correspondingly augmenting the dataset with corpora to vastly increase the vocabulary at training time. Like earlier work that selectively masked slot values, this prevents the system from overfitting to specific values found in the training data. Furthermore, however, it forces the system to learn a wider range of values, rather than syntactic features only, vastly improving the performance. Second, we do this in the context of a language model based Transformer, that due to the language-based nature of its representation – slots are simply represented as tokens concatenated to user utterances – is capable of transferring seamlessly between and working jointly on different datasets without the need to change the underlying architecture. In the future, we would like to address other forms of targeted data augmentation, addressing grammatical differences in addition to vocabulary modifications.

7 Acknowledgements

The information provided in this document is derived from an effort sponsored by the Defense Advanced Research Projects Agency (DARPA) and Air Force Research Laboratory (AFRL), and awarded to Raytheon BBN Technologies under contract number FA865018-C-7885.

References

David Bamman, Brendan OConnor, and Noah A Smith. 2013. Learning latent personas of film characters. In *Proceedings of the 51st Annual Meeting of the Association for Computational Linguistics (Volume 1: Long Papers)*, pages 352–361.

Guan-Lin Chao and Ian Lane. 2019. BERT-DST: Scalable end-to-end dialogue state tracking with bidirectional encoder representations from transformer. In *INTERSPEECH*.

Junyoung Chung, Caglar Gulcehre, Kyunghyun Cho, and Yoshua Bengio. 2014. Empirical evaluation of gated recurrent neural networks on sequence modeling. In *NIPS 2014 Workshop on Deep Learning, December 2014*.

Jacob Devlin, Ming-Wei Chang, Kenton Lee, and Kristina Toutanova. 2019. BERT: Pre-training of deep bidirectional transformers for language understanding. In *Proceedings of the 2019 Conference of the North American Chapter of the Association for Computational Linguistics: Human Language Technologies, Volume 1 (Long and Short Papers)*, pages 4171–4186, Minneapolis, Minnesota. Association for Computational Linguistics.

Matthew Henderson, Blaise Thomson, and Jason D Williams. 2014a. The second dialog state tracking challenge. In *Proceedings of the 15th Annual Meeting of the Special Interest Group on Discourse and Dialogue (SIGDIAL)*, pages 263–272.

Matthew Henderson, Blaise Thomson, and Jason D Williams. 2014b. The third dialog state tracking challenge. In *2014 IEEE Spoken Language Technology Workshop (SLT)*, pages 324–329. IEEE.

Sepp Hochreiter and Jürgen Schmidhuber. 1997. Long short-term memory. *Neural computation*, 9(8):1735–1780.

Yutai Hou, Yijia Liu, Wanxiang Che, and Ting Liu. 2018. Sequence-to-sequence data augmentation for dialogue language understanding. In *Proceedings of the 27th International Conference on Computational Linguistics*, pages 1234–1245, Santa Fe, New Mexico, USA. Association for Computational Linguistics.

Bing Liu, Gokhan Tur, Dilek Hakkani-Tur, Pararth Shah, and Larry Heck. 2018. Dialogue learning with human teaching and feedback in end-to-end trainable task-oriented dialogue systems. *arXiv preprint arXiv:1804.06512*.

Yinhan Liu, Myle Ott, Naman Goyal, Jingfei Du, Mandar Joshi, Danqi Chen, Omer Levy, Mike Lewis, Luke Zettlemoyer, and Veselin Stoyanov. 2019. Roberta: A robustly optimized bert pretraining approach. *arXiv preprint arXiv:1907.11692*.

Jun Quan and Deyi Xiong. 2019. Effective data augmentation approaches to end-to-end task-oriented dialogue. In *2019 International Conference on Asian Language Processing (IALP 2019)*.

Abhinav Rastogi, Raghav Gupta, and Dilek Hakkani-Tur. 2018. Multi-task learning for joint language understanding and dialogue state tracking. In *Proceedings of the 19th Annual SIGdial Meeting on Discourse and Dialogue*, pages 376–384, Melbourne, Australia. Association for Computational Linguistics.

Abhinav Rastogi, Dilek Hakkani-Tür, and Larry Heck. 2017. Scalable multi-domain dialogue state tracking. In *2017 IEEE Automatic Speech Recognition and Understanding Workshop (ASRU)*, pages 561–568. IEEE.

Ben Samuel, James Ryan, Adam J Summerville, Michael Mateas, and Noah Wardrip-Fruin. 2016. Bad news: An experiment in computationally assisted performance. In *International Conference on Interactive Digital Storytelling*, pages 108–120. Springer.

Pararth Shah, Dilek Hakkani-Tür, Gokhan Tür, Abhinav Rastogi, Ankur Bapna, Neha Nayak, and Larry Heck. 2018. Building a conversational agent overnight with dialogue self-play. *arXiv preprint arXiv:1801.04871*.

Jason Williams, Antoine Raux, Deepak Ramachandran, and Alan Black. 2013. The dialog state tracking challenge. In *Proceedings of the SIGDIAL 2013 Conference*, pages 404–413.

Thomas Wolf, Lysandre Debut, Victor Sanh, Julien Chaumond, Clement Delangue, Anthony Moi, Pierric Cistac, Tim Rault, R'emi Louf, Morgan Funtowicz, and Jamie Brew. 2019. Huggingface's transformers: State-of-the-art natural language processing. *ArXiv*, abs/1910.03771.

Puyang Xu and Ruhi Sarikaya. 2014. Targeted feature
dropout for robust slot filling in natural language understanding. In *Fifteenth Annual Conference of the
International Speech Communication Association.*

Efficient Intent Detection with Dual Sentence Encoders

github.com/PolyAI-LDN/polyai-models

Iñigo Casanueva, **Tadas Temčinas,** **Daniela Gerz, Matthew Henderson, and Ivan Vulić**
PolyAI Limited
London, United Kingdom
{inigo,dan,matt,ivan}@poly-ai.com

Abstract

Building conversational systems in new domains and with added functionality requires resource-efficient models that work under low-data regimes (i.e., in few-shot setups). Motivated by these requirements, we introduce intent detection methods backed by pretrained dual sentence encoders such as USE and ConveRT. We demonstrate the usefulness and wide applicability of the proposed intent detectors, showing that: **1)** they outperform intent detectors based on fine-tuning the full BERT-Large model or using BERT as a fixed black-box encoder on three diverse intent detection data sets; **2)** the gains are especially pronounced in few-shot setups (i.e., with only 10 or 30 annotated examples per intent); **3)** our intent detectors can be trained in a matter of minutes on a single CPU; and **4)** they are stable across different hyperparameter settings. In hope of facilitating and democratizing research focused on intention detection, we release our code, as well as a new challenging single-domain intent detection dataset comprising 13,083 annotated examples over 77 intents.

1 Introduction

Task-oriented conversational systems allow users to interact with computer applications through conversation in order to solve a particular task with well-defined semantics, such as booking restaurants, hotels and flights (Hemphill et al., 1990; Williams, 2012; El Asri et al., 2017), providing tourist information (Budzianowski et al., 2018), or automating customer support (Xu et al., 2017).

Intent detection is a vital component of any task-oriented conversational system (Hemphill et al., 1990; Coucke et al., 2018). In order to understand the user's current goal, the system must leverage its intent detector to classify the user's utterance (provided in varied natural language) into one of several predefined classes, that is, *intents*.[1] Scaling intent detectors (as well as conversational systems in general) to support new target domains and tasks is a very challenging and resource-intensive process (Wen et al., 2017; Rastogi et al., 2019). The need for expert domain knowledge and domain-specific labeled data still impedes quick and wide deployment of intent detectors. In other words, one crucial challenge is enabling effective intent detection in *low-data scenarios* typically met in commercial systems, with only several examples available per intent (i.e., the so-called *few-shot learning setups*).

Transfer learning on top of pretrained sentence encoders (Devlin et al., 2019; Liu et al., 2019b, *inter alia*) has now established as the mainstay paradigm aiming to mitigate the bottleneck with scarce in-domain data. However, directly applying the omnipresent sentence encoders such as BERT to intent detection may be sub-optimal. **1)** As shown by Henderson et al. (2019b), pretraining on a general language-modeling (LM) objective for conversational tasks is less effective than *conversational pretraining* based on the response selection task and conversational data (Henderson et al., 2019c; Mehri et al., 2019). **2)** Fine-tuning BERT and its variants is very resource-intensive as it assumes the adaptation of the full large model. Moreover, in few-shot setups fine-tuning may result in overfitting. From a commercial perspective, these properties lead to extremely slow, cumbersome, and expensive development cycles.

Therefore, in this work we propose to use efficient *dual sentence encoders* such as Universal Sentence Encoder (USE) (Cer et al., 2018) and ConveRT (Henderson et al., 2019b) to support intent detection. These models are in fact neural

---

[1]For instance, in the e-banking domain intents can be *lost card* or *failed top-up* (see Table 2). The importance of intent detection is also illustrated by the fact that getting the intent wrong is the first point of failure of any conversational agent.

*Equal contribution. TT is now at the Oxford University.

Proceedings of the 2nd Workshop on Natural Language Processing for Conversational AI, pages 38–45
July 9, 2020. ©2020 Association for Computational Linguistics

architectures tailored for modeling sentence pairs (Henderson et al., 2019c; Humeau et al., 2020), and are trained on a conversational response selection task. As such, they inherently encapsulate conversational knowledge needed for (few-shot) intent detection. We discuss their advantage over LM-based encoders, and empirically validate the usefulness of conversational pretraining for intent detection. We show that intent detectors based on fixed USE and ConveRT encodings outperform BERT-backed intent detectors across the board on three diverse intent detection datasets, with prominent gains especially in few-shot scenarios. Another advantage of dual models is their compactness:[2] we demonstrate that our state-of-the-art USE+ConveRT intent detectors can be trained even on a regular laptop's CPU in only several minutes.

We also show that intent classifiers based on dual sentence encoders are largely invariant to hyperparameter changes. This finding is extremely important for real-life low-data regimes: due to the invariance, the expensive hyperparameter tuning step can be bypassed, and a limited number of annotated examples can be used directly as additional training data (instead of held-out validation data).

Another contribution of this work is a new and challenging intent detection dataset in the banking domain, dubbed BANKING77. It follows the very recent endeavor of procuring high-quality intent detection data (Liu et al., 2019a; Larson et al., 2019), but is very different in nature than the other datasets. Unlike prior work which scatters a set of coarse-grained intents across a multitude of domains (i.e., 10+ domains, see Table 1 later), we present a challenging single-domain dataset comprising 13,083 examples over 77 fine-grained intents. We release the code as part of the growing PolyAI's repository: `github.com/PolyAI-LDN/polyai-models`. The BANKING77 dataset is available at: `github.com/PolyAI-LDN/task-specific-datasets`.

2   Methodology: Intent Detection with Dual Sentence Encoders

Pretrained Sentence Encoders. Large-scale pretrained models have benefited a wide spectrum of NLP applications immensely (Devlin et al., 2019; Liu et al., 2019b; Radford et al., 2019). Their core strength lies in the fact that, through consuming large general-purpose corpora during pretraining,

they require smaller amounts of domain-specific training data to adapt to a particular task and/or domain (Ruder et al., 2019). The adaptation is typically achieved by adding a task-specific output layer to a large pretrained sentence encoder, and then fine-tuning the entire model (Devlin et al., 2019). However, the fine-tuning process is computationally intensive (Zafrir et al., 2019; Henderson et al., 2019b), and still requires sufficient task-specific data (Arase and Tsujii, 2019; Sanh et al., 2019). As such, the standard full fine-tuning approach is both unsustainable in terms of resource consumption (Strubell et al., 2019), as well as suboptimal for few-shot scenarios.

Dual Sentence Encoders and Conversational Pretraining. A recent branch of sentence encoders moves beyond the standard LM-based pretraining objective, and proposes an alternative objective: *conversational response selection*, typically on Reddit data (Al-Rfou et al., 2016; Henderson et al., 2019a). As empirically validated by Henderson et al. (2019c); Mehri et al. (2019), conversational (instead of LM-based) pretraining aligns better with conversational tasks such as dialog act prediction or next utterance generation.

Pretraining on response selection also allows for the use of efficient *dual* models: the neural response selection architectures are instantiated as dual-encoder networks that learn the interaction between inputs/contexts and their relevant (follow-up) responses. Through such response selection pretraining regimes they organically encode useful conversational cues in their representations.

In this work, we propose to use such efficient conversational dual models as the main source of (general-purpose) conversational knowledge to inform domain-specific intent detectors. We empirically demonstrate their benefits over other standard sentence encoders such as BERT in terms of **1)** performance, **2)** efficiency, and **3)** applicability in few-shot scenarios. We focus on two prominent dual models trained on the response selection task: Universal Sentence Encoder (USE) (Cer et al., 2018), and Conversational Representations from Transformers (ConveRT) (Henderson et al., 2019b). For further technical details regarding the two models, we refer the interested reader to the original work.

Intent Detection with dual Encoders. We implement a simple yet effective model (see §5 later) for intent detection which is based on the two dual models. Unlike with BERT, we do not fine-tune

---

[2] For instance, ConveRT is only 59MB in size, pretrained in less than a day on 12 GPUs (Henderson et al., 2019b).

the entire model, but use fixed sentence representations encoded by USE and ConveRT. We simply stack a Multi-Layer Perceptron (MLP) with a single hidden layer with ReLU non-linear activations (Maas et al., 2013) on top of the fixed representations, followed by a softmax layer for multi-class classification. This simple formulation also allows us to experiment with the combination of USE and ConveRT representations: we can feed the concatenated vectors to the same classification architecture without any further adjustment.

3 New Dataset: BANKING77

In spite of the crucial role of intent detection in any task-oriented conversational system, publicly available intent detection datasets are still few and far between, even for English. The previous standard datasets such as Web Apps, Ask Ubuntu, the Chatbot Corpus (Braun et al., 2017) or SNIPS (Coucke et al., 2018) are limited to only a small number of classes (< 10), which oversimplifies the intent detection task and does not emulate the true environment of commercial systems. Therefore, more recent work has recognized the need for improved and more challenging intent detection datasets. **1)** The dataset of Liu et al. (2019a), dubbed HWU64, contains 25,716 examples for 64 intents in 21 domains. **2)** The dataset of Larson et al. (2019), dubbed CLINC150, spans 150 intents and 23,700 examples across 10 domains.

However, the two recent English datasets are *multi-domain*, and the examples per each domain may not sufficiently capture the full complexity of each domain as encountered "in the wild". Therefore, to complement the recent effort on data collection for intent detection, we propose a new *single-domain* dataset: it provides a very fine-grained set of intents in a banking domain, not present in HWU64 and CLINC150. The new BANKING77 dataset comprises 13,083 customer service queries labeled with 77 intents. Its focus on fine-grained single-domain intent detection makes it complementary to the two other datasets: we believe that any comprehensive intent detection evaluation should involve both coarser-grained multi-domain datasets such as HWU64 and CLINC150, and a fine-grained single-domain dataset such as BANKING77. The data statistics are summarized in Table 1.

The single-domain focus of BANKING77 with a large number of intents makes it more challenging. Some intent categories partially overlap with others,

Dataset	Intents	Examples	Domains
HWU64	64	25,716	21
CLINC150	150	23,700	10
BANKING77 (ours)	77	13,083	1

Table 1: Intent detection datasets: key statistics.

which requires fine-grained decisions, see Table 2 (e.g., *reverted top-up* vs. *failed top-up*). Furthermore, as other examples from Table 2 suggest, it is not always possible to rely on the semantics of individual words to capture the correct intent.[3]

4 Experimental Setup

Few-Shot Setups. We conduct all experiments on the three intent detection datasets described in §3. We are interested in wide-scale few-shot intent classification in particular: we argue that this setup most closely resembles the development process of a commercial conversational system, which typically starts with only a small number of data points when expanding to a new domain or task. We simulate such low-data settings by sampling smaller subsets from the full data. We experiment with setups where only 10 or 30 examples are available for each intent, while we use the same standard test sets for each experimental run.[4]

MLP Design. Unless stated otherwise (e.g., in experiments where we explicitly vary hyperparameters), for the MLP classifier, we use a single 512-dimensional hidden layer. We train with stochastic gradient descent (SGD), with the learning rate of 0.7 and linear decay. We rely on very aggressive dropout (0.75) and train for 500 iterations to reach convergence. We show how this training regime can improve the model's generalization capability, and we also probe its (in)susceptibility to diverse hyperparameter setups later in §5. Low-data settings are balanced, which is especially easy to guarantee in few-shot scenarios.

Models in Comparison. We compare intent detectors supported by the following pretrained sentence encoders. First, in the BERT-FIXED model we use pretrained BERT in the same way as dual encoders, in the so-called *feature mode*: we treat BERT as a black-box fixed encoder and use it to compute encodings/features for training the classifier.[5] We use

---

[3]The examples in BANKING77 are also longer on average (12 words) than in HWU64 (7 words) or CLINC150 (8).

[4]For reproducibility, we release all training subsets.

[5]We have also experimented with ELMo embeddings (Pe-

Intent Class	Example Utterance
Card Lost	*Could you assist me in finding my lost card?*
Link to Existing Card	*I found my lost card. Am I still able to use it?*
Reverted Top-up	*Hey, I thought my topup was all done but now the money is gone again – what's up with that?*
Failed Top-up	*Tell me why my topup wouldn't go through?*

Table 2: Intent classes and example utterances from BANKING77.

Model	BANKING77			CLINC150			HWU64		
	10	30	Full	10	30	Full	10	30	Full
BERT-FIXED	67.55	80.07	87.19	80.16	87.99	91.79	72.61	79.78	85.77
BERT-TUNED	83.42	90.03	**93.66**	91.93	95.49	96.93	84.86	88.27	92.10
USE	84.23	89.74	92.81	90.85	93.98	95.06	83.75	89.03	91.25
CONVERT	83.32	89.37	93.01	92.62	95.78	**97.16**	82.65	87.88	91.24
USE+CONVERT	**85.19**	**90.57**	93.36	**93.26**	**96.13**	**97.16**	**85.83**	**90.16**	**92.62**

Table 3: Accuracy scores ($\times 100\%$) on all three intent detection data sets with varying number of training examples (**10** examples per intent; **30** examples per intent; **Full** training data). The peak scores per column are in bold.

the mean-pooled "sequence ouput" (i.e., the pooled mean of the sub-word embeddings) as the sentence representation.[6] In the BERT-TUNED model, we rely on the standard BERT-based fine-tuning regime for classification tasks (Devlin et al., 2019) which adapts the full model. We train a softmax layer on top of the [CLS] token output. We use the Adam optimizer with weight decay and a learning rate of 4×10^{-4}. For low-data (10 examples per intent), mid-data (30 examples) and full-data settings we train for 50, 18, and 5 epochs, respectively, which is sufficient for the model to converge, while avoiding overfitting or catastrophic forgetting.

We use the two publicly available pretrained dual encoders: **1)** the multilingual large variant of USE (Yang et al., 2019),[7] and **2)** the single-context CONVERT model trained on the full 2015-2019 Reddit data comprising 654M *(context, response)* training pairs (Henderson et al., 2019b).[8] In all experimental runs, we compare against the pretrained cased BERT-large model: 24 Transformer layers, embedding dimensionality 1024, and a total of 340M parameters. Note that e.g. ConveRT is much lighter in its design and is also pretrained more quickly than BERT (Henderson et al., 2019b): it relies on 6 Transfomer layers with embedding dimensionality of 512. We report accuracy as the main evaluation measure for all experimental runs.

5   Results and Discussion

Table 3 summarizes the main results; we show the accuracy scores of all models on all three datasets, and for different training data setups. As one crucial finding, we report competitive performance of intent detectors based on the two dual models, and their relative performance seems to also depend on the dataset at hand: USE has a slight edge over CONVERT on HWU64, but the opposite holds on CLINC150. The design based on fixed sentence representations, however, allows for the straightforward combination of USE and CONVERT. The results suggest that the two dual models in fact capture complementary information, as the combined USE+CONVERT-based intent detectors result in peak performance across the board. As discussed later, due to its pretraining objective, BERT is competitive only in its fine-tuning mode of usage, and cannot match other two sentence encoders in the feature-based (i.e., fixed) usage mode.

Few-Shot Scenarios. The focus of this work is on low-data few-shot scenarios often met in production, where only a handful of annotated examples per intent are available. The usefulness of dual sentence encoders comes to the fore especially in this setup: 1) the results indicate gains over the fine-tuned BERT model especially for few-shot scenarios, and the gains are more pronounced in our "fewest-shot" setup (with only 10 annotated examples per intent). The respective improvements of USE+CONVERT over BERT-TUNED are +1.77, +1.33, and +0.97 for BANKING77, CLINC150, and HWU64 (10 examples per intent), and we also see

---

ters et al., 2018) in the same feature mode, but they are consistently outperformed by all other models in comparison.

[6]This performed slightly better than using the [CLS] token embedding as sentence representation.

[7]https://tfhub.dev/google/universal-sentence-encoder-multilingual-large/1

[8]https://github.com/PolyAI-LDN/polyai-models

Model	BANKING77		CLINC150		HWU64	
	10	Full	10	Full	10	Full
BERT-FIXED	64.9 (67.8) [57.0]	86.2 (88.4) [74.9]	78.1 (80.6) [70.2]	91.2 (92.6) [84.7]	71.5 (72.8) [68.0]	85.9 (86.8) [81.5]
USE	83.9 (84.4) [83.0]	92.6 (92.9) [91.4]	90.6 (91.0) [89.9]	95.0 (95.3) [93.9]	83.6 (83.9) [83.0]	91.6 (92.1) [90.7]
CONVERT	83.1 (83.4) [82.4]	92.6 (93.0) [91.6]	92.4 (92.8) [92.0]	97.1 (97.2) [96.3]	82.5 (83.1) [82.0]	91.3 (91.6) [90.8]
USE+CONVERT	85.2 (85.5) [84.8]	93.3 (93.5) [92.8]	93.2 (93.5) [92.8]	97.0 (97.2) [96.5]	85.9 (86.2) [85.7]	92.5 (92.8) [91.6]

Table 4: Variation in accuracy scores ($\times 100\%$) with different hyperparameter regimes for all the models in comparison and on all three datasets. **10** again means 10 training examples per intent as opposed to **Full** training data. The scores are provided as *avg (max) [min]*: *avg* is the average over all runs with different hyperparameter settings for each encoder model and each setup, *max* and *min* are the respective maximum and minimum scores.

Encoder	CPU	GPU
BERT (Large)	2.4	235.9
USE	53.5	785.4
CONVERT	58.3	866.7

Table 5: Average number of sentences encoded *per second* with the three sentence encoders. The data is fed to each encoder in batches of 15 sentences.

Classifer	CPU	GPU	TPU
BERT-TUNED	n/a	n/a	567s
USE	65s	57s	n/a
CONVERT	73s	53s	n/a

Table 6: Time to train and evaluate an intent classification model based on two dual models and fine-tuning BERT on BANKING77 in a few-shot scenario with 10 examples per intent. The CPU is a 2.3 GHz Dual-Core Intel Core i5. The GPU is a GeForce RTX 2080 Ti, 11 GB. The TPU is a v2-8, 8 cores, 64 GB.

better results with the combined model when 30 examples per intent are available on all three datasets. Overall, this proves the suitability of dual sentence encoders for the few-shot intent classification task.

Invariance to Hyperparameters. A prominent risk in few-shot setups concerns overfitting to small data sets (Srivastava et al., 2014; Olson et al., 2018). Another issue concerns the sheer lack of training data, which gets even more pronounced if a subset of the (already scarce) data must be reserved for validation and hyper-parameter tuning. Therefore, a desirable property of any few-shot intent detector is its invariance to hyperparameters and, consequently, its off-the-shelf usage without further tuning on the validation set. This effectively means that one could use all available annotated examples directly for training. In order to increase the reliability of the intent detectors and prevent overfitting in few-shot scenarios, we suggest to use the aggressive dropout regularization (i.e., the dropout rate is 0.75), and a very large number of iterations

(500), see §4.

We now demonstrate that the intent detectors based on dual encoders are very robust with respect to different hyper-parameter choices, starting from this basic assumption that a high number of iterations and high dropout rates r are needed. For each classifier, we fix the *base/pivot* configuration from §4: the number of hidden layers is $H = 1$, its dimensionality is $h = 512$, the SGD optimizer is used with the learning rate of 0.75. Starting from the pivot configuration, we create other configurations by altering one hyper-parameter at the time from the pivot. We probe the following values: $r = \{0.75, 0.5, 0.25\}$, $H = \{0, 1, 2\}$, $h = \{128, 256, 512, 1024\}$, and we also try out all the configurations with another optimizer: Adam with the linearly decaying learning rate of 4×10^{-4}.

The results with all hyperparameter configs are summarized in Table 4. They suggest that intent detectors based on dual models are indeed very robust. Importantly, we do not observe any experimental run which results in substantially lower performance with these models. In general, the peak scores with dual-based models are reported with higher r rates (0.75), and with larger hidden layer sizes h (1,024). On the other side of the spectrum are variants with lower r rates (0.25) and smaller h-s (128). However, the fluctuation in scores is not large, as illustrated by the results in Table 4. This finding does not hold for BERT-FIXED where in Table 4 we do observe "outlier" runs with substantially lower performance compared to its peak and average scores. Finally, it is also important to note BERT-TUNED does not converge to a good solution for 2% of the runs with different seeds, and such runs are not included in the final reported numbers with that baseline in Table 3.

Resource Efficiency. Besides strong performance established in Table 3 and increased stability (see Table 4), another advantage of the two dual models is their *encoding efficiency*. In Table 5 we report the average times needed by each fixed encoder to encode sentences fed in the batches of size 15 on both CPU (2.3 GHz Dual-Core Intel Core i5) and GPU (GeForce RTX 2080 Ti, 11 GB). The encoding times reveal that BERT, when used as a sentence encoder, is around 20 times slower on the CPU and roughly 3 times slower on the GPU.[9]

Furthermore, in Table 6 we present the time required to train and evaluate an intent classification model for BANKING77 in the lowest-data regime (10 instances per intent).[10] Note that the time reduction on GPU over CPU for the few-shot scenario is mostly due to the reduced encoding time on GPU (see Table 5 again). However, when operating in the *Full* data regime, the benefits of GPU training vanish: using a neural net with a single hidden layer the overhead of the GPU usage is higher than the speed-up achieved due to faster encoding and network computations. Crucially, the reported training and execution times clearly indicate that effective intent detectors based on pretrained dual models can be constructed even without large resource demands and can run even on CPUs, without huge models that require GPUs or TPUs. In sum, we hope that our findings related to improved resource efficiency of dual models, as well as the shared code will facilitate further and wider research focused on the intent classification task.

Further Discussion. The results from Tables 3 and 4 show that transferring representations from conversational pretraining based on the response selection task (and conversational data) is useful for conversational tasks such as intent detection. This corroborates the main findings from prior work (Humeau et al., 2020; Henderson et al., 2019b). The results also suggest that using the current pretrained BERT as an off-the-shelf sentence encoder is sub-optimal for an application such as intent detection: BERT is much more powerful when used in the fine-tuning mode instead of the less expensive "feature-based" mode (Peters et al., 2019). This might be due to its pretraining LM objective: while both USE and ConveRT are forced to reason at the level of full sentences during the re-

sponse selection pretraining, BERT is primarily a (local) language model. It seems that the next sentence prediction objective is not sufficient to learn a universal sentence encoder which can be applied off-the-shelf to unseen sentences in conversational tasks (Mehri et al., 2019). However, BERT's competitive performance in the fine-tuning mode, at least in the *Full* data scenarios, suggests that it still captures knowledge which is useful for intent detection. Given strong performance of both fine-tuned BERT and dual models in the intent detection task, in future work we plan to investigate hybrid strategies that combine dual sentence encoders and LM-based encoders. Note that it is also possible to combine BERT-FIXED with the two dual encoders, but such ensembles, besides yielding reduced performance, also substantially increase training times (see again Table 5).

We also believe that further gains can be achieved by increasing the overall size and depth of dual models such as ConveRT, but this comes at the expense of its efficiency and training speed: note that the current architecture of ConveRT relies on only 6 Transformer layers and embedding dimensionality of 512 (cf., BERT-Large with 24 layers and 1024-dim embeddings).

6 Conclusion

We have presented intent classification models that rely on sentence encoders which were pretrained on a conversational response selection task. We have demonstrated that using dual encoder models such as USE and ConveRT yield state-of-the-art intent classification results on three diverse intent classification data sets in English. One of these data sets is another contribution of this work: we have proposed a fine-grained single-domain data set spanning 13,083 annotated examples across 77 intents in the banking domain.

The gains with the proposed models over fully fine-tuned BERT-based classifiers are especially pronounced in few-shot scenarios, typically encountered in commercial systems, where only a small set of annotated examples per intent can be guaranteed. Crucially, we have shown that the proposed intent classifiers are extremely lightweight in terms of resources, which makes them widely usable: they can be trained on a standard laptop's CPU in several minutes. This property holds promise to facilitate the development of intent classifiers even without access to large computational

---

[9]We provide a *colab* script to reproduce these experiments.

[10]Note that we cannot evaluate BERT-TUNED on GPU as it runs out of memory. Similar problems were reported in prior work; see https://github.com/google-research/bert/blob/master/README.md#squad-11 for a reference. USE and CONVERT cannot be evaluated on TPUs as they currently lack TPU-specific code.

resources, which in turn also increases equality and fairness in research (Strubell et al., 2019).

In future work we will port the efficient intent detectors based on dual encoders to other languages, leveraging multilingual pretrained representations (Chidambaram et al., 2019). This work has also empirically validated that there is still ample room for improvement in the intent detection task especially in low-data regimes. Therefore, similar to recent work (Upadhyay et al., 2018; Khalil et al., 2019; Liu et al., 2019c), we will also investigate how to transfer intent detectors to low-resource target languages in few-shot and zero-shot scenarios. We also plan to extend the models to handle out-of-scope prediction (Larson et al., 2019).

We have released the code and the data sets online at: `github.com/PolyAI-LDN/polyai-models`.

Acknowledgments

We thank our colleagues at PolyAI, especially Paweł Budzianowski, Sam Coope, and Shawn Wen for many fruitful discussions. We also thank the anonymous reviewers for their helpful suggestions.

References

Rami Al-Rfou, Marc Pickett, Javier Snaider, Yun-Hsuan Sung, Brian Strope, and Ray Kurzweil. 2016. Conversational contextual cues: The case of personalization and history for response ranking. *CoRR*, abs/1606.00372.

Yuki Arase and Jun'ichi Tsujii. 2019. Transfer finetuning: A BERT case study. In *Proceedings of EMNLP-IJCNLP*, pages 5392–5403.

Daniel Braun, Adrian Hernandez Mendez, Florian Matthes, and Manfred Langen. 2017. Evaluating natural language understanding services for conversational question answering systems. In *Proceedings of SIGDIAL*, pages 174–185.

Paweł Budzianowski, Tsung-Hsiang Wen, Bo-Hsiang Tseng, Iñigo Casanueva, Stefan Ultes, Osman Ramadan, and Milica Gašić. 2018. MultiWOZ - A large-scale multi-domain wizard-of-oz dataset for task-oriented dialogue modelling. In *Proceedings of EMNLP*, pages 5016–5026.

Daniel Cer, Yinfei Yang, Sheng-yi Kong, Nan Hua, Nicole Limtiaco, Rhomni St. John, Noah Constant, Mario Guajardo-Cespedes, Steve Yuan, Chris Tar, Yun-Hsuan Sung, Brian Strope, and Ray Kurzweil. 2018. Universal sentence encoder. *CoRR*, abs/1803.11175.

Muthuraman Chidambaram, Yinfei Yang, Daniel Cer, Steve Yuan, Yun-Hsuan Sung, Brian Strope, and Ray Kurzweil. 2019. Learning cross-lingual sentence representations via a multi-task dual-encoder model. In *Proceedings of the 4th Workshop on Representation Learning for NLP*, pages 250–259.

Alice Coucke, Alaa Saade, Adrien Ball, Théodore Bluche, Alexandre Caulier, David Leroy, Clément Doumouro, Thibault Gisselbrecht, Francesco Caltagirone, Thibaut Lavril, et al. 2018. Snips Voice Platform: An embedded spoken language understanding system for private-by-design voice interfaces. *arXiv preprint arXiv:1805.10190*, pages 12–16.

Jacob Devlin, Ming-Wei Chang, Kenton Lee, and Kristina Toutanova. 2019. BERT: Pre-training of deep bidirectional transformers for language understanding. In *Proceedings of NAACL-HLT*, pages 4171–4186.

Layla El Asri, Hannes Schulz, Shikhar Sharma, Jeremie Zumer, Justin Harris, Emery Fine, Rahul Mehrotra, and Kaheer Suleman. 2017. Frames: A corpus for adding memory to goal-oriented dialogue systems. In *Proceedings of SIGDIAL*, pages 207–219.

Charles T. Hemphill, John J. Godfrey, and George R. Doddington. 1990. The ATIS Spoken Language Systems Pilot Corpus. In *Proceedings of the Workshop on Speech and Natural Language*, pages 96–101.

Matthew Henderson, Pawel Budzianowski, Iñigo Casanueva, Sam Coope, Daniela Gerz, Girish Kumar, Nikola Mrkšić, Georgios Spithourakis, Pei-Hao Su, Ivan Vulić, and Tsung-Hsien Wen. 2019a. A repository of conversational datasets. In *Proceedings of the 1st Workshop on Natural Language Processing for Conversational AI*, pages 1–10.

Matthew Henderson, Iñigo Casanueva, Nikola Mrkšić, Pei-Hao Su, Ivan Vulić, et al. 2019b. ConveRT: Efficient and accurate conversational representations from transformers. *arXiv preprint arXiv:1911.03688*.

Matthew Henderson, Ivan Vulić, Daniela Gerz, Iñigo Casanueva, Paweł Budzianowski, Sam Coope, Georgios Spithourakis, Tsung-Hsien Wen, Nikola Mrkšić, and Pei-Hao Su. 2019c. Training neural response selection for task-oriented dialogue systems. In *Proceedings of ACL*, pages 5392–5404.

Samuel Humeau, Kurt Shuster, Marie-Anne Lachaux, and Jason Weston. 2020. Poly-encoders: Transformer architectures and pre-training strategies for fast and accurate multi-sentence scoring. In *Proceedings of ICLR*, volume abs/1905.01969.

Talaat Khalil, Kornel Kiełczewski, Georgios Christos Chouliaras, Amina Keldibek, and Maarten Versteegh. 2019. Cross-lingual intent classification in a low resource industrial setting. In *Proceedings of EMNLP-IJCNLP*, pages 6418–6423.

Stefan Larson, Anish Mahendran, Joseph J. Peper, Christopher Clarke, Andrew Lee, Parker Hill, Jonathan K. Kummerfeld, Kevin Leach, Michael A. Laurenzano, Lingjia Tang, and Jason Mars. 2019. An evaluation dataset for intent classification and out-of-scope prediction. In *Proceedings of EMNLP-IJCNLP*, pages 1311–1316.

Xingkun Liu, Arash Eshghi, Pawel Swietojanski, and Verena Rieser. 2019a. Benchmarking natural language understanding services for building conversational agents. In *Proceedings of IWSDS*.

Yinhan Liu, Myle Ott, Naman Goyal, Jingfei Du, Mandar Joshi, Danqi Chen, Omer Levy, Mike Lewis, Luke Zettlemoyer, and Veselin Stoyanov. 2019b. RoBERTa: A robustly optimized BERT pretraining approach. *CoRR*, abs/1907.11692.

Zihan Liu, Jamin Shin, Yan Xu, Genta Indra Winata, Peng Xu, Andrea Madotto, and Pascale Fung. 2019c. Zero-shot cross-lingual dialogue systems with transferable latent variables. In *Proceedings of EMNLP-IJCNLP*, pages 1297–1303.

Andrew L. Maas, Awni Y. Hannun, and Andrew Y. Ng. 2013. Rectifier nonlinearities improve neural network acoustic models. In *Proceedings of ICML*.

Shikib Mehri, Evgeniia Razumovskaia, Tiancheng Zhao, and Maxine Eskenazi. 2019. Pretraining methods for dialog context representation learning. In *Proceedings of ACL*, pages 3836–3845.

Matthew Olson, Abraham J. Wyner, and Richard Berk. 2018. Modern neural networks generalize on small data sets. In *Proceedings of NeurIPS*, pages 3623–3632.

Matthew Peters, Mark Neumann, Mohit Iyyer, Matt Gardner, Christopher Clark, Kenton Lee, and Luke Zettlemoyer. 2018. Deep contextualized word representations. In *Proceedings of NAACL-HLT*, pages 2227–2237.

Matthew E. Peters, Sebastian Ruder, and Noah A. Smith. 2019. To tune or not to tune? Adapting pretrained representations to diverse tasks. In *Proceedings of the 4th Workshop on Representation Learning for NLP*, pages 7–14.

Alec Radford, Jeffrey Wu, Rewon Child, David Luan, Dario Amodei, and Ilya Sutskever. 2019. Language models are unsupervised multitask learners. *OpenAI Blog*, 1(8).

Abhinav Rastogi, Xiaoxue Zang, Srinivas Sunkara, Raghav Gupta, and Pranav Khaitan. 2019. Towards scalable multi-domain conversational agents: The schema-guided dialogue dataset. *arXiv preprint arXiv:1909.05855*.

Sebastian Ruder, Matthew E. Peters, Swabha Swayamdipta, and Thomas Wolf. 2019. Transfer learning in natural language processing. In *Proceedings of NAACL-HLT: Tutorials*, pages 15–18.

Victor Sanh, Lysandre Debut, Julien Chaumond, and Thomas Wolf. 2019. DistilBERT, a distilled version of BERT: Smaller, faster, cheaper and lighter. *CoRR*, abs/1910.01108.

Nitish Srivastava, Geoffrey E. Hinton, Alex Krizhevsky, Ilya Sutskever, and Ruslan Salakhutdinov. 2014. Dropout: A simple way to prevent neural networks from overfitting. *Journal of Machine Learning Research*, 15(1):1929–1958.

Emma Strubell, Ananya Ganesh, and Andrew McCallum. 2019. Energy and policy considerations for deep learning in NLP. In *Proceedings of ACL*, pages 3645–3650.

Shyam Upadhyay, Manaal Faruqui, Gökhan Tür, Dilek Hakkani-Tür, and Larry P. Heck. 2018. (almost) zero-shot cross-lingual spoken language understanding. In *Proceedings of ICASSP*, pages 6034–6038.

Tsung-Hsien Wen, David Vandyke, Nikola Mrkšić, Milica Gašić, Lina M. Rojas-Barahona, Pei-Hao Su, Stefan Ultes, and Steve Young. 2017. A network-based end-to-end trainable task-oriented dialogue system. In *Proceedings of EACL*, pages 438–449.

Jason Williams. 2012. A critical analysis of two statistical spoken dialog systems in public use. In *Proceedings of SLT*.

Anbang Xu, Zhe Liu, Yufan Guo, Vibha Sinha, and Rama Akkiraju. 2017. A new chatbot for customer service on social media. In *Proceedings of the 2017 CHI Conference on Human Factors in Computing Systems*, pages 3506–3510.

Yinfei Yang, Daniel Cer, Amin Ahmad, Mandy Guo, Jax Law, Noah Constant, Gustavo Hernández Ábrego, Steve Yuan, Chris Tar, Yun-Hsuan Sung, Brian Strope, and Ray Kurzweil. 2019. Multilingual universal sentence encoder for semantic retrieval. *CoRR*, abs/1907.04307.

Ofir Zafrir, Guy Boudoukh, Peter Izsak, and Moshe Wasserblat. 2019. Q8BERT: Quantized 8bit BERT. *CoRR*, abs/1910.06188.

Accelerating Natural Language Understanding in Task-Oriented Dialog

Ojas Ahuja and **Shrey Desai**
Department of Computer Science
The University of Texas at Austin
{ojas, shreydesai}@utexas.edu

Abstract

Task-oriented dialog models typically leverage complex neural architectures and large-scale, pre-trained Transformers to achieve state-of-the-art performance on popular natural language understanding benchmarks. However, these models frequently have in excess of tens of millions of parameters, making them impossible to deploy on-device where resource-efficiency is a major concern. In this work, we show that a simple convolutional model compressed with structured pruning achieves largely comparable results to BERT (Devlin et al., 2019) on ATIS and Snips, with under 100K parameters. Moreover, we perform acceleration experiments on CPUs, where we observe our multi-task model predicts intents and slots nearly $63\times$ faster than even DistilBERT (Sanh et al., 2019).

1 Introduction

The advent of smart devices like Amazon Alexa, Facebook Portal, and Google Assistant has increased the necessity of resource-efficient task-oriented systems (Coucke et al., 2018; Zhang et al., 2020; Desai et al., 2020). These systems chiefly perform two natural language understanding tasks, intent detection and slot filling, where the goals are to understand what the user is trying to accomplish and the metadata associated with the request, respectively (Gupta et al., 2018). However, there remains a disconnect between state-of-the-art task-oriented systems and their deployment in real-world applications. Recent top performing systems have largely saturated performance on ATIS (Hemphill et al., 1990) and Snips (Coucke et al., 2018) by leveraging complex neural architectures and large-scale, pre-trained language models (Devlin et al., 2019), but their usability in on-device settings remains suspect (Qin et al., 2019; Cheng et al., 2017). Mobile phones, for example, have

sharp hardware constraints and limited memory capacities, implying systems must optimize for both accuracy and resource-efficiency as possible to be able to run in these types of environments (Lin et al., 2010; McIntosh et al., 2018).

In this work, we present a vastly simplified, single-layer convolutional model (Kim, 2014; Bai et al., 2018) that is highly compressible but nonetheless achieves competitive results on task-oriented natural language understanding benchmarks. In order to compress the model, we use structured magnitude-based pruning (Anwar et al., 2017; Li et al., 2017), a two-step approach where (1) entire convolutional filters are deleted according to their ℓ_2 norms; and (2) remaining portions of the underlying weight matrix are spliced together. The successive reduction in the number of convolutional output connections permits downstream weight matrices to reduce their number of input connections as well, collectively resulting in a smaller model. Structured pruning and re-training steps are then interleaved to ensure the model is able to reconstruct lost filters that may contribute valuable information. During test-time, however, we use the pruned model as-is without further fine-tuning.

Our simple convolutional model with structured pruning obtains strong results despite having less than 100K parameters. On ATIS, our multi-task model achieves 95% intent accuracy and 94% slot F1, only about 2% lower than BERT (Devlin et al., 2019). Structured pruning also admits significantly faster inference: on CPUs, we show our model is $63\times$ faster than DistilBERT. Unlike compression methods based on unstructured pruning (Frankle and Carbin, 2019), our model enjoys speedups *without* having to rely on a sparse tensor library at test-time (Han et al., 2016), thus we demonstrate the potential for usage in resource-constrained, on-device settings. Our code is publicly available at `https://github.com/oja/pruned-nlu`.

Proceedings of the 2nd Workshop on Natural Language Processing for Conversational AI, pages 46–53
July 9, 2020. ©2020 Association for Computational Linguistics

2 Related Work

Task-Oriented Dialog. Dialog systems perform a range of tasks, including language understanding, dialog state tracking, content planning, and text generation (Bobrow et al., 1977; Henderson, 2015; Yu et al., 2016; Yan et al., 2017; Gao et al., 2018). For smart devices, specifically, intent detection and slot filling form the backbone of natural language understanding (NLU) modules, which can either be used in single-turn or multi-turn conversations (Coucke et al., 2018; Rastogi et al., 2020). We contribute a single-turn, multi-task NLU system especially tailored for on-device settings, as demonstrated through acceleration experiments.

Model Compression. In natural language processing, numerous works have used compression techniques like quantization (Wróbel et al., 2018; Zafrir et al., 2019), distillation (Sanh et al., 2019; Tang et al., 2019; Jiao et al., 2020), pruning (Yoon et al., 2018; Gordon et al., 2020), and smaller representations (Ravi and Kozareva, 2018; Kozareva and Ravi, 2018; Desai et al., 2020). Concurrently, Desai et al. (2020) develop lightweight convolutional representations for on-device task-oriented systems, related to our goals, but they do not compare with other compression methods and solely evaluate on a proprietary dataset. In contrast, we compare the efficacy of structured pruning against strong baselines—including BERT (Devlin et al., 2019)—on the open-source ATIS and Snips datasets.

3 Convolutional Model

Convolutions for On-Device Modeling. State-of-the-art task-oriented models are largely based on recurrent neural networks (RNNs) (Wang et al., 2018) or Transformers (Qin et al., 2019). However, these models are often impractical to deploy in low-resource settings. Recurrent models must sequentially unroll sequences during inference, and self-attention mechanisms in Transformers process sequences with quadratic complexity (Vaswani et al., 2017). High-performing, pre-trained Transformers, in particular, also have upwards of tens of millions of parameters, even when distilled (Tang et al., 2019; Sanh et al., 2019).

Convolutional neural networks (CNNs), in contrast, are highly parallelizable and can be significantly compressed with structured pruning (Li et al., 2017), while still achieving competitive performance on a variety of NLP tasks (Kim, 2014;

Gehring et al., 2017). Furthermore, the core convolution operation has enjoyed speedups with dedicated digital signal processors (DSPs) and field programmable gate arrays (FPGAs) (Ahmad and Pasha, 2020). Model compatibility with on-device hardware is one of the most important considerations for practitioners as, even if a model works well on high throughput GPUs, its components may saturate valuable resources like memory and power (Lin et al., 2010).

Model Description. Model inputs are encoded as a sequence of integers $\mathbf{w} = (w_1, \cdots, w_n)$ and right-padded up to a maximum sequence length. The embedding layer replaces each token w_i with a corresponding d-dimensional vector $\mathbf{e}_i \in \mathbb{R}^d$ sourced from pre-trained GloVe embeddings (Pennington et al., 2014). A feature map $\mathbf{c} \in \mathbb{R}^{n-h+1}$ is then calculated by applying a convolutional filter of height h over the embedded input sequence. We apply max-over-time pooling $\hat{c} = \max(\mathbf{c})$ (Collobert et al., 2011) to simultaneously reduce the dimensionality and extract the most salient features. The pooled features are then concatenated and fed through a linear layer with dropout (Srivastava et al., 2014). The objective is to maximize the log likelihood of intents, slots, or both (under a multi-task setup), and is optimized with Adam (Kingma and Ba, 2015).

To ensure broad applicability, our model emphasizes simplicity, and therefore minimizes the number of extraneous architectural decisions: there is only a single convolutional block, no residual connections, and no normalization layers.

Temporal Padding. The model described above is capable of predicting an intent that encompasses the entire input sequence, but cannot be used for sequence labeling tasks, namely slot filling. To create a one-to-one correspondence between input tokens and output slots, Bai et al. (2018) left-pad the input sequence by $k - 1$, where k is the kernel size. We modify this by loosening the causality constraint and instead padding each side by $\frac{k-1}{2}$. Visually, this results in a "centered" convolution that inculcates bidirectional context when computing a feature map. Note that this padding is unnecessary for intent detection, therefore we skip it when training a single-task intent model.

Multi-Task Training. Intent detection and slot filling can either be disjointly learned with dedicated single-task models or jointly learned with a unified multi-task model (Liu and Lane, 2016). In the latter model, we introduce task-specific heads on top of the common representation layer and simultaneously optimize both objectives:

$$\mathcal{L}_{\text{joint}} = \alpha \mathcal{L}_{\text{intent}} + (1 - \alpha)\mathcal{L}_{\text{slot}}$$

for α where $0 \leq \alpha \leq 1$. Empirically, we observe that weighting $\mathcal{L}_{\text{slot}}$ more than $\mathcal{L}_{\text{intent}}$ results in higher performance ($\alpha \approx 0.2$). Our hypothesis is that, because of the comparative difficulty of the slot filling task, the model is required to learn a more robust representation of each utterance, which is nonetheless useful for intent detection.

4 Structured Pruning

Structured vs. Unstructured Pruning. Pruning is one compression technique that removes weights from an over-parameterized model (LeCun et al., 1990), often relying on a heuristic function that ranks weights (or groups of weights) by their importance. Methods for pruning are broadly categorized as unstructured and structured: unstructured pruning allows weights to be removed haphazardly without geometric constraints, but structured pruning induces well-defined sparsity patterns, for example, dropping entire filters in a convolutional layer according to their norm (Molchanov et al., 2016; Li et al., 2017; Anwar et al., 2017). Critically, **the model's true size is not diminished with unstructured pruning**, as without a sparse tensor library, weight matrices with scattered zero *elements* must still be stored (Han et al., 2016). In contrast, structurally pruned models do not rely on such libraries at test-time since non-zero *units* can simply be spliced together.

Pruning Methodology. The structured pruning process is depicted in Figure 1. In each pruning iteration, we rank each filter by its ℓ_2 norm, greedily remove filters with the smallest magnitudes, and splice together non-zero filters in the underlying weight matrix. The deletion of a single filter results in one less output channel, implying we can also remove the corresponding input channel of the subsequent linear layer with a similar splicing operation. Repetitions of this process result in an objectively smaller model because of reductions in the convolutional and linear layer weight matrices. Furthermore, this process does not lead to irregular sparsity patterns, resulting in a general speedup on all hardware platforms.

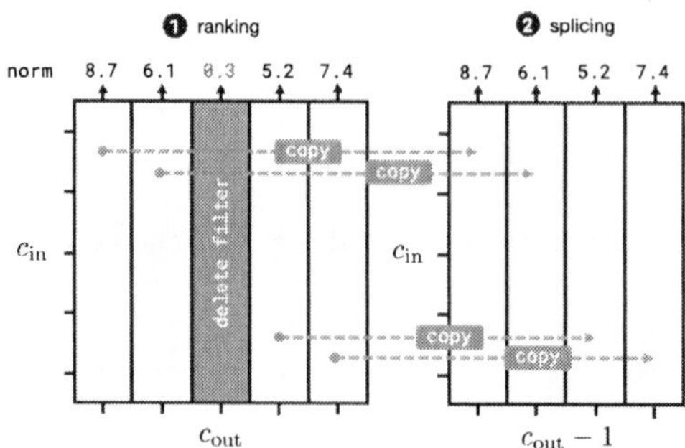

Figure 1: Structured pruning of convolutional models by (1) ranking filters by their ℓ_2 norm, then (2) splicing out the lowest norm filter, resulting in a successively smaller weight matrix. Because each filter convolves input filters c_{in} into one output filter c_{out}, removing a single filter results in $c_{\text{out}} - 1$ output channels.

The heuristic function for ranking filters and whether to re-train the model after a pruning step are important hyperparameters. We experimented with both ℓ_1 and ℓ_2 norms for selecting filters, and found that ℓ_2 slightly outperforms ℓ_1. More complicated heuristic functions, such as deriving filter importance according to gradient saliency (Persand et al., 2020), can also be dropped into our pipeline without modification.

One-Shot vs. Iterative Pruning. Furthermore, when deciding to re-train the model, we experiment with one-shot and iterative pruning (Frankle and Carbin, 2019). One-shot pruning involves repeatedly deleting filters until reaching a desired sparsity level without re-training, whereas iterative pruning interleaves pruning and re-training, such that the model is re-trained to convergence after each pruning step. These re-training steps increase overall training time, but implicitly help the model "reconstruct" deleted filter(s), resulting in significantly better performance. During test-time, however, the pruned model uses significantly fewer resources, as we demonstrate in our acceleration experiments.

5 Tasks and Datasets

We build convolutional models for intent detection and slot filling, two popular natural language understanding tasks in the task-oriented dialog stack. Intent detection is a multi-class classification problem, whereas slot filling is a sequence labeling problem. Formally, given utterance tokens $\mathbf{w} = (w_1, \cdots, w_n)$, models induce a joint distribution $P(y^*_{\text{intent}}, \mathbf{y}^*_{\text{slot}} | \mathbf{w})$ over an intent label y^*_{intent}

Models	ATIS		Snips	
	Intent	Slot	Intent	Slot
Baselines				
Slot-Gated RNN	94.10	95.20	97.00	88.80
Stack Propagation	96.90	95.90	98.00	94.20
DistilBERT (66M)	96.98	95.44	97.94	94.59
BERT (110M)	97.16	96.02	98.26	95.05
Method: No Compression				
Single-Task	94.94	94.01	96.54	85.06
Multi-Task (195K/174K)	94.98	94.30	96.97	84.38
Method: Structured Pruning				
Single-Task	95.45	94.61	96.94	85.11
Multi-Task (97K/87K)	95.39	94.42	97.17	83.81

Table 1: Intent accuracy and slot F1 of baseline models (Goo et al., 2018; Qin et al., 2019; Sanh et al., 2019; Devlin et al., 2019) and our systems on ATIS and Snips. We experiment with single-task and multi-task models. Number of model parameters are shown in parentheses where applicable; multi-task models use the format (ATIS/Snips).

and slot labels $\mathbf{y}^*_{\text{slot}} = (\mathbf{y}^{*(1)}_{\text{slot}}, \cdots, \mathbf{y}^{*(n)}_{\text{slot}})$. These models are typically multi-task: intent and slots predictions are derived with task-specific heads but share a common representation (Liu and Lane, 2016). However, since the intent and slots of an utterance are independent, we can also learn single-task models, where an intent model optimizes $P(y^*_{\text{intent}}|\mathbf{w})$ and a slot model optimizes $P(\mathbf{y}^*_{\text{slot}}|\mathbf{w})$. We experiment with both approaches, although our ultimate compressed model is multi-tasked as aligned with on-device use cases.

Following previous work, we evaluate on ATIS (Hemphill et al., 1990) and Snips (Coucke et al., 2018), both of which are single-turn dialog benchmarks with intent detection and slot filling. ATIS has 4,478/500/893 train/validation/test samples, respectively, with 21 intents and 120 slots. Snips has 13,084/700/700 samples with 7 intents and 72 slots. Our setup follows the same preparation as Zhang et al. (2019).

6 Experiments and Results

We evaluate the performance, compression, and acceleration of our structured pruning approach against several baselines. Note that we do not employ post-hoc compression methods like quantization (Guo, 2018), as they are orthogonal to our core method, and can be utilized at no additional cost to further improve performance on-device.

Params	CR (%)	Pruning		Distillation	
		Intent	Slot	Intent	Slot
195K	0%	94.98	94.30	93.84	94.12
156K	20%	95.39	94.19	94.85	94.22
117K	40%	95.03	94.14	94.51	94.13
78K	60%	95.10	94.12	92.27	94.32
39K	80%	94.40	93.91	90.48	94.05
19K	90%	92.23	93.20	78.28	92.46
9K	95%	88.35	92.19	70.89	89.54
2K	99%	79.49	87.17	70.89	64.75

Table 2: ATIS performance of multi-task models compressed with structured pruning (ours) and knowledge distillation (Hinton et al., 2015) as the compression rate (CR; %) increases. We report intent accuracy and slot F1. Darker shades of red indicate higher absolute performance drops with respect to 100%.

6.1 Benchmark Results

We experiment with both single-task and multi-task models, with and without structured pruning, on ATIS and Snips. The results are displayed in Table 1. Our multi-task model with structured pruning, even with over a 50% reduction in parameters, performs on par with our NO COMPRESSION baselines. On ATIS, our model is comparable to SLOT-GATED RNN (Goo et al., 2018) and is only about 2% worse in accuracy/F1 than BERT. However, we note that our model's slot F1 severely drops off on Snips, possibly because it is a much larger dataset spanning a myriad of domains. Whether our pre-trained embeddings have sufficient explanatory power to scale past common utterances is an open question.

Furthermore, to approximate what information is lost after compression, we analyze which samples' predictions flip from correct to incorrect after structured pruning. We observe that sparser models tend to prefer larger classes; for example, in slot filing, tags are often mislabeled as "outside" in IOB labeling (Tjong and Sang, 2000). This demonstrates a trade-off between preserving non-salient features that work on average for all classes or salient features that accurately discriminate between the most prominent classes. Our model falls on the right end of this spectrum, in that it greedily de-prioritizes representations for inputs that do not contribute as much to aggregate dataset log likelihood.

6.2 Comparison with Distillation

In addition, we compare structured pruning with knowledge distillation, a popular compression technique where a small, student model learns from a large, teacher model by minimizing the KL diver-

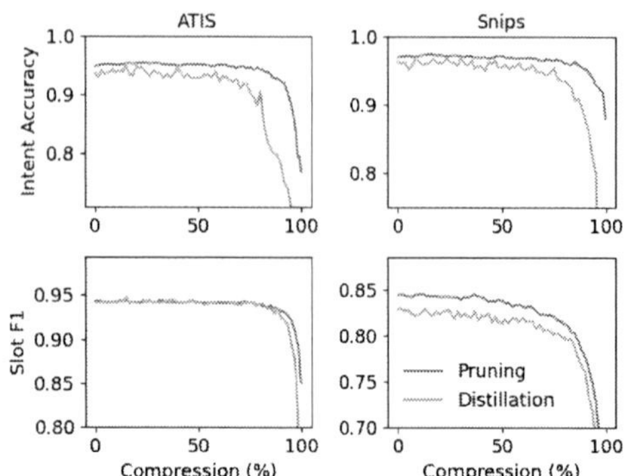

Figure 2: Performance-compression tradeoff curves on ATIS and Snips, comparing multi-task models compressed with structured pruning (ours) and knowledge distillation (Hinton et al., 2015). Pruning curves denote the mean of five compression runs with random restarts. Note that the y-axis ticks are *not* uniform across graphs.

gence between their output distributions (Hinton et al., 2015). Using a multi-task model on ATIS, we compress it with structured pruning and distillation, then examine its performance at varying levels of compression. The results are shown in Table 2. Distillation achieves similar results as structured pruning with 0-50% sparsity, but its performance largely drops off after 80%. Surprisingly, even with extreme compression (99%), structured pruning is about 10% and 20% better on intents and slots, respectively.

Our results show that, in this setting, the iterative refinement of a sparse topology admits an easier optimization problem; learning a smaller model directly is not advantageous, even when it is supervised with a larger model. Furthermore, the iterative nature of structured pruning means it is possible to select a model that optimizes a particular performance-compression trade off along a sparsity curve, as shown in Figure 2. To do the same with distillation requires re-training for a target compression level each time, which is intractable with a large set of hyperparameters.

6.3 Acceleration Experiments

Lastly, to understand how our multi-task model with structured pruning performs without significant computational resources, we benchmark its test-time performance on a CPU and GPU. Specifically, we measure several models' inference times on ATIS and Snips (normalized by the total number of test samples) using an Intel Xeon E3-1270

System	ATIS		Snips	
	CPU ↓	GPU ↓	CPU ↓	GPU ↓
DistilBERT	22.15 ms	1.87 ms	21.81 ms	1.76 ms
BERT	43.19 ms	2.80 ms	43.04 ms	2.72 ms
Pruning	**0.35** ms	**0.37** ms	**0.33** ms	**0.36** ms
Distillation	0.40 ms	0.37 ms	0.38 ms	0.37 ms

Table 3: Average CPU and GPU inference time (in milliseconds) of baselines (Sanh et al., 2019; Devlin et al., 2019) and our multi-task models on ATIS and Snips.

v3 CPU and NVIDIA GTX 1080-TI GPU. Results are shown in Table 3. Empirically, we see that our pruned model results in significant speedups without a GPU compared to both a distilled model and BERT. DistilBERT, which is a strong approximation of BERT, is still $63\times$ slower than our model. We expect that latency disparities on weaker CPUs will be even more extreme, therefore selecting a model that maximizes both task performance and resource-efficiency will be an important consideration for practitioners.

7 Conclusion

In this work, we show that structurally pruned convolutional models achieve competitive performance on intent detection and slot filling at only a fraction of the size of state-of-the-art models. Our method outperforms popular compression methods, such as knowledge distillation, and results in large CPU speedups compared to BERT and DistilBERT.

Acknowledgments

Thanks to our anonymous reviewers for their helpful comments and feedback.

References

Afzal Ahmad and Muhammad Adeel Pasha. 2020. FF-Conv: An FPGA-Based Accelerator for Fast Convolution Layers in Convolutional Neural Networks. *ACM Transactions on Embedded Computing Systems.*

Sajid Anwar, Kyuyeon Hwang, and Wonyong Sung. 2017. Structured Pruning of Deep Convolutional Neural Networks. *ACM Journal on Emerging Technologies in Computing Systems (JETC).*

Shaojie Bai, J. Zico Kolter, and Vladlen Koltun. 2018. An Empirical Evaluation of Generic Convolutional and Recurrent Networks for Sequence Modeling. *arXiv preprint arXiv:1803.01271.*

Daniel G. Bobrow, Ronald M. Kaplan, Martin Kay, Donald A. Norman, Henry S. Thompson, and Terry Winograd. 1977. GUS, A Frame-Driven Dialog System. *Artificial Intelligence*.

Yu Cheng, Duo Wang, Pan Zhou, and Tao Zhang. 2017. A Survey of Model Compression and Acceleration for Deep Neural Networks. *arXiv preprint arXiv:1710.09282*.

Ronan Collobert, Jason Weston, Léon Bottou, Michael Karlen, Koray Kavukcuoglu, and Pavel P. Kuksa. 2011. Natural Language Processing (Almost) from Scratch. *Journal of Machine Learning Research (JMLR)*.

Alice Coucke, Alaa Saade, Adrien Ball, Théodore Bluche, Alexandre Caulier, David Leroy, Clément Doumouro, Thibault Gisselbrecht, Francesco Caltagirone, Thibaut Lavril, Maël Primet, and Joseph Dureau. 2018. Snips Voice Platform: an embedded Spoken Language Understanding system for private-by-design voice interfaces. *arXiv preprint arXiv:1805.10190*.

Shrey Desai, Geoffrey Goh, Arun Babu, and Ahmed Aly. 2020. Lightweight Convolutional Representations for On-Device Natural Language Processing. *arXiv preprint arXiv:2002.01535*.

Jacob Devlin, Ming-Wei Chang, Kenton Lee, and Kristina Toutanova. 2019. BERT: Pre-training of Deep Bidirectional Transformers for Language Understanding. In *Proceedings of the Conference of the North American Chapter of the Association for Computational Linguistics: Human Language Technologies (NAACL-HLT)*.

Jonathan Frankle and Michael Carbin. 2019. The Lottery Ticket Hypothesis: Finding Sparse, Trainable Neural Networks. In *Proceedings of the International Conference on Learning Representations (ICLR)*.

Jianfeng Gao, Michel Galley, and Lihong Li. 2018. Neural Approaches to Conversational AI. In *Proceedings of the 56th Annual Meeting of the Association for Computational Linguistics (NAACL): Tutorial Abstracts*.

Jonas Gehring, Michael Auli, David Grangier, Denis Yarats, and Yann N. Dauphin. 2017. Convolutional Sequence to Sequence Learning. In *Proceedings of the International Conference on Machine Learning (ICML)*.

Chih-Wen Goo, Guang Gao, Yun-Kai Hsu, Chih-Li Huo, Tsung-Chieh Chen, Keng-Wei Hsu, and Yun-Nung Chen. 2018. Slot-Gated Modeling for Joint Slot Filling and Intent Prediction. In *Proceedings of the Conference of the North American Chapter of the Association for Computational Linguistics: Human Language Technologies (NAACL-HLT)*.

Mitchell A Gordon, Kevin Duh, and Nicholas Andrews. 2020. Compressing BERT: Studying the Effects of Weight Pruning on Transfer Learning. *arXiv preprint arXiv:2002.08307*.

Yunhui Guo. 2018. A Survey on Methods and Theories of Quantized Neural Networks. *arXiv preprint arXiv:1808.04752*.

Sonal Gupta, Rushin Shah, Mrinal Mohit, Anuj Kumar, and Mike Lewis. 2018. Semantic Parsing for Task Oriented Dialog using Hierarchical Representations. In *Proceedings of the Conference on Empirical Methods in Natural Language Processing (EMNLP)*.

Song Han, Huizi Mao, and William J. Dally. 2016. Deep Compression: Compressing Deep Neural Network with Pruning, Trained Quantization and Huffman Coding. In *Proceedings of the International Conference on Learning Representations (ICLR)*.

Charles T. Hemphill, John J. Godfrey, and George R. Doddington. 1990. The ATIS Spoken Language Systems Pilot Corpus. In *Speech and Natural Language: Proceedings of a Workshop Held at Hidden Valley, Pennsylvania*.

Matthew Henderson. 2015. Machine Learning for Dialog State Tracking: A Review. In *Proceedings of The First International Workshop on Machine Learning in Spoken Language Processing*.

Geoffrey E. Hinton, Oriol Vinyals, and Jeffrey Dean. 2015. Distilling the Knowledge in a Neural Network. *arXiv preprint arXiv:1503.02531*.

Xiaoqi Jiao, Yichun Yin, Lifeng Shang, Xin Jiang, Xiao Chen, Linlin Li, Fang Wang, and Qun Liu. 2020. TinyBERT: Distilling BERT for Natural Language Understanding. *arXiv preprint arXiv:1909.10351*.

Yoon Kim. 2014. Convolutional Neural Networks for Sentence Classification. In *Proceedings of the Conference on Empirical Methods in Natural Language Processing (EMNLP)*.

Diederik P. Kingma and Jimmy Ba. 2015. Adam: A Method for Stochastic Optimization. *Proceedings of the International Conference on Learning Representations (ICLR)*.

Zornitsa Kozareva and Sujith Ravi. 2018. Fast & Small On-device Neural Networks for Short Text Natural Language Processing. In *Proceedings of the NeurIPS Workshop on Machine Learning on the Phone and other Consumer Devices (MLPCD)*.

Yann LeCun, John S. Denker, and Sara A. Solla. 1990. Optimal Brain Damage. In *Proceedings of the Conference on Neural Information Processing Systems (NeurIPS)*.

Hao Li, Asim Kadav, Igor Durdanovic, Hanan Samet, and Hans Peter Graf. 2017. Pruning Filters for Efficient ConvNets. In *Proceedings of the International Conference on Learning Representations (ICLR)*.

Ziheng Lin, Yan Gu, and Samarjit Chakraborty. 2010. Tuning Machine-Learning Algorithms for Battery-Operated Portable Devices. In *Proceedings of the Asia Information Retrieval Symposium (AIRS)*.

Bing Liu and Ian Lane. 2016. Attention-Based Recurrent Neural Network Models for Joint Intent Detection and Slot Filling. In *Proceedings of the Annual Conference of the International Speech Communication Association (INTERSPEECH)*.

Andrea K. McIntosh, Safwat Hassan, and Abram Hindle. 2018. What can Android mobile app developers do about the energy consumption of machine learning? *Empirical Software Engineering*.

Pavlo Molchanov, Stephen Tyree, Tero Karras, Timo Aila, and Jan Kautz. 2016. Pruning Convolutional Neural Networks for Resource Efficient Inference. In *Proceedings of the International Conference on Learning Representations (ICLR)*.

Jeffrey Pennington, Richard Socher, and Christopher Manning. 2014. GloVe: Global Vectors for Word Representation. In *Proceedings of the Conference on Empirical Methods in Natural Language Processing (EMNLP)*.

Kaveena Persand, Andrew Anderson, and David Gregg. 2020. Composition of Saliency Metrics for Channel Pruning with a Myopic Oracle. *arXiv preprint arXiv:2004.03376*.

Libo Qin, Wanxiang Che, Yangming Li, Haoyang Wen, and Ting Liu. 2019. A Stack-Propagation Framework with Token-Level Intent Detection for Spoken Language Understanding. In *Proceedings of the Conference on Empirical Methods in Natural Language Processing and the International Joint Conference on Natural Language Processing (EMNLP-IJCNLP)*.

Abhinav Rastogi, Xiaoxue Zang, Srinivas Sunkara, Raghav Gupta, and Pranav Khaitan. 2020. Towards Scalable Multi-domain Conversational Agents: The Schema-Guided Dialogue Dataset. In *Proceedings of the AAAI Conference on Artificial Intelligence (AAAI)*.

Sujith Ravi and Zornitsa Kozareva. 2018. Self-Governing Neural Networks for On-Device Short Text Classification. In *Proceedings of the Conference on Empirical Methods in Natural Language Processing (EMNLP)*.

Victor Sanh, Lysandre Debut, Julien Chaumond, and Thomas Wolf. 2019. DistilBERT, a distilled version of BERT: smaller, faster, cheaper and lighter. *arXiv preprint: arXiv:1910.01108*.

Nitish Srivastava, Geoffrey E. Hinton, Alex Krizhevsky, Ilya Sutskever, and Ruslan Salakhutdinov. 2014. Dropout: A Simple Way to Prevent Neural Networks from Overfitting. *Journal of Machine Learning Research (JMLR)*.

Raphael Tang, Yao Lu, Linqing Liu, Lili Mou, Olga Vechtomova, and Jimmy Lin. 2019. Distilling Task-Specific Knowledge from BERT into Simple Neural Networks. *arXiv preprint arXiv:1903.12136*.

Erik F. Tjong and Kim Sang. 2000. Transforming a chunker to a parser. In *Proceedings of the Meeting of Computational Linguistics in the Netherlands (CLIN)*.

Ashish Vaswani, Noam Shazeer, Niki Parmar, Jakob Uszkoreit, Llion Jones, Aidan N. Gomez, Lukasz Kaiser, and Illia Polosukhin. 2017. Attention is All you Need. In *Proceedings of the Conference on Neural Information Processing Systems (NeurIPS)*.

Yu Wang, Yilin Shen, and Hongxia Jin. 2018. A Bi-Model Based RNN Semantic Frame Parsing Model for Intent Detection and Slot Filling. In *Proceedings of the Conference of the North American Chapter of the Association for Computational Linguistics: Human Language Technologies (NAACL-HLT)*.

Krzysztof Wróbel, Marcin Pietroń, Maciej Wielgosz, Michal Karwatowski, and Kazimierz Wiatr. 2018. Convolutional neural network compression for natural language processing. *arXiv preprint arXiv:1805.10796*.

Zhao Yan, Nan Duan, Peng Chen, Ming Zhou, Jianshe Zhou, and Zhoujun Li. 2017. Building Task-Oriented Dialogue Systems for Online Shopping. In *Proceedings of the AAAI Conference on Artificial Intelligence (AAAI)*.

Hong-Jun Yoon, Sarah Robinson, J. Blair Christian, John X. Qiu, and Georgia D. Tourassi. 2018. Filter pruning of Convolutional Neural Networks for text classification: A case study of cancer pathology report comprehension. In *Proceedings of the IEEE EMBS International Conference on Biomedical & Health Informatics (BHI)*.

Zhou Yu, Ziyu Xu, Alan W Black, and Alexander Rudnicky. 2016. Strategy and Policy Learning for Non-Task-Oriented Conversational Systems. In *Proceedings of the Annual Meeting of the Special Interest Group on Discourse and Dialogue (SIGDIAL)*.

Ofir Zafrir, Guy Boudoukh, Peter Izsak, and Moshe Wasserblat. 2019. Q8BERT: Quantized 8Bit BERT. *arXiv preprint arXiv:1910.06188*.

Chenwei Zhang, Yaliang Li, Nan Du, Wei Fan, and Philip Yu. 2019. Joint Slot Filling and Intent Detection via Capsule Neural Networks. In *Proceedings of the Annual Meeting of the Association for Computational Linguistics (ACL)*.

Zheng Zhang, Ryuichi Takanobu, Minlie Huang, and Xiaoyan Zhu. 2020. Recent Advances and Challenges in Task-oriented Dialog System. *arXiv preprint arXiv:2003.07490.*

DLGNet: A Transformer-based Model for Dialogue Response Generation

Oluwatobi Olabiyi
Capital One Conversation Research
Vienna VA
oluwatobi.olabiyi@capitalone.com

Erik T. Mueller
Capital One Conversation Research
Vienna VA
erik.mueller@capitalone.com

Abstract

Neural dialogue models, despite their successes, still suffer from lack of relevance, diversity, and in many cases coherence in their generated responses. On the other hand, transformer-based models such as GPT-2 have demonstrated an excellent ability to capture long-range structures in language modeling tasks. In this paper, we present DLGNet, a transformer-based model for dialogue modeling. We specifically examine the use of DLGNet for multi-turn dialogue response generation. In our experiments, we evaluate DLGNet on the open-domain Movie Triples dataset and the closed-domain Ubuntu Dialogue dataset. DLGNet models, although trained with only the maximum likelihood objective, achieve significant improvements over state-of-the-art multi-turn dialogue models. They also produce best performance to date on the two datasets based on several metrics, including BLEU, ROUGE, and distinct n-gram. Our analysis shows that the performance improvement is mostly due to the combination of (1) the long-range transformer architecture with (2) the injection of random informative paddings. Other contributing factors include the joint modeling of dialogue context and response, and the 100% tokenization coverage from the byte pair encoding (BPE).

1 Introduction

Recent successes of pretrained transformer-based language models, such as BERT (Devlin et al., 2019), GPT(-2) (Radford and Salimans, 2018; Radford et al., 2019), Transformer-XL (Dai et al., 2019), XLNet (Yang et al., 2019), and ERNIE(2.0) (Sun et al., 2019a,b), have led to state-of-the-art performance on many natural language understanding (NLU) tasks including sentence classification, named entity recognition, sentence similarity, and question answering. The exceptional performance

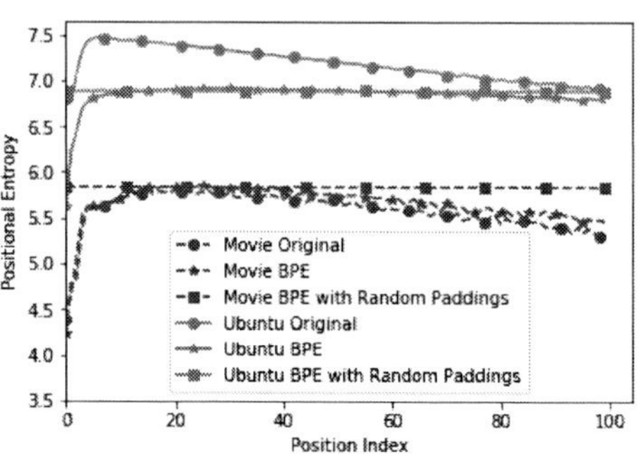

Figure 1: **Positional Entropy for Movie and Ubuntu datasets -** Applying a greedy training objective to the original and BPE datasets can achieve low overall entropy just by overfitting to low entropy regions, resulting in short and generic responses. Injecting random paddings into the data does not suffer from this problem and can be used to train transformer architectures due to their lack of recurrent propagations.

of transformer-based language models is due to their ability to capture long-term temporal dependencies in the input sequence. This attribute should be very beneficial to dialogue modeling, especially in multi-turn scenarios. Most of the existing neural dialogue response generation models are based on recurrent neural networks (Sutskever et al., 2014; Vinyals and Le, 2015; Li et al., 2016a; Serban et al., 2016; Xing et al., 2017; Serban et al., 2017b,a; Li et al., 2016b; Zhang et al., 2018a; Olabiyi et al., 2018, 2019a).

These models have yielded promising results by generating mostly coherent responses given the dialogue context. However, most of them, including the state-of-the-art models trained with naturalistic dialogue data, still perform well below the human level. Generated responses tend to be either generic, out-of-context, or disproportionately short. Previous work points to some causes of these limitations:

54

Proceedings of the 2nd Workshop on Natural Language Processing for Conversational AI, pages 54–62
July 9, 2020. ©2020 Association for Computational Linguistics

i) Training data: The presence of high frequency generic utterances (utterance-level semantic redundancy), such as "I don't know", "I'm not sure", and high frequency generic n-gram tokens (word-level syntactic redundancy), such as "I", "I am", leading to the concave positional entropy profile of dialogue datasets, see Fig. 1), which makes learning difficult, resulting in short and generic responses. *ii) Short-range Model Architecture:* Short-range model architectures that capture limited temporal dependencies. *iii) Out-of-vocabulary Problem:* Less frequent (usually more informative) words mapped to the out-of-vocabulary token <UNK>, leading to generation of a large number of <UNK> tokens. *iv) Exposure Bias:* The discrepancy in model behavior between training and inference, which limits the informativeness of the responses *iv) Training Objective:* The limitations of the maximum likelihood training objective.

In this paper, we propose DLGNet, a transformer-based model for multi-turn dialogue modeling that addresses some of the highlighted problems above. The use of a transformer architecture allows DLGNet to capture long-term temporal dependencies in the dialogue data better than the existing RNN-based architectures (Vaswani et al., 2017). However, applying a vanilla Seq2Seq transformer (Vaswani et al., 2017) and its multi-turn variants, such as ReCoSa (Zhang et al., 2019), for dialogue modeling does not work well because of the semantic redundancy in dialogue data. To overcome this, DLGNet models the joint distribution of the context and response instead of the conditional distribution of the response given the context, usually employed in Seq2Seq frameworks (Vinyals and Le, 2015; Serban et al., 2016; Olabiyi et al., 2018; Vaswani et al., 2017). DLGNet also addresses the syntactic redundancy in dialogue data by appending random paddings before and after the input data. This helps to break down the learning barrier from the concave entropy profile of human conversation data, as shown in Fig. 1. The flattening of the entropy profile also provides regularization during training, and reduces even the extent of the exposure bias problem. Finally, to avoid the out-of-vocabulary problem, DLGNet uses byte pair encoding (BPE) similar to GPT-2 (Radford et al., 2019) to provide 100% coverage for any Unicode input and output texts. Given all these proposed changes, we train DLGNet models using only the maximum likelihood objective. DLGNet models,

Table 1: Example of generated responses from DLGNet models

Item	Utterance
Movie	
Context_0	says he wanted food . <person> . he wanted the gold .
Context_1	how ' s he going to want the gold ? he couldn ' t even know we had it .
Groundtruth	he . he could have been watching us .
DLGNet-117M [1]	he knew we did .
DLGNet-345M	<person> ' s just say he doesn ' t have enough to buy a trailer and seeds . i ' ll write him up as a decorated veteran of the united states army .
DLGNet-117M_Random [2]	<person> , you know the break-in , i might not be able to afford it .
DLGNet-345M_Random	are you going to preach now ?
Context_0	what are you thinking ?
Context_1	that i want you to take me home .
Groundtruth	now ? we just –
DLGNet-117M	now ? we ' re going now ? what about tomorrow ?
DLGNet-345M	now ? we ' re on the run !
DLGNet-117M_Random	now ?
DLGNet-345M_Random	no . keep me company . <person> offers its rewards . <person> appetit .
Ubuntu	
Context_0	The netboot one is suppose to download packages from the net.
Context_1	like the ones to be installed? or the installed to be run?
Groundtruth	Installed. The netbook also features the non-graphical installer.
DLGNet-117M	the installed to be run.
DLGNet-345M	the ones to be installed.
DLGNet-117M_Random	I think the netboot one is the one that is installed to the net.
DLGNet-345M_Random	the ones to be installed to.
Context_0	DJones: update manager won't detect 12.04.1 as a new version if you are already running 12.04, because 12.04.1 = 12.04 + lots of package updates
Groundtruth	DJones I am running 10.04.
DLGNet-117M	I'm not sure what you mean by "update manager won't detect"
DLGNet-345M	I see. I guess I'll just do a fresh install.
DLGNet-117M_Random	I'm running 12.04.1, and I'm not running 12.04.1.
DLGNet-345M_Random	I'm not sure what you mean by "update manager"

despite being trained with only the maximum likelihood objective, demonstrate state-of-the-art performance on the Movie and Ubuntu datasets, as measured in terms of BLEU, ROUGE, and distinct n-gram scores.

2 Task Description

Consider a dialogue sample consisting of a sequence of N utterances, $\mathbf{x} = (x_1, x_2, \cdots, x_N)$, where each utterance $x_i = (x_i^1, x_i^2, \cdots, x_i^{M_i})$ contains a variable-length sequence of M_i word tokens such that $x_i^j \in V$ for vocabulary V. At any time step i, the dialogue history is given by $\mathbf{x}_i = (x_1, x_2, \cdots, x_i)$. The dialogue response generation task can be defined as follows: Given a dialogue history $\mathbf{x}_i$, generate a response $y_i = (y_i^1, y_i^2, \cdots, y_i^{T_i})$, where T_i is the number of generated tokens such that the distribution of the generated response $P(y_i)$ is indistinguishable from that of the ground truth $P(x_{i+1})$. The distribution of the model output sequence can be factored by the

---

[1] Model with pretraining

[2] Model with random initialization (without pretraining)

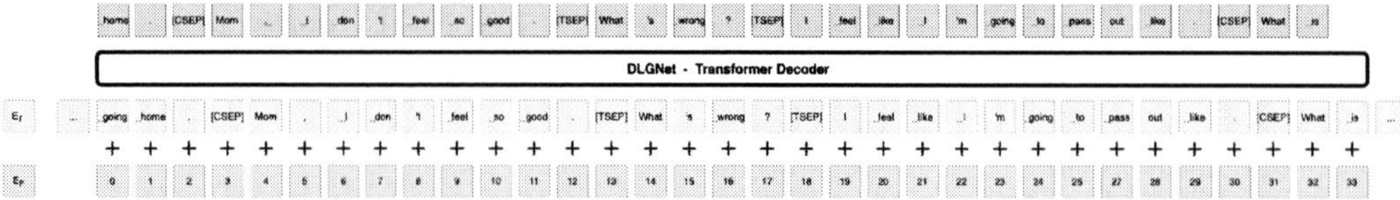

Figure 2: **An example of DLGNet input and output** consisting of a 3-turn conversation sample separated by [TSEP] tokens, combined with random informative paddings, before and after. Paddings and conversations are separated by [CSEP] tokens.

product rule:

$$P(y_i|\mathbf{x}_i) = \prod_{j=2}^{T_i} P\big(y_i^j | y_i^{1:j-1}, \mathbf{x}_i\big) \qquad (1)$$

where $y_i^{1:j-1} = (y_i^1, \cdots, y_i^{j-1})$.

The MLE objective based on the conditional distribution of (1) can be expressed as

$$L_{\text{Cond}} = -\log P_\theta(y_i|\mathbf{x}_i) \qquad (2)$$

where θ are the model parameters.

This formulation, known as Seq2Seq, originated from machine translation (Sutskever et al., 2014) and assumes that the context-response pair in the training examples are fairly unique. Seq2Seq is the basis of most of the previous work on dialogue modeling. The framework, however, does not account for the semantic and syntactic redundancy in human conversations as pointed out by Li et al. (2016a).

3 DLGNet Model Description

In order to address the semantic redundancy, we propose to jointly model both the context and the response as an alternative to the mutual information objective (Li et al., 2016a; Zhang et al., 2018b). The resulting distribution and the objective function can then be respectively expressed as

$$P(y_i, \mathbf{x}_i) = P(y_i|\mathbf{x}_i)P(\mathbf{x}_i) \qquad (3)$$

$$L_{\text{Joint}} = -\log P_\theta(y_i|\mathbf{x}_i) - \log P_\theta(\mathbf{x}_i) \qquad (4)$$

While (3) addresses the semantic redundancy, it does not address the syntactic redundancy coming from the concave positional entropy profile of dialogue data. To circumvent this, we append random informative paddings (sampled from the dataset) before ($\mathbf{x}_i^b$) and after ($\mathbf{x}_i^a$), the dialogue example of interest, leading to

$$P(\mathbf{x}_i^a, y_i, \mathbf{x}_i, \mathbf{x}_i^b) = P(\mathbf{x}_i^a)P(y_i|\mathbf{x}_i)P(\mathbf{x}_i)P(\mathbf{x}_i^b) \qquad (5)$$

and

$$L_{\text{DLGNet}} = -\log P_\theta(\mathbf{x}_i^a) - \log P_\theta(y_i|\mathbf{x}_i) \\ -\log P_\theta(\mathbf{x}_i) - \log P_\theta(\mathbf{x}_i^b) \qquad (6)$$

since $\mathbf{x}_i^b$ and $\mathbf{x}_i^a$ are independent of $(y_i, \mathbf{x}_i)$. As we see from the resulting entropy profile in Fig. 1, appending random paddings circumvents the adverse effect of syntactic redundancy in dialogue data on model training. The conditional distribution $P(y_i|\mathbf{x}_i)$ in (1) is then just an inference on the joint distribution of (5).

DLGNet adopts GPT-2's autoregressive transformer architecture (Radford et al., 2019) using only the decoder part of the original transformer architecture (Vaswani et al., 2017) since there is no need for a separate encoder network (see Fig. 2). Autoregressive transformer models use multiple layers of masked multi-head self-attention to map a sequence of input tokens to a sequence of output tokens (i.e., the input sequence token shifted one position to the right). During inference, at each step, the model is autoregressive, consuming the previously generated token as additional input when generating the next. There are some basic conceptual differences between autoregressive architectures based on transformers and those based on recurrent neural networks (RNNs). For instance, while the output of an RNN layer depends on only the immediate previous output, a transformer layer output consists of attention over all previous outputs. Due to this lack of ordering in transformer architectures, the position representation is usually passed along with the input tokens into the model (Vaswani et al., 2017).

In order to take advantage and evaluate the impact of pretrained parameters, we use two model configurations i.e., (i) **DLGNet-117M** - with 117M parameters, 12 attention layers, and a hidden state size of 767, and (ii) **DLGNet-345M** - with 345M parameters, 24 attention layers, and a hidden state size of 1024; similar to the publicly available GPT-2 models (Radford et al., 2019).

Table 2: Automatic Evaluation of Model Performance

Model	Movie				Ubuntu			
	Relevance		Diversity		Relevance		Diversity	
	BLEU	ROUGE	DIST-1/2	NASL	BLEU	ROUGE	DIST-1/2	NASL
HRED	0.0474	0.0384	0.0026/0.0056	0.535	0.0177	0.0483	0.0203/0.0466	0.892
VHRED	0.0606	0.1181	0.0048/0.0163	0.831	0.0171	0.0855	0.0297/0.0890	0.873
hredGAN_u	0.0493	0.2416	0.0167/0.1306	0.884	0.0137	0.0716	0.0260/0.0847	1.379
hredGAN_w	0.0613	0.3244	0.0179/0.1720	**1.540**	0.0216	0.1168	0.0516/0.1821	1.098
DAIM	0.0155	0.0077	0.0005/0.0006	0.721	0.0015	0.0131	0.0013/0.0048	**1.626**
aBoots_u_cat	0.0880	0.4063	0.0624/0.3417	0.918	0.0210	0.1491	0.0523/0.1795	1.040
aBoots_w_cat	0.0940	0.3973	0.0613/0.3476	1.016	0.0233	0.2292	0.1288/0.5190	1.208
DLGNet-117M_Random	0.1796	0.4338	0.1198/0.4578	1.011	0.0215	0.1978	0.1827/0.4074	0.829
DLGNet-345M_Random	0.2682	0.4881	0.1286/0.4612	0.907	**0.0315**	0.2041	0.1927/0.4468	0.794
DLGNet-117M	0.1872	0.4346	0.1232/0.4506	0.982	0.0279	0.2191	0.2228/0.4953	0.746
DLGNet-345M	**0.2742**	**0.4945**	**0.1282/0.4736**	0.895	**0.0309**	**0.2409**	**0.2436/0.5632**	0.759

4 Model Training

We trained the small DLGNet-117M and the medium DLGNet-345M models on multi-turn dialogue datasets initialized with either random noise or pretrained language model parameters. The models are trained end-to-end using the Adaptive Moment Estimation (Adam) stochastic gradient descent algorithm with a learning rate of 0.001. The maximum sequence length is 1024. Due to GPU memory limitations, we use a batch size of 2 and accumulate gradients over 5 iterations, making the effective batch size 10. Both models are trained until the training perplexity on the dialogue datasets reaches a steady state. Finally, the models are implemented, trained, and evaluated using Python and the TensorFlow deep learning framework.

5 Experiments

5.1 Setup

We evaluated DLGNet models on the Movie Triples and Ubuntu Dialogue corpora randomly split into training, validation, and test sets, using 90%, 5%, and 5% proportions. Since we use BPE with 100% tokenization coverage, we performed no preprocessing of the datasets whatsoever. For each training example, however, we randomly sample a target conversation and two independent padding chunks from the dataset to fill up the maximum input sequence length. We append the paddings to the target conversation, one before, and one after, separated by token [C_SEP]. The target conversation in each training example in turn consists of utterances that are separated by token [T_SEP] as shown in Fig. 2.

The Movie dataset (Serban et al., 2016) spans a wide range of topics with few spelling mistakes and contains about 240,000 dialogue triples, which makes it suitable for studying the relevance-diversity tradeoff in multi-turn conversations (Zhang et al., 2018b). The Ubuntu dialog dataset extracted from the Ubuntu Relay Chat Channel (Serban et al., 2017b) contains about 1.85 million conversations with an average of 5 utterances per conversation. This dataset is ideal for training dialogue models that can provide expert knowledge/recommendation in domain-specific conversations.

We compare DLGNet multi-turn dialogue performance with existing state-of-the-art dialogue models including (V)HRED[3] (Serban et al., 2016, 2017b), DAIM[4] (Zhang et al., 2018b), hredGAN (Olabiyi et al., 2018), and aBoots (Olabiyi et al., 2019b). Note that DAIM is single turn and does not use a multi-turn dialogue context, but we have included it here for completeness. We compare how the models perform based on informativeness (a combination of relevance and diversity metrics) of generated responses. For relevance, we adopted BLEU-2 (Papineni et al., 2002) and ROUGE-2 (Lin, 2014) scores. For diversity, we adopted distinct unigram (DIST-1) and bigram (DIST-2) (Li et al., 2016a) scores as well as normalized average sequence length (NASL), similar to Olabiyi et al. (2018).

All models are evaluated in autoregressive mode, i.e., we pass a multi-turn dialogue context to the model inputs and the models generate a sequence of response tokens using the context and all the previously generated tokens until the end-of-sequence

---

[3]implementation obtained from https://github.com/julianser/hed-dlg-truncated

[4]implementation obtained from https://github.com/dreasysnail/converse_GAN

token is reached. All models are greedily sampled to generate the model outputs. It is worth noting that, for DLGNet models, we search for the optimum top_k between 0 and 20 inclusive that maximizes the overall BLEU-2 (relevance) score of the validation set using the top_k sampling strategy (Radford et al., 2019). It turns out that for all DLGNet models, the optimum top_k is 1 across datasets, which is equivalent to greedy sampling.

6 Results and Discussion

6.1 Quantitative Evaluation

We report the quantitative measures in Table 2. The transformer-based DLGNet provides a significant improvement in response generation performance over existing methods such as (V)HRED, hredGAN, DAIM, and adversarial bootstrapping (aBoots), all of which are based on recurrent neural networks. In fact, DLGNet achieves the best performance to date on the Movie triples and Ubuntu dialogue datasets in terms of BLEU, ROUGE, and distinct n-gram scores. This indicates that, despite being trained only with the maximum likelihood objective, the autoregressive transformer architecture in conjunction with the random padding injection, is able to overcome some of the problems that have plagued existing dialogue models such as semantic and syntactic redundancy, and exposure bias. Also contributing to the models' performance improvement is the 100% input coverage from the BPE encoding, which eliminates the generation of <UNK> tokens (this is especially helpful for the Ubuntu dataset with a large number of out-of-vocabulary tokens) as well as the joint modeling of the context and response. Also, in contrast to existing work reporting a trade-off between relevance and diversity (Zhang et al., 2018b; Li et al., 2016a,b), we observe that relevance performance improves with diversity performance in DLGNet models. It is worth pointing out, however, that DLGNet models tend to generate shorter responses than adversarially trained models (hredGAN and aBoots). This indicates that the models still suffer from the impact of using only the maximum likelihood training objective. Alleviating this problem with an adversarial training objective similar to aBoots and or hredGAN should further improve performance and will be considered in our future work.

6.2 Qualitative Evaluation

Random samples of the model outputs are shown in Tables 1 and 4. One striking observation is the high level of coherence in the generated responses from DLGNet models. The models are able to capture both short- and long-term temporal dependencies in their responses. The models give responses that are relevant to the topic of the discussion, and are able to answer posed questions with answer choices. Also, they don't simply generate the all-too-common phrase "I'm not sure" like existing models; they are able to point to areas of the context they are uncertain about (see the Ubuntu section of Table 1).

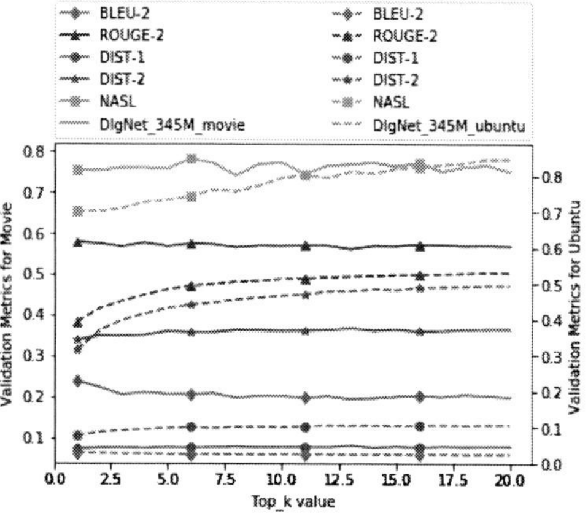

Figure 3: Relevance vs. diversity tradeoff with top_k sampling for DLGNet-345M models.

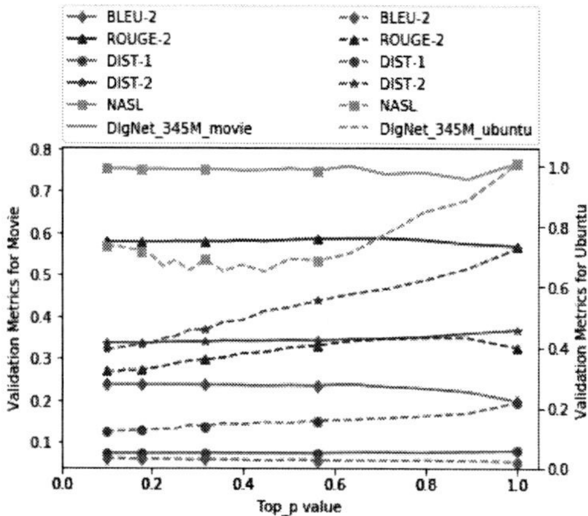

Figure 4: Relevance vs. diversity tradeoff with top_p sampling for DLGNet-345M models.

7 Ablation Studies on DLGNet Models with Random Informative Padding

In this section, we carry out a more detailed analysis and discussion of different configurations of DLGNet models as well as their performance across datasets, using the evaluation results in Table 2.

7.1 Open vs. Closed Domain Dataset

From Table 2, we observe that the performance improvement achieved by DLGNet models over existing models is higher for the open-domain Movie Triples dataset than for the closed-domain Ubuntu Dialogue dataset with or without pretraining. While the performance difference could be due to the size of the dataset, it could also indicate that closed-domain dialogue responses are inherently more difficult to learn, even for large and expressive models such as the DLGNet transformer.

7.2 Effect of Model Pretraining

Although models with pretraining generally perform better than ones trained with random initialization, we observe that the performance difference is not significant. This shows that the performance of the DLGNet is mostly due to the multi-layer self attention model architecture rather than the scaffolding achieved from language model pretraining. We observe similar behavior across datasets. However, pretraining seems to be consistently more helpful for open-domain datasets versus closed-domain datasets. This might be because the distribution of the language data used for pretraining is similar to the open-domain dataset but different from the closed-domain dataset. Also, models without pretraining tend to generate longer responses on average compare to those with pretraining. This indicates that model pretraining also plays a role in the relevance-diversity tradeoff.

7.3 Effect of Model Size

We also compare the small (DLGNet-117M) and large (DLGNet-345M) models. We observe that there is a significant performance improvement of the larger over the smaller model on the Movie dataset (about 50%), but a smaller performance improvement on the Ubuntu dataset. It's also surprising that the larger model doesn't overfit to the Movie dataset. Overfitting might have been prevented by the injection of random padding into the input data, which regularizes the model training by artificially inducing high entropy into the data.

7.4 Relevance vs. Diversity Tradeoff

The results in Table 2 show state-of-the-art relevance performance with some compromise on the response length. Here, we explore the possibility of generating longer and more diverse responses with the trained models and estimate the effect on the relevance scores. For this experiment, we chose the larger DLGNet-345M models of both datasets and tried two sampling techniques, i.e., top_k (Radford et al., 2019) and top_p nucleus (Holtzman et al., 2019; Zellers et al., 2019) sampling strategies on the validation sets. The trajectory of the evaluation metrics with increasing top_k and top_p values are shown Figs. 3 and 4 respectively. With top_k sampling, increasing the top_k value increases the response length at the expense of relevance metrics like BLEU for both datasets, as expected. However, the response length increase is more significant on the Ubuntu dataset than the Movie dataset. It is also surprising that the ROGUE-2 score for Ubuntu increases with increasing top_k value, which is the reverse of the case for the Movie dataset. Also, Fig. 3 shows that it is more advantageous to trade off relevance for diversity on the Ubuntu dataset compare to the Movie dataset. This is probably due to the size and closed-domain nature of the Ubuntu dataset, which makes it more difficult to learn with the maximum likelihood estimation only.

We observe a similar pattern with the top_p nucleus sampling in Fig. 4. This reinforces the fact that greedy sampling may be sufficient for open-domain datasets such as Movie.

8 Further Ablation Studies on DLGNet Models

We also set out to analyze the features of DLGNet that make it suitable for multi-turn dialogue modeling. We train both DLGNet-117M and DLGNet-345M models on both datasets, but replace the random informative paddings with static paddings using a pad token. Below are the definitions of the model configuration factors considered:

1.) Multi-turn Data (M): Training data is variable-length multi-turn data padded to a fixed length. This helps to evaluate the effect of using random informative padding.

2.) Single-turn Data (S): Training data is variable-length single-turn data padded to a fixed length. This helps to evaluate the effect of number of turns.

3.) Joint model (Joint): DLGNet models are

Table 3: Ablation Performance of DLGNet Models with Static Padding

| Model | Movie | | | | Ubuntu | | | |
| | Relevance | | Diversity | | Relevance | | Diversity | |
	BLEU	ROUGE	DIST-1/2	NASL	BLEU	ROUGE	DIST-1/2	NASL
DLGNet-117M								
S-Joint with BPE	~0.0	~0.0	0.0400/0.1502	0.072	~0.0	0.0004	0.1946/0.4636	0.064
S-Cond with BPE	0.0013	0.0296	0.0134/0.0482	3.582	~0.0	0.0083	0.0723/0.1470	0.890
M-Joint with BPE	0.1825	0.1321	0.0346/0.0838	0.610	0.0012	0.1172	0.1719/0.3482	0.2937
M-Cond with BPE	0.0096	0.0628	0.0088/0.0394	3.425	0.0048	0.0766	0.0500/0.1454	2.372
M-Joint with Basic Tokenizer	0.0518	0.0630	0.0176/0.0540	1.101	0.0030	0.0384	0.0465/0.0949	0.566
M-Cond with Basic Tokenizer	0.0149	0.1628	0.0394/0.1770	1.472	~0.0	0.0136	0.2211/0.4192	0.281
DLGNet-345M								
S-Joint with BPE	~0.0	~0.0	~0.0/~0.0	0.072	~0.0	0.0006	0.4741/0.9760	0.061
S-Cond with BPE	0.0006	0.0212	0.0010/0.0419	3.582	0.0004	0.0158	0.0721/0.1671	3.437
M-Joint with BPE	0.0449	0.1931	0.0460/0.1273	0.531	~0.0	0.0121	0.3323/0.4406	0.227
M-Cond with BPE	0.0010	0.0125	0.0091/0.0422	3.918	0.0004	0.0158	0.0721/0.1671	4.108
M-Joint with Basic Tokenizer	0.0376	0.1389	0.0232/0.0654	0.543	0.0042	0.0341	0.0568/0.1299	0.552
M-Cond with Basic Tokenizer	0.0057	0.0970	0.1568/0.3785	0.331	0.0015	0.0345	0.1555/0.3990	0.470

trained by jointly modeling the dialogue context and response.

4.) Conditional model (Cond): DLGNet models are trained in the traditional sequence-to-sequence mode with a bidirectional encoder and an autoregressive decoder for a conditional modeling of the dialogue response given the context (Vaswani et al., 2017; Zhang et al., 2019).

5.) Basic Tokenizer: We use a basic tokenization traditionally used in dialogue modeling instead of BPE tokenization to evaluate the effect of tokenization coverage. It also provides an apples-to-apples comparison between the transformer-based and RNN-based architectures.

8.1   Effect of Random Padding Injection

The results in Table 3 are from models trained with static paddings. The models perform significantly worse than those of Table 2. Without random padding injection, the models quickly overfit to the low entropy regions of the training data, which leads generic and/or short responses.

8.2   Single Turn vs. Multi-turn

We also observe that the multi-turn models perform better than single-turn models on BPE tokenized data. This is expected because the multi-turn models capture longer temporal dependencies in the input data. It is also worth mentioning that the single-turn performance is further hurt by BPE tokenization since it tends to work better with long input sequences.

8.3   Joint vs. Conditional Models

For multi-turn models, the joint modeling architecture yields better performance than the conditional Seq2Seq architecture. This trend is however reversed for single-turn models. This is because a model that focuses on jointly modeling both the context and the response performs better with longer contextual information compared to a model that focuses on modeling only the conditional distribution of the response given the context. Therefore, multi-turn dialogue model should rather employ the joint structure instead of the conditional Seq2Seq structure.

8.4   Effect of Tokenization Coverage

For a more fair comparison with previous work on multi-turn dialogue not using random padding injection and 100% BPE tokenization, we trained the DLGNet models on multi-turn data with basic tokenization. The tokenization coverages of the basic tokenizer used are 83.9% and 4.19% for Movie and Ubuntu datasets respectively. Basically, most of the Ubuntu tokens are mapped to the <UNK> token. In comparison with previous work on HRED, the results in Table 3 show that the transformer-based DLGNet models under the same conditions perform better than the basic HRED model but worse than the improved HRED models (such as VHRED, hredGAN, and aBoots). In comparison with other transformer-based configurations, the smaller size multi-turn models perform better than their BPE counterparts but the larger size models perform worse. This is probably due to the overfitting of the larger models.

9 Conclusion

In this paper, we have proposed DLGNet, an extension of autoregressive transformer models such as GPT-2 for multi-turn dialogue modeling. Our experiments show that DLGNet models perform better than existing state-of-the-art multi-turn dialogue models. They also achieve the best performance to date on open-domain Movie and closed-domain Ubuntu datasets based on BLEU, ROUGE and distinct n-gram scores. Our experiments reveal that the combination of (i) the transformer architecture with (ii) the injection of random paddings exploiting the large maximum input sequence is responsible for the performance improvement over existing methods. Other contributing factors include joint modeling of dialogue context and response, and the 100% tokenization coverage from the byte pair encoding (BPE). Our analysis also reveals some tradeoffs between response relevance and response length, and we showed how different sampling strategies can be used to make an informed decision about such response relevance-diversity compromises. In our future work, we plan to investigate how to improve on the length of the generated responses without necessarily sacrificing their coherence and their relevance to the dialogue context.

References

Z. Dai, Z. Yang, Y. Yang, J. Carbonell, Q. V. Le, and R. Salakhutdinov. 2019. Transformer-xl: Attentive language models beyond a fixed-length context. In *ACL*.

J. Devlin, M. Chang, K. Lee, and K. Toutanova. 2019. Bert: Pre-training of deep bidirectional transformers for language understanding. In *NAACL-HLT*.

A. Holtzman, J. Buys, M. Forbes, and Y. Choi. 2019. The curious case of neural text degeneration. In *arXiv preprint arXiv:1904.09751*.

J. Li, M. Galley, C. Brockett, J. Gao, and B. Dolan. 2016a. A diversity-promoting objective function for neural conversation models. In *Proceedings of NAACL-HLT*.

J. Li, W. Monroe, A. Ritter, M. Galley, J. Gao, and D. Jurafsky. 2016b. Deep reinforcement learning for dialogue generation. In *arXiv preprint arXiv:1606.01541v4*.

C. Y. Lin. 2014. Rouge: a package for automatic evaluation of summaries. In *Proceedings of the Workshop on Text Summarization Branches Out*.

Table 4: Sample responses of DAIM, (V)HRED, hredGAN, aBoots and DLGNet models.

Model	Response
Movie	
Context_0	we ' re grateful , <person> . it ' s not that . those craftsman tools . they ' re a dream come true .
Context_1	your dad and i were raised with a certain work ethic , that ' s all .
Groundtruth	we can ' t start living like we ' re the rockerfellers or something .
HRED	<person> .
VHRED	<person> , mr . <person> . <person> , i ' m not going to tell you , <person> . i ' m sorry . i ' m sorry , <person> . i ' m sorry
hredGAN_w	<person> , i know you ' re see . < continued_utterance > <person> , please .
aBoots_w_cat	you ' re a liar !
DLGNet-117M	<person> , come on , hang on . how do you like that ? i can barely believe you ' re doing this .
DLGNet-345M	i have some very bad dreams .
DLGNet-117M_Random	i ' m sorry about all this . <person> , this is all their house .
DLGNet-345M_Random	remember that shoe you lost .
Context_0	<person> i ' ve raised my rate . i might even cut my sessions to forty minutes .
Context_1	<person> , i know you don ' t like flattery but if anybody i know is going to win a nobel prize , it ' s you . you got ta be thinking about your next book so i know you ' ll find this case particularly interesting .
Groundtruth	what sort of case is it , <person> ?
HRED	i ' m sorry , < person> .
VHRED:	it ' s not a lot of <unk> . i ' m not going to tell you , <person> . i ' m not going to help you .
hredGAN_w	i ' m a little nervous , but i don ' t care if there ' s something more important than <person> .
aBoots_w_cat	if i ' m sure they ' ll call it ' s place <person> .
DLGNet-117M	what sort of case is it , <person> ?
DLGNet-345M	what sort of case is it , <person> ?
DLGNet-117M_Random	what sort of case is your next ?
DLGNet-345M_Random	like what ?
Context_0	what was that for ?
Context_1	i ' d forgotten how exciting it is working together .
Groundtruth	you ' ve been so quiet lately , <person> , i thought you no longer cared .
HRED	i ' m sorry , <person> .
VHRED:	<person> , <person> . i don ' t know .
hredGAN_w	i ' m sorry , <person> . so many people are so interested , but you ' re a very nice guy .
aBoots_w_cat	we ' re going to take a look ?
DLGNet-117M	you look like working with <person> .
DLGNet-345M	you ' re a helluva translator .
DLGNet-117M_Random	you ' ve been so nice to <person> ach .
DLGNet-345M_Random	oh .
Ubuntu	
Context_0	DJones: update manager won't detect 12.04.1 as a new version if you are already running 12.04, because 12.04.1 = 12.04 + lots of package updates
Context_1	DJones I am running 10.04.
Context_2	what does 'gksu update-manager c' report?
Groundtruth	does not report that there is a new version out. So I am just holding. No rush.
HRED	I don't know what the problem is
VHRED	you mean ?
hredGAN_w	yes , I get the new one , I just want to get the new one
aBoots_w_cat	it says : no such file or directory , that is what it says
DLGNet-117M	gksu: command not found
DLGNet-345M	it says No new release found
DLGNet-117M_Random	http://pastebin.com/m7e8e0e7c
DLGNet-345M_Random	it says "update-manager: error: no new version is available"
Context_0	libgnome2-dev is the package that has that pkgconfig file
Context_1	After I installed libgnome2-dev I got a different output. http://pastebin.com/zpDeGs81 sorry it is so long.
Context_2	I thought that was what was going on thanks. :) I ran the command ./configure && sudo make && sudo make install would that have worked.
Groundtruth	you shouldn't run: sudo make; but yes
HRED	I don't know what the problem is
VHRED	what do you mean ? _eou_ what are you trying ?
hredGAN_w	I have no idea , I can just copy the files and copy files to the other one
aBoots_w_cat	yeah , if you have a few times to put things in the ' make ' command it is not in a file you can install it by hand .
DLGNet-117M	no, that's not what you want to do
DLGNet-345M	no, you need to run it as root
DLGNet-117M_Random	no, it won't.
DLGNet-345M_Random	yes, that's what I did

O. Olabiyi, A. Khazan, A. Salimov, and E.T. Mueller. 2019a. An adversarial learning framework for a persona-based multi-turn dialogue model. In *NAACL NeuralGen Workshop*.

O. Olabiyi, E.T. Mueller, C. Larson, and T. Lahlou. 2019b. Adversarial bootstrapping for dialogue model training. In *arXiv preprint arXiv:1909.00925*.

O. Olabiyi, A. Salimov, A. Khazane, and E. Mueller. 2018. Multi-turn dialogue response generation in an adversarial learning framework. In *arXiv preprint arXiv:1805.11752*.

K. Papineni, S. Roukos, T. Ward, and W. Zhu. 2002. Bleu: A method for automatic evalution of machine translation. In *Proceedings of the 40th Annual Meeting of the Association for Computational Linguistics*, pages 311–318.

A. Radford and T. Salimans. 2018. Improving language understanding by generative pre-training. In *https://s3-us-west-2.amazonaws.com/openai-assets/research-covers/language-unsupervised/language_understanding_paper.pdf*.

A. Radford, J. Wu, R. Child, D. Luan, D. Amodei, and I. Sutskever. 2019. Language models are unsupervised multitask learners. In *https://d4mucfpksywv.cloudfront.net/better-language-models*.

I. Serban, A. Sordoni, Y. Bengio, A. Courville, and J. Pineau. 2016. Building end-to-end dialogue systems using generative hierarchical neural network models. In *Proceedings of The Thirtieth AAAI Conference on Artificial Intelligence (AAAI 2016)*, pages 3776–3784.

I. V. Serban, T. Klinger, G. Tesauro, K. Talamadupula, B. Zhou, Y. Bengio, and A. Courville. 2017a. Multiresolution recurrent neural networks: An application to dialogue response generation. In *Proceedings of The Thirty-first AAAI Conference on Artificial Intelligence (AAAI 2017)*.

I. V. Serban, A. Sordoni, R. Lowe, L. Charlin, J. Pineau, A. Courville, and Y. Bengio. 2017b. A hierarchical latent variable encoder-decoder model for generating dialogue. In *Proceedings of The Thirty-first AAAI Conference on Artificial Intelligence (AAAI 2017)*.

Y. Sun, S. Wang, Y. Li, S. Feng, X. Chen, H. Zhang, X. Tian, D. Zhu, H. Tian, and H. Wu. 2019a. Ernie: Enhanced representation through knowledge integration. In *arXiv preprint arXiv:1904.09223*.

Y. Sun, S. Wang, Y. Li, S. Feng, H. Tian, H. Wu, and H. Wang. 2019b. Ernie 2.0: A continual pre-training framework for language understanding. In *arXiv preprint arXiv:1907.12412*.

I. Sutskever, O. Vinyals, and Q. Le. 2014. Sequence to sequence learning with neural networks. In *Proceedings of Advances in Neural Information Processing Systems (NIPS)*, pages 3104–3112.

A. Vaswani, N. Shazeer, N. Parmar, J. Uszkoreit, L. Jones, A. N. Gomez, L. Kaiser, and I. Polosukhin. 2017. Attention is all you need. In *NIPS*.

O. Vinyals and Q. Le. 2015. A neural conversational model. In *Proceedings of ICML Deep Learning Workshop*.

C. Xing, W. Wu, Y. Wu, M. Zhou, Y. Huang, and W. Ma. 2017. Hierarchical recurrent attention network for response generation. In *arXiv preprint arXiv:1701.07149*.

Z. Yang, Z. Dai, Y. Yang, J. Carbonell, R. Salakhutdinov, and Q. V. Le. 2019. Xlnet: Generalized autoregressive pretraining for language understanding. In *arXiv preprint arXiv:1906.08237*.

R. Zellers, A. Holtzman, H. Rashkin, Y. Bisk, A. Farhadi, F. Roesner, and Y. Choi. 2019. Defending against neural fake news. In *arXiv preprint arXiv:1905.12616*.

H. Zhang, Y. Lan, L. Pang, J. Guo, and Xueqi Cheng. 2019. Recosa: Detecting the relevant contexts with self-attention for multi-turn dialogue generation. In *arXiv preprint arXiv:1907.05339*.

S. Zhang, E. Dinan, J. Urbanek, A. Szlam, D. Kiela, and J. Weston. 2018a. Personalizing dialogue agents: I have a dog, do you have pets too? In *arXiv preprint arXiv:1801.07243v3*.

Y. Zhang, M. Galley, J. Gao, Z. Gan, X. Li, C. Brockett, and B. Dolan. 2018b. Generating informative and diverse conversational responses via adversarial information maximization. In *NeurIPS*.

Data Augmentation for Training Dialog Models Robust to Speech Recognition Errors

Longshaokan Wang   Maryam Fazel-zarandi   Aditya Tiwari
Spyros Matsoukas   Lazaros Polymenakos
Alexa AI, Amazon
{longsha, fazelzar, aditiwar, matsouka, polyml}@amazon.com

Abstract

Speech-based virtual assistants, such as Amazon Alexa, Google assistant, and Apple Siri, typically convert users' audio signals to text data through automatic speech recognition (ASR) and feed the text to downstream dialog models for natural language understanding and response generation. The ASR output is error-prone; however, the downstream dialog models are often trained on error-free text data, making them sensitive to ASR errors during inference time. To bridge the gap and make dialog models more robust to ASR errors, we leverage an ASR error simulator to inject noise into the error-free text data, and subsequently train the dialog models with the augmented data. Compared to other approaches for handling ASR errors, such as using ASR lattice or end-to-end methods, our data augmentation approach does not require any modification to the ASR or downstream dialog models; our approach also does not introduce any additional latency during inference time. We perform extensive experiments on benchmark data and show that our approach improves the performance of downstream dialog models in the presence of ASR errors, and it is particularly effective in the low-resource situations where there are constraints on model size or the training data is scarce.

1   Introduction

Speech-based virtual assistants, such as Amazon Alexa, Google Assistant, and Apple Siri, have become increasingly powerful and popular in our everyday lives, offering a wide range of functionality including controlling smart home devices, booking movie tickets, and even chit-chatting. These speech-based virtual assistants typically contain the following components: an automatic speech recognition (ASR) module that converts audio signals from a user to a sequence of words, a natural language understanding (NLU) module that extracts semantic meaning from the user utterance, a dialog management (DM) module that controls the dialog flow and communicates with external applications if necessary, a natural language generation (NLG) module that converts the system response to natural language, and a text-to-speech (TTS) module that converts the text response to an audio response (Jurafsky and Martin, 2009). The errors made by the ASR module can propagate to the downstream dialog models in NLU and DM and degrade their performances (Serdyuk et al., 2018; Shivakumar et al., 2019).

One straightforward approach to improve the downstream dialog models' robustness to ASR errors is to train them with ASR hypotheses with potential ASR errors in addition to the error-free reference texts. However, the training data might not always have corresponding ASR hypotheses available, for example, when the training data are created in written forms from the beginning. Such training data include online reviews, forums, and data collected in a Wizard-of-Oz (WOZ) setting (Rieser and Lemon, 2011). Additionally, even when there are ASR hypotheses available, transcribing and annotating the ASR hypotheses to create the training data is a slow and expensive process due to human involvement, limiting the size of available training data.

To address these challenges, we propose a simple data augmentation method leveraging a confusion-matrix-based ASR error simulator (Fazel-Zarandi et al., 2019; Schatzmann et al., 2007). Our method can be used on training data with or without existing ASR hypotheses, does not require modifying the ASR model or downstream dialog models, and consequently does not introduce additional latency during inference time. We assess the method's effectiveness on a multi-label classification task on a public dataset from DSTC2 (Henderson et al., 2014). We show that our method can improve the

63

Proceedings of the 2nd Workshop on Natural Language Processing for Conversational AI, pages 63–70
July 9, 2020. ©2020 Association for Computational Linguistics

dialog models' performances in the presence of ASR errors, particularly in the low resource situations where there are model size or latency constraints, or the training data is scarce.

2 Related Work

Existing approaches for handling ASR errors generally fall into four categories: 1) pre-training word embeddings such that acoustically similar words are close to each other in the embedding space (Shivakumar et al., 2019; Shivakumar and Georgiou, 2018; Ghannay et al., 2016); 2) using multi-task training to jointly correct ASR errors in addition to performing the original NLU tasks (Schumann and Angkititrakul, 2018; Weng et al., 2020); 3) using n-best ASR hypotheses, word confusion networks, or ASR lattice produced by the ASR system as the input for the downstream dialog models, allowing the models to consider all the alternatives instead of only the 1-best ASR hypothesis (Weng et al., 2020; Ladhak et al., 2016; Hakkani-Tür et al., 2006); and 4) using an end-to-end approach that combines ASR and NLU systems into one, extracting semantics directly from audio signals (Serdyuk et al., 2018; Haghani et al., 2018). These approaches often either require significant modifications to ASR model and/or downstream dialog models, or require access to additional information from the ASR model, such as ASR n-best or ASR lattice, during inference time. In comparison, data augmentation is much simpler because it does not modify the existing model architecture or introduce additional latency during inference time. Data augmentation has a long history in image processing (Shorten and Khoshgoftaar, 2019). In language processing, researchers have proposed back-translation (Einolghozati et al., 2019) and simple operations such as synonym replacement and random swap (Wei and Zou, 2019) to increase the variations of training data. These data augmentation approaches aim to improve dialog models' robustness to surface form variations in general, whereas our approach focuses on robustness to ASR errors in particular. Note that our data augmentation approach can be complimentary to using acoustic embeddings (first category), multi-task training (second category), and the other mentioned data augmentation approaches, and it is possible to combine them for further performance gains.

3 Method

We propose to use simulated ASR hypotheses to augment the training data of dialog models. To this end, we adopt the confusion-matrix-based ASR error simulator initially proposed by Schatzmann et al. (2007) and improved by Fazel-Zarandi et al. (2019). Here we describe the error simulator at a high level, while leaving the details to the mentioned references. The main component of the error simulator is an n-gram confusion matrix constructed from a corpus of ASR hypotheses and corresponding reference texts: Each ASR hypothesis and its reference text are aligned at the word level by minimizing the Levenshtein distance between them, then the frequencies of n-gram confusions are added to the confusion matrix for $n \in [1, M]$, where M is a pre-specified constant. During inference time, the error simulator first partitions a reference text into n-grams where n can vary, then for each n-gram it samples a replacement from the confusion matrix with sampling probabilities proportional to the frequencies of confusions. Note that the sampled "confusion" can be the original n-gram itself, which means correct recognition for this n-gram in the simulated hypothesis.

We refer to the corpus used to construct the n-gram confusion matrix as the *ASR corpus* to distinguish it from the training data for the dialog models that we want to apply the error simulator to. By design, if the reference texts that the error simulator is applied to have the same distribution as the reference texts in the *ASR corpus*, then the simulated ASR hypotheses will have the same error distribution as the ASR hypotheses in the *ASR corpus* (Schatzmann et al., 2007), where the error distribution includes word-error-rate (WER) and proportions of insertion, deletion, and substitution errors. However, in practice it can be useful to simulate ASR hypotheses with a pre-specified WER different from that of the *ASR corpus*. Adjusting the WER is non-trivial, because each word's individual WER is often different from the overall WER of the *ASR corpus*; i.e., some words are more easily confusable than others. We introduce a heuristic to adjust each word's individual WER during inference time of the error simulator so that the overall WER in the simulated ASR hypotheses is close to the pre-specified target overall WER based on the following formula (see Appendix A):

$$\frac{1 - \text{target individual WER}}{1 - \text{original individual WER}} = \frac{1 - \text{target overall WER}}{1 - \text{original overall WER}}.$$

This heuristic has the following desired properties: 1) If w_1 has a higher original individual WER than that of w_2 before the adjustment, then w_1 will have a higher target individual WER than that of w_2 from this adjustment, for arbitrary words w_1 and w_2 under certain simplifying conditions (Appendix A); i.e., we mostly preserve the property that some words are more easily confusable than others. 2) In the trivial case where all words have the same individual WER as the overall WER, this heuristic is equivalent to setting all individual WER to the target overall WER.

We apply data augmentation to the training data of dialog models in two different cases: **S1**) The training data only have reference texts and no corresponding ASR hypotheses. In this case, we construct the confusion matrix used by the ASR error simulator with an *ASR corpus* ideally close to the training data of dialog models in terms of vocabulary overlap, or a large generic *ASR corpus* such as Fisher English Training Speech Corpora (Cieri et al., 2004; Shivakumar and Georgiou, 2018). We simulate multiple ASR hypotheses for each reference sentence with different WER, and combine all the simulated ASR hypotheses with the reference text as the augmented training data – the motivation behind this is to create more variations, make dialog models robust to different levels of WER, and avoid degradation on error-free data. **S2**) The training data have both reference texts and corresponding ASR hypotheses. In this case, we can directly use the training data as the *ASR corpus* to construct the confusion matrix, then simulate ASR hypotheses with different WER and combine them with the original ASR hypotheses and reference texts as the augmented training data. Note that during inference time of the ASR error simulator, it partitions a sentence and samples n-gram replacements probabilistically, so even though we use the training data of dialog models as the *ASR corpus*, the error simulator can still create new variations in the simulated ASR hypotheses.

4 Experiments

We experiment our proposed data augmentation method on the dialog act classification task.

4.1 Data

We use the public dataset from DSTC2 (Henderson et al., 2014), which has reference texts, ASR hypotheses, and dialog act annotations. We choose DSTC2 because the other commonly used NLU datasets often don't have ASR hypotheses available. This dataset consists of human-computer dialogs in a restaurant domain collected using Amazon Mechanical Turk. We follow the same data preprocessing steps as in Weng et al.'s (2020) work. After preprocessing, the dataset has 10,876/3,553/9,153 training/validation/test samples and 25 unique dialog act labels. Each user utterance may have multiple dialog act labels, thus we treat this problem as a multi-label classification problem. More specifically, in the training set, 7,516 utterances have 1 dialog act label each, 3,254 utterances have 2 dialog act labels each, and 106 utterances have 3 dialog act labels each. The ASR hypotheses for the user utterances have a WER of 27.89%, where the errors consist of 58.96% substitutions, 15.66% insertions, and 25.38% deletions. Additionally, in 45% of the test cases, the ASR hypothesis has perfect recognition.

4.2 Setup

We measure the effectiveness of data augmentation in both cases mentioned in Section 3. In the first use case, we assume that the training and validation sets have no ASR hypotheses, and we need to construct the n-gram confusion matrix with a separate *ASR corpus*. The *ASR corpus* used for constructing the confusion matrix for the error simulator is a separate dataset of 10,000 transcribed utterances from different domains such as movie recommendation, ticket booking, and restaurant booking. As a measure of similarity, this *ASR corpus* contains 43.3% of unique words, 12.6% of unique bigrams, and 4.4% of unique trigrams from DSTC2. In addition to experimenting with data augmentation with the confusion-matrix-based ASR error simulator, we consider data augmentation with a much simpler error simulator which we call *the uniform error simulator*, to see whether a simpler error simulator would suffice. The uniform error simulator samples word replacements from the training data vocabulary uniformly with a pre-specified WER. The training and validation data in each setting are as follows:

S1-1 Reference utterances only (baseline);

S1-2 Reference utterances + simulated ASR hypotheses by the uniform error simulator with 27.9% WER;

S1-3 Reference utterances + simulated ASR hy-

Table 1: Accuracy (%) and F1-score results on ASR hypotheses and reference texts from the DSTC2 test set for different settings described in Section 4.2. "Uniform" refers to the uniform error simulator, and "Conf. Mat." refers to the confusion-matrix-based error simulator.

	Training Setup	Validation Setup	Hypothesis		Reference	
			Accuracy	F1-Score	Accuracy	F1-Score
S1-1	ref	ref	80.76	0.8935	96.98	0.9847
S1-2	ref + sim hyp (Uniform, 27.9% WER)	ref + sim hyp (Uniform, 27.9% WER)	80.80	0.8938	96.36	0.9814
S1-3	ref + sim hyp (Conf. Mat., 27.9% WER)	ref + sim hyp (Conf. Mat., 27.9% WER)	80.98	0.8950	96.95	0.9845
S1-4	ref + sim hyp (Conf. Mat., mixed WER)	ref + sim hyp (Conf. Mat., mixed WER)	81.05	0.8953	97.19	0.9857
S2-1	ref + hyp	ref + hyp	83.03	0.9073	96.88	0.9841
S2-2	ref + hyp + sim hyp (Uniform, 27.9% WER)	ref + hyp	82.73	0.9054	96.49	0.9821
S2-3	ref + hyp + sim hyp (Conf. Mat., 27.9% WER)	ref + hyp	83.16	0.9080	96.59	0.9827
S2-4	ref + hyp + sim hyp (Conf. Mat., mixed WER)	ref + hyp	83.19	0.9082	96.80	0.9837

potheses by the confusion-matrix-based error simulator with 27.9% WER[1];

S1-4 Reference utterances + three sets of simulated ASR hypotheses by the confusion-matrix-based error simulator with 27.9%, 20%, 15% WER, respectively.

Note that the ratios between reference utterances and simulated hypotheses are 1:1 for S1-2 and S1-3 and 1:3 for S1-4.

In the second use case, the training and validation sets have both reference utterances and ASR hypotheses. We use the training set itself as the *ASR corpus* to construct the confusion matrix. Compared to the first case, we include the original ASR hypotheses in the training and validation sets for each setting, but we do not include the simulated ASR hypotheses in the validation set to keep this set as close to the test set as possible. We refer to the settings for the second case as S2-1, S2-2, S2-3 and S2-4.

We use the FLAIR package (Akbik et al., 2018) to build the multi-label classifier, tune the hyperparameters on the validation set with hyperopt (Bergstra et al., 2015) under the baseline setting S1-1, and keep the same model architecture across all settings. The final model architecture selected by hyperopt is BERT embeddings (Devlin et al., 2019) + embedding re-projection + 1 layer bidirectional LSTM with 256 hidden size. In each setting, we use the validation set for learning rate decay and early stopping, and test the trained model on the ASR hypotheses and reference utterances in the test set separately. We measure the model performance with micro-averaged accuracy and F1-score. Because each sample only has one or a few class labels out of the 25 possible labels, we follow FLAIR's convention in calculating the accuracy for multi-label classification by excluding the number of true negatives from both the numerator and denominator:

$$\text{Accuracy} = \frac{(\text{\# true pos.})}{(\text{\# true pos.}) + (\text{\# false pos.}) + (\text{\# false neg.})}.$$

4.3 Results

The results are shown in Table 1. We see that in both cases, the proposed data augmentation settings (S1-4 and S2-4) yield the best performance when tested on ASR hypotheses. However, the improvements over the baselines (S1-1 and S2-1) are very marginal (0.29% absolute improvement for S1 and 0.16% for S2), which could be due to the baseline performances already being close to optimal, or data augmentation being less effective for models with powerful pre-trained embeddings like BERT, which Shleifer (2019) also observed in his work. For S1-4, we also experiment with using the DSTC2 ASR hypotheses as the *ASR corpus* as an oracle/upper bound setting for S1, where we assume that the training data have no ASR hypotheses but the *ASR corpus* is perfectly in-domain, which yields an accuracy of 82.90% testing on hypotheses and 96.87% on references.

Examining the errors made by S1-1, S1-4, S2-1, and S2-4 settings on the ASR hypotheses, we see that more than 90% of the errors are common among the four settings. Furthermore, in about 54% of the cases there is no overlap between the words in the references and the corresponding ASR hypotheses. For example, the user utterance "Danish" is recognized as "the address", and "seafood" is recognized as "is serve". This indicates that these ASR hypotheses are distorted to the extent that it

---

[1] We use 27.9% WER to match the WER of DSTC2. Note that in this case even though we assume that we don't have ASR hypotheses in the training data, we may still know the overall WER of the ASR system. If the overall WER is unknown, we can always use a combination of different WER similar to S1-4.

Table 2: Accuracy (%) and F1-score results for reduced model architectures. Except for model architecture, the settings are exactly the same as those of Table 1. "without BERT" refers to the model architecture from Table 1 with BERT replaced with GloVe embeddings; "Simple NN" refers to the GloVe embeddings + 1 layer unidirectional LSTM with 128 hidden size architecture.

Training Setup	Model Architecture	Hypothesis Acc.	Hypothesis F1	Reference Acc.	Reference F1
S1-1	without BERT	80.34	0.8910	94.09	0.9695
S1-2	without BERT	81.12	0.8958	94.55	0.9720
S1-3	without BERT	80.81	0.8939	94.33	0.9709
S1-4	without BERT	81.19	0.8962	95.36	0.9762
S2-1	without BERT	80.40	0.8913	92.18	0.9593
S2-2	without BERT	81.47	0.8979	93.88	0.9685
S2-3	without BERT	81.32	0.8969	93.24	0.9650
S2-4	without BERT	82.63	0.9049	95.14	0.9751
S1-1	Simple NN	76.92	0.8695	87.74	0.9347
S1-2	Simple NN	77.01	0.8701	87.11	0.9311
S1-3	Simple NN	79.66	0.8868	91.82	0.9573
S1-4	Simple NN	80.81	0.8939	94.28	0.9706
S2-1	Simple NN	79.35	0.8848	89.65	0.9454
S2-2	Simple NN	79.65	0.8867	90.63	0.9508
S2-3	Simple NN	81.76	0.8996	93.87	0.9684
S2-4	Simple NN	81.69	0.8992	94.16	0.9699

would be very unlikely to correctly predict the label, even for a human annotator. In an additional 32% of the common errors, the ASR hypotheses have changed the semantics of the reference texts. For example, "Spanish food" is recognized as "which food", "no Thai" is recognized as "no hi", and "no Italian food" is recognized as "would like Italian food". In these cases, it would also be almost impossible to predict the ground-truth labels.

4.4 Follow-up Experiments

To investigate whether data augmentation is more effective for models without large pre-trained embeddings like BERT, we run one set of follow-up experiments where we replace BERT with GloVe embeddings (Pennington et al., 2014) from the previous model architecture (a 99.79% reduction in number of parameters), and another set where we further reduce the model architecture to a much simpler one: GloVe embeddings + 1 layer unidirectional LSTM with 128 hidden size (a further 83.05% reduction in number of parameters). The results are shown in Table 2. We see that for the reduced model architectures, the improvements from data augmentation are much larger (e.g., 3.89% absolute improvement in S1 and 2.34% in S2 for Simple NN). The promising results on simpler model architectures have practical implications, because in certain use cases we may not be able to use large model architectures due to constraints on model size, computing power, or latency.

Lastly, hypothesizing that data augmentation could be particularly effective for limited training data even with the best model architecture found by hyperopt, we randomly subsample 1%, 5%, 10%, 25%, 50%, and 75% of the training and validation sets (without changing the test sets) and apply the

Table 3: Accuracy (%) results for training on different sub-samples of the data with different model architecture on the hypothesis test set. We compare the baselines (S1-1 and S2-1) with the proposed data augmentation settings (S1-4 and S2-4) and show the absolute improvements in accuracy.

Model Architecture	Subsample Proportion	S1 Setting S1-1	S1-4	Gain	S2 Setting S2-1	S2-4	Gain
With BERT	1%	43.67	64.94	+21.27	61.81	62.32	+0.51
	5%	71.79	77.65	+5.86	74.51	78.62	+4.11
	10%	78.29	79.41	+1.12	79.90	80.23	+0.33
	25%	79.37	80.15	+0.78	80.88	81.56	+0.68
	50%	80.54	80.8	+0.26	82.00	82.40	+0.40
	75%	81.05	81.27	+0.22	82.58	83.16	+0.58
Without BERT	1%	5.72	4.48	−1.24	6.17	0.81	−5.36
	5%	0.88	73.01	+72.13	0.02	70.33	+70.31
	10%	0.12	76.16	+76.04	69.91	76.65	+6.74
	25%	70.75	78.47	+7.72	76.71	80.55	+3.84
	50%	78.73	80.59	+1.86	80.15	82.10	+1.95
	75%	78.04	81.38	+3.34	80.92	82.11	+1.19
Simple NN	1%	15.90	16.68	+0.78	16.55	15.59	−0.96
	5%	11.11	41.10	+29.99	8.28	41.47	+33.19
	10%	8.55	74.10	+65.55	0.07	72.61	+72.54
	25%	12.11	77.37	+65.26	75.84	77.70	+1.90
	50%	75.72	80.08	+4.36	76.99	79.54	+2.55
	75%	76.69	80.54	+3.85	78.32	81.53	+3.21

Table 4: Accuracy (%) results for training on different sub-samples of the data with different model architecture on the reference test set. Except for testing on reference utterances instead of ASR hypotheses, the settings are exactly the same as in Table 3.

Model Architecture	Subsample Proportion	S1 Setting			S2 Setting		
		S1-1	S1-4	Gain	S2-1	S2-4	Gain
With BERT	1%	53.57	73.75	+20.18	70.30	71.90	+1.60
	5%	83.58	90.12	+6.54	85.11	90.47	+5.36
	10%	91.62	92.80	+1.18	91.93	92.99	+1.06
	25%	93.34	95.49	+2.15	93.84	94.99	+1.15
	50%	96.01	96.68	+0.67	95.82	95.96	+0.14
	75%	96.54	96.90	+0.36	96.12	96.49	+0.37
Without BERT	1%	5.66	4.38	−1.28	4.35	0.81	−3.54
	5%	0.75	83.56	+82.81	0.04	79.14	+79.10
	10%	0.21	87.03	+86.82	79.08	86.67	+7.59
	25%	81.9	90.25	+8.35	86.85	91.37	+4.52
	50%	90.45	93.77	+3.32	91.27	94.52	+3.25
	75%	89.7	94.97	+5.27	92.87	94.66	+1.79
Simple NN	1%	17.44	18.61	+1.17	18.37	16.96	−1.41
	5%	12.32	45.19	+32.87	10.01	45.21	+35.20
	10%	8.82	84.83	+76.01	0.07	82.91	+82.84
	25%	17.55	87.76	+70.21	85.05	87.4	+2.35
	50%	86.17	92.66	+6.49	86.17	90.17	+4.00
	75%	88.46	93.88	+5.42	88.16	94.00	+5.84

proposed data augmentation with different model architectures. The comparisons between the baselines (S1-1 and S2-1) and proposed settings (S1-4 and S2-4) on the reduced data are shown in Tables 3 and 4. As expected, the improvements from data augmentation are generally larger for smaller datasets and simpler model architectures, except for most cases on the smallest subset (1% of training data).

5 Conclusion

In this paper, we proposed a method for data augmentation in order to make downstream dialog models more robust to ASR errors. We leveraged a confusion-matrix-based ASR error simulator to inject noise into the error-free text data, and subsequently trained dialog act classification models with the augmented data. Compared to other approaches of handling ASR errors, our data augmentation approach does not require any modification to the ASR models or downstream dialog models, thus our approach also does not introduce any additional latency during inference time of the dialog models. We performed extensive experiments on benchmark data and showed that our approach improves the performance of downstream dialog models in the presence of ASR errors, and it is particularly effective in the low-resource situations where the model size needs to be small or the training data is scarce.

For future work, we plan to investigate the effect of our proposed method on additional tasks such as dialog state tracking and response generation. Additionally, we believe that our data augmentation approach is complimentary to using acoustic embeddings, multi-task training, and other mentioned data augmentation approaches, and we plan to combine them for further performance gains.

Acknowledgments

We thank Angeliki Metallinou, Sajjad Beygi, Josep Valls Vargas, and the ACL workshop reviewers for the constructive feedback.

References

Alan Akbik, Duncan Blythe, and Roland Vollgraf. 2018. Contextual string embeddings for sequence labeling. In *COLING 2018, 27th International Conference on Computational Linguistics*, pages 1638–1649.

James Bergstra, Brent Komer, Chris Eliasmith, Dan Yamins, and David D Cox. 2015. Hyperopt: a python library for model selection and hyperparameter optimization. *Computational Science & Discovery*, 8(1):014008.

C. Cieri, D. Miller, and K. Walker. 2004. The fisher corpus: a resource for the next generations of speech-to-text. *LREC*, 4:69–71.

Jacob Devlin, Ming-Wei Chang, Kenton Lee, and Kristina Toutanova. 2019. Bert: Pre-training of deep bidirectional transformers for language understanding. In *NAACL-HLT*.

Arash Einolghozati, Sonal Gupta, Mrinal Mohit, and Rushin Shah. 2019. Improving robustness of task oriented dialog systems. *ArXiv*, abs/1911.05153.

Maryam Fazel-Zarandi, Longshaokan Wang, Aditya Tiwari, and Spyros Matsoukas. 2019. Investigation of error simulation techniques for learning dialog policies for conversational error recovery. *2019 Conversational Agents Workshop (NeurIPS)*, abs/1911.03378.

Sahar Ghannay, Yannick Estève, Nathalie Camelin, and Paul Deléglise. 2016. Acoustic word embeddings for asr error detection. In *INTERSPEECH*.

Parisa Haghani, Arun Narayanan, Michiel Bacchiani, Galen Chuang, Neeraj Gaur, Pedro J. Moreno, Rohit Prabhavalkar, Zhongdi Qu, and Austin Waters. 2018. From audio to semantics: Approaches to end-to-end spoken language understanding. *2018 IEEE Spoken Language Technology Workshop (SLT)*, pages 720–726.

Dilek Hakkani-Tür, Frédéric Béchet, Giuseppe Riccardic, and Gokhan Tur. 2006. Beyond asr 1-best: Using word confusion networks in spoken language understanding. *Computer Speech & Language*, 20.

Matthew Henderson, Blaise Thomson, and Jason D. Williams. 2014. The second dialog state tracking challenge. In *Proceedings of the 15th Annual Meeting of the Special Interest Group on Discourse and Dialogue (SIGDIAL)*, pages 263–272, Philadelphia, PA, U.S.A. Association for Computational Linguistics.

Daniel Jurafsky and James H. Martin. 2009. *Speech and Language Processing (2nd Edition)*. Prentice-Hall, Inc., USA.

Faisal Ladhak, Ankur Gandhe, Markus Dreyer, Lambert Mathias, Ariya Rastrow, and Björn Hoffmeister. 2016. Latticernn: Recurrent neural networks over lattices. In *Interspeech 2016*, pages 695–699.

Xuezhe Ma and Eduard H. Hovy. 2016. End-to-end sequence labeling via bi-directional lstm-cnns-crf. *CoRR*, abs/1603.01354.

Jeffrey Pennington, Richard Socher, and Christopher D. Manning. 2014. Glove: Global vectors for word representation. In *EMNLP*.

Verena Rieser and Oliver Lemon. 2011. Data collection in a wizard-of-oz experiment. *Reinforcement Learning for Adaptive Dialogue Systems*, page 85–99.

Jost Schatzmann, Blaise Thomson, and Steve Young. 2007. Error simulation for training statistical dialogue systems. In *2007 IEEE Workshop on Automatic Speech Recognition Understanding (ASRU)*, pages 526–531.

R. Schumann and P. Angkititrakul. 2018. Incorporating asr errors with attention-based, jointly trained rnn for intent detection and slot filling. In *2018 IEEE International Conference on Acoustics, Speech and Signal Processing (ICASSP)*, pages 6059–6063.

Dmitriy Serdyuk, Yongqiang Wang, Christian Fuegen, Anuj Kumar, Baiyang Liu, and Yoshua Bengio. 2018. Towards end-to-end spoken language understanding. *2018 IEEE International Conference on Acoustics, Speech and Signal Processing (ICASSP)*, pages 5754–5758.

Prashanth Gurunath Shivakumar and Panayiotis G. Georgiou. 2018. Confusion2vec: Towards enriching vector space word representations with representational ambiguities. *CoRR*, abs/1811.03199.

Prashanth Gurunath Shivakumar, Mu Yang, and Panayiotis G. Georgiou. 2019. Spoken language intent detection using confusion2vec. *CoRR*, abs/1904.03576.

Sam Shleifer. 2019. Low resource text classification with ulmfit and backtranslation. *CoRR*, abs/1903.09244.

Connor Shorten and Taghi M. Khoshgoftaar. 2019. A survey on image data augmentation for deep learning. *J Big Data*, 6.

Tomohiro Tanaka, Ryo Masumura, Hirokazu Masataki, and Yushi Aono. 2018. Neural error corrective language models for automatic speech recognition. In *INTERSPEECH*.

Erik F. Tjong Kim Sang and Fien De Meulder. 2003. Introduction to the CoNLL-2003 shared task: Language-independent named entity recognition. In *Proceedings of the Seventh Conference on Natural Language Learning at HLT-NAACL 2003*, pages 142–147.

Jason W. Wei and Kai Zou. 2019. EDA: easy data augmentation techniques for boosting performance on text classification tasks. *CoRR*, abs/1901.11196.

Yue Weng, Sai Sumanth Miryala, Chandra Khatri, Runze Wang, Huaixiu Zheng, Piero Molino, Mahdi Namazifar, Alexandros Papangelis, Hugh Williams, Franziska Bell, and Gokhan Tur. 2020. Joint contextual modeling for asr correction and language understanding. *ArXiv*, abs/2002.00750.

A Adjusting Word-Error-Rate when Applying the ASR Error Simulator

Please refer to the work by Schatzmann et al. (Schatzmann et al., 2007) and Fazel-Zarandi et al. (Fazel-Zarandi et al., 2019) for details on how the ASR error simulator is applied during inference time, which include how out-of-vocabulary words are handled. Here we focus on the newly introduced heuristic of adjusting word-error-rate (WER).

Note that a single word can be contained in multiple n-grams in the confusion matrix, and when an n-gram is confused with an m-gram for arbitrary n, and m, the actual number of word errors introduced could be greater than, equal to, or less than n. Thus, making a precise adjustment of a single word's individual WER can be difficult. Instead, for simplicity, we treat each n-gram in the confusion matrix as a single word for all n when applying this heuristic. Under the simplifying condition, the individual WER of a word w can be computed with

$$1 - \frac{\text{frequency of correct recognition for } w}{\text{sum of frequencies of confusions for } w},$$

where the correct recognition is the same as "confusing" with the original word itself.

Now, assume that we sample from the confusion matrix without any adjustment on the test set when applying the error simulator, and the resulting overall WER is R_1. The target overall WER we want to have is R_2. We adjust each word's individual WER by changing its frequency of correction recognition based on the following formula:

$$\frac{1 - \text{target individual WER}}{1 - \text{original individual WER}} = \frac{1 - \text{target overall WER}}{1 - \text{original overall WER}}.$$

Then we can derive how many additional correct recognitions, denoted as X, to add for a word w as follows:

$$1 - \text{target individual WER}$$
$$= (1 - \text{original individual WER}) \cdot \frac{1 - R_2}{1 - R_1}.$$

In practice, the right-hand-side of the above equation can be greater than 1, so we add an upper bound constant $U < 1$:

$$1 - \text{target individual WER}$$
$$= \min\left[(1 - \text{original individual WER}) \cdot \frac{1 - R_2}{1 - R_1}, U\right].$$

Expanding the original and target individual WER:

$$\frac{(\text{freq. of correct recognition for } w) + X}{(\text{sum of freq. of confusions for } w) + X}$$
$$= \min\left[\frac{\text{freq. of correct recognition for } w}{\text{sum of freq. of confusions for } w} \cdot \frac{1 - R_2}{1 - R_1}, U\right].$$

R_1 and R_2 are known, and the frequencies are stored in the confusion matrix, hence we can solve for X. Denoting the right-hand-side of the above equation as H, we have:

$$X = [H \cdot (\text{sum of freq. of confusions for } w)$$
$$- (\text{freq. of correct recognition for } w)]/(1 - H).$$

Note that X can be negative, which corresponds to having a lower target WER.

During the inference time of the error simulator, for each word w we sample replacement for, we adjust its individual WER by computing X using the last equation and adding it to the frequency of correct recognition for w before sampling.

Automating Template Creation for Ranking-Based Dialogue Models

Jingxiang Chen   **Heba Elfardy**   **Simi Wang**   **Andrea Kahn**   **Jared Kramer**
`{jxchen,helfardy,simiwang,kahna,jaredkra}@amazon.com`
Amazon
Seattle, WA, USA

Abstract

Dialogue response generation models that use template ranking rather than direct sequence generation allow model developers to limit generated responses to pre-approved messages. However, manually creating templates is time-consuming and requires domain expertise. To alleviate this problem, we explore automating the process of creating dialogue templates by using unsupervised methods to cluster historical utterances and selecting representative utterances from each cluster. Specifically, we propose an end-to-end model called Deep Sentence Encoder Clustering (DSEC) that uses an auto-encoder structure to jointly learn the utterance representation and construct template clusters. We compare this method to a random baseline that randomly assigns templates to clusters as well as a strong baseline that performs the sentence encoding and the utterance clustering sequentially.

To evaluate the performance of the proposed method, we perform an automatic evaluation with two annotated customer service datasets to assess clustering effectiveness, and a human-in-the-loop experiment using a live customer service application to measure the acceptance rate of the generated templates. DSEC performs best in the automatic evaluation, beats both the sequential and random baselines on most metrics in the human-in-the-loop experiment, and shows promising results when compared to gold/manually created templates.

1 Introduction

Dialogue response generation has been an active area of research in recent years. Response generation can be used in human-to-bot conversational systems (Qiu et al., 2017) or to generate quick replies in human-to-human conversational systems (Kannan et al., 2016; Pasternack et al., 2017).

Response generation approaches fall under two broad categories: (1) direct sequence generation using an encoder-decoder architecture (Vinyals and Le, 2015; Serban et al., 2016) or (2) response ranking, in which the model developer specifies a pre-defined template pool and an encoder model is used to score pairs of conversation history and candidate template response (Liu et al., 2018; Zhou et al., 2018; Kannan et al., 2016). Using template ranking rather than direct sequence generation allows model developers to limit generated responses to pre-approved messages, preventing the model from producing impolite or ungrammatical responses. In addition, sequence generation models have a tendency to favor safe, generic responses (Baheti et al., 2018; Shao et al., 2017; Zhang et al., 2018; Li et al., 2016), and template ranking models can be used to ensure that the system generates information-rich responses that drive the conversation towards an end goal. However, manually creating templates is time-consuming and requires domain expertise. For certain use cases such as customer service, templates need to be continually updated to reflect policy changes, further adding to this cost. In addition, manually created templates may differ subtly from actual agent utterances in model training data and thus may not be selected by the ranking model.

In this paper, we explore automating the creation of a template pool for a customer service chat application through clustering historical agent utterances and choosing representative utterances from each cluster. To the best of our knowledge, research on automatic template creation using utterance clustering has been limited.

The structure of this paper is as follows. In section 2, we describe the data and text preprocessing methods we used to extract template candidates from historical chat transcripts. In section 3, we describe our proposed approach for template generation: an end-to-end approach that uses an auto-

Proceedings of the 2nd Workshop on Natural Language Processing for Conversational AI, pages 71–78
July 9, 2020. ©2020 Association for Computational Linguistics

encoder structure to jointly learn the utterance representation and construct template clusters. In addition, we describe a strong baseline that we propose for comparison: a sequential approach in which we first learn the utterance representation and then construct template clusters. In section 4, we describe the automatic and human-in-the-loop evaluations that we conducted and our findings, and in section 5 we draw conclusions and propose future research directions.

2 Data

We select template responses from a dataset of agent utterances extracted from historical chat transcripts. To construct this dataset, we collect anonymized transcripts of conversations between customers and customer service agents (CSAs) in two domains: (1) Cancel Membership (CM), and (2) Tracking shows delivered but order not received (DNR). In the anonymized transcripts, all unique customer identifiers (UCI) are replaced with a special token: "*GENERIC_SLOT*". We further extract all agent utterances[1] in these transcripts and exclude those occurring only once in the data. The intuition behind this is that if an utterance only occurred once, it is not likely to be useful as a template. We end up with approximately 550K agent utterances in each domain. The DNR domain contains longer utterances than the CM domain (an average of 12 words per sentence vs. 11 for CM) and a larger vocabulary size (22.9K for DNR vs. 19.2K for CM).

2.1 Annotation Guidelines

To create our evaluation data, we select a random sample of approximately 1,000 utterances from each domain and have it annotated for "Cluster ID". For the annotation task, we ask the annotators to come up with cluster IDs as they are annotating the utterances and then consolidate these clusters after they are done assigning all utterances to clusters. We have one annotator per domain and a gold annotator that further refines the clusters for both domains. For each domain we ask the annotator to do the following:

1. Starting with the first utterance, define the first cluster to convey the semantic meaning of this utterance and give a descriptive name for the cluster.

---

2. For each utterance in the list, either assign it to an existing cluster (if appropriate) or define a new cluster.
3. When assigning utterances to clusters, ignore the tense and utterance type (statement versus question).
   E.g., *"I canceled your membership"*, *"I will cancel your membership"*, and *"Should I cancel your membership?"* will all belong to the same cluster.
4. All noisy/unneeded utterances that are not related to the current domain or that do not contain information that can be useful for resolving the customer's issue should be excluded.
5. After finishing all of the utterances, go through the list of clusters to merge redundant ones and map the utterances to the new list of cluster IDs.

The annotation process resulted in 44 and 43 clusters for the CM and DNR domains respectively. Table 1 shows sample utterances from some clusters.

3 Approach

We cluster agent utterances using a novel end-to-end approach, Deep Sentence Encoder Clustering (DSEC), in which the utterance representation and the clustering model are jointly learned. We compare this against two baselines: (1) a weak baseline in which templates are sampled randomly from the dataset, and (2) a sequential baseline in which the utterance representation and the clustering model are learned sequentially. For the baseline system, we use dense features to represent each utterance and explore the use of different embedding types—GloVe (Pennington et al., 2014), ELMo (Peters et al., 2018b,a), and BERT (Devlin et al., 2018)—as well as the effect of using in-domain data on the performance of the system.

For both DSEC and the sequential baseline, after the clusters have been obtained, we create the template pool by selecting the highest-confidence utterance in each cluster. The confidence is either the probability that the utterance falls in the cluster (for DSEC), or the distance between the utterance and its cluster centroid (for the sequential baseline).

Domain	Cluster Description	Utterances
CM	Informing the customer of confirmation e-mail	Your refund of GENERIC_SLOT will be credited to your original payment method within 7 to 10 business days.
CM	Confirming refund request	I see that you have used the membership benefits, and because of that I can offer GENERIC_SLOT refund. Sounds good?
CM	Greeting	Good afternoon.
CM	Asking for confirmation	Can you please confirm the last four digits and the expiration date of the payment method that has been charged?
DNR	Confirming refund options	Would you like the refund to be back on your gift or credit card?
DNR	Apology	I do apologize for the inconvenience if it was tagged as delivered but nowhere to be found.
DNR	Confirming order status	It seems that the package was already lost and mismarked as delivered.

Table 1: Sample agent utterances for our two domains: Cancel membership (CM) and Tracking shows delivered but item not received (DNR)

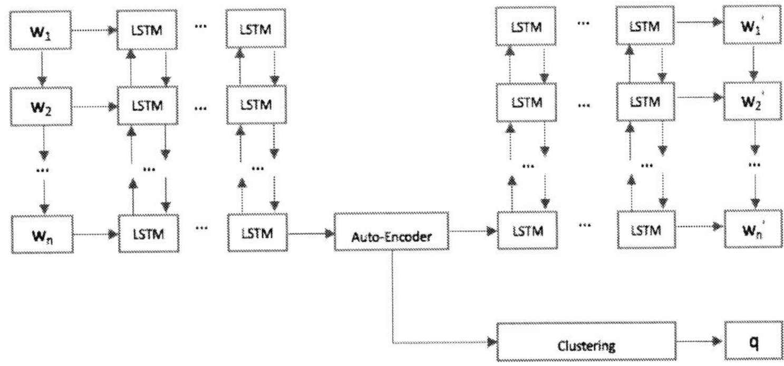

Figure 1: DSEC: An LSTM auto-encoder representing the sentence encoder and a clustering layer

3.1 Deep Sentence Encoder Clustering (DSEC)

We propose an end-to-end auto-encoder structure (Figure 1) that learns a sentence encoding layer that aims to achieve two goals simultaneously: (1) generate a feature representation from which the input utterance can be reconstructed as accurately as possible, and (2) construct template clusters by introducing a clustering-oriented loss. To achieve these two goals, we minimize a weighted (w) sum of reconstruction loss (L_r) and clustering loss (L_c).

$$L = L_r + \omega * L_c$$

To build the auto-encoder structure, we utilize a deep bi-directional Long Short-Term Memory (LSTM) network (Hochreiter and Schmidhuber, 1997). We first use a word embedding layer, and then train a multi-layer bi-directional LSTM as the encoder. We choose a bi-directional network since subsequent words can sometimes facilitate the prediction of previous words. For example, it is easy to infer that the previous word has a high probability of being "*I*" if we know that the current word is "*am*". The final output of the hidden layer is then used as the input to the decoder. Padding is used to normalize sentence length, and a softmax function is added on top of the decoder to reconstruct the input. It is intuitive that the vectors generated by the encoder are good representations of the sentences they encode if they contain enough information to reconstruct these sentences.

For clustering, we define the loss using a soft assignment between the sentence embedding and the cluster centroids, similar to Xie et al. (2016). In particular, we first use the Student's *t-distribution* as a kernel to measure the similarity between the sentence encoder z_i and each of the centroid points

μ_j:

$$q_{ij} = \frac{(1 + \|z_i - \mu_j\|^2/\alpha)^{-(\alpha+1)/2}}{\sum_{j'}(1 + \|z_i - \mu_{j'}\|^2/\alpha)^{-(\alpha+1)/2}}$$

where q_{ij} indicates the probability of assigning sentence i to cluster j. The degree of freedom α is set to be 1. The sentence clustering loss is defined as:

$$L = KL(P\|Q) = \sum_i \sum_j p_{ij} \log \frac{p_{ij}}{q_{ij}}$$

in which the soft target distribution P is defined as:

$$p_{ij} = \frac{q_{ij}^2/\sum_i q_{ij}}{\sum_j (q_{ij}^2/\sum_i q_{ij})}$$

One potential deficiency of using the target distribution, as Guo et al. (2017) pointed out, is that such a loss emphasizes data points with large p_{ij} (i.e. high confidence) hence is less impacted by mistakes for the points farther away from the centroid or ones that are close to the decision boundary hence can lead to underfitting if many such points exist. This problem can be more severe in sentence clustering than image clustering since image clustering usually has a more well defined objective whereas sentence clustering can be ambiguous and subjective. We find that different annotators often suggest different cluster labels for many of the sentences. To alleviate this issue, we suggest setting a threshold on the probability q_{ij} to filter out utterances with weak cluster signals when tuning or evaluating the model. Note that our goal is to select representative utterances from each cluster to form a reliable template pool. In this way it is most important to maximize the quality of utterances with high estimated confidences.

In practice, we initialize the reconstruction coefficients by first training the auto-encoder separately, i.e. setting $\omega = 0$. This *"warm-start"* approach helps accelerate the convergence rate.

Our proposed method borrows the loss from Xie et al. (2016) but addresses a different problem. First, Xie et al. (2016) use a convolutional network to learn an image representation. We target sentence reconstruction along with clustering, and thus propose an LSTM structure to capture the time series aspect of the sequence. Second, we use a pre-trained model fit on our own customer service data to initialize the parameters, and thus our model does not have to be very deep, which makes it less computationally intensive to train.

3.2 Sequential Baseline

Since there is no prior research targeting the task of automating template creation for ranking-based dialogue models, we propose a strong baseline that embeds the utterances and clusters them sequentially. To ensure that the baseline we are comparing against is effective, we explore the use of publicly available/pretrained embedding models versus models that are trained on in-domain customer service data. Additionally, we experiment with a traditional word embedding model, GloVe, in which the representation of each word in the vocabulary is the same regardless of the context it is appearing in, as well as contextual embeddings in which the representation depends on the entire context in which a word is used, namely ELMo and BERT. For in-domain data, we use approximately 118 million utterances to train a customer service (CS) GloVe model and an attention-based ELMo model. Once we obtain the representation for each utterance using a specific embedding model, we then use a pooling layer to obtain the utterance representation. For the pooling layer, we use weighted-mean pooling, in which each word is weighted by the "Term Frequency Inverse Document Frequency" (tf-idf) score (Aizawa, 2003), with documents defined as utterances in this case.[2]

Finally, we cluster the utterance representations. We experiment with K-means (MacQueen et al., 1967), AffinityPropagation (Frey and Dueck, 2007), spectral (Shi and Malik, 2000), Ward's (Murtagh and Legendre, 2014), Agglomerative (Müllner, 2011) and Birch (Zhang et al., 1997) clustering. For K-means, we use the centroid as the representation of the cluster, while for other algorithms, we take the mean pooling for all templates in the cluster as the centroid, compute the distance from each template to the centroid, and choose the template that is the shortest distance from the centroid. In the experiments described in Section 4, we select the clustering method with the best normalized mutual information score (NMI) as our baseline. We find that this is always achieved by either Ward's or Birch.

---

[2]We also experimented with max and unweighted-mean pooling but achieved better results using weighted-mean pooling.

4   Experiments & Results

We evaluate clustering performance using both automatic and human-in-the-loop evaluations. For all experiments, we fix the cluster number at 50 for all models to ensure that the template pool has good coverage of common situations.

4.1   Automatic Evaluation

To evaluate the quality of the generated clusters, we compare the ground truth—from our gold labeled data—with predicted labels using normalized mutual information score (NMI), unsupervised clustering accuracy (ACC; Xie et al. (2016)), and Rand index adjusted for chance (ARI; Hubert and Arabie (1985)). We evaluate the performance of DSEC when compared to (1) the sequential baseline and (2) a weak baseline that randomly assigns each utterance to one of the clusters.

Tables 2 and 3 show the results of the automatic evaluation on the labeled CM and DNR datasets. For DSEC, the validation accuracy of reconstruction is approximately 93% for both datasets, indicating that the auto-encoder vector extracts the sentence information well. On CM, DSEC achieves the best NMI and ACC, while the sequential method, with the ELMo-CS embedding and weighted mean pooling of tf-idf features, has the best ARI results overall. The models using in-domain embeddings outperform others with pre-trained embeddings. Note that the metrics NMI, ACC, and ARI are not always consistent when compared across different methods. For example, Glove-CS has a high ARI score but under-performs with all the other automatic metrics.

In addition, clustering performs better on DNR dataset than on CM. This is potentially because the CM domain contains a broader range of customer issues corresponding to different membership types and hence is more challenging to represent using utterance clustering. For example, the templates can be quite different for canceling a free trial, a regular subscription, and certain memberships with an additional subscription attached.

Overall, none of the proposed methods achieve the accuracy of some image clustering work, such as Guo et al. (2017). As discussed before, image clustering and text clustering are very different tasks, and sentence clustering can be quite subjective. Rephrasing or adding content to sentences can make such clustering challenging even for humans. For example, it is non-trivial to decide whether the following sentences should be clustered together: "I will cancel your membership", "I'll cancel your membership and issue a refund", and "The membership will be canceled starting today and you will not be able to use the free subscription". Note that the second and third sentences both contain additional information as opposed to the first sentence. In practice, we encourage annotators to define each cluster as precisely as possible, even if it results in a large number of clusters. This can increase the coverage of the generated template pool but decrease the performance of clustering in the automatic evaluation. To determine the true impact of clustering on our downstream task, response generation, we conduct a human-in-the-loop evaluation in which we use the generated template pool along with a neural response ranking model to recommend responses to CSAs handling customer service contacts.

4.2   Human-in-the-Loop Evaluation

To evaluate the effectiveness of clustering for the downstream task of response generation, we use a human-in-the-loop research platform through which CSAs handle live customer contacts. Specifically, we train template-based neural response ranking models for CM and DNR similar to the model proposed by Lu et al. (2019), and then use them to select responses from the template pools generated using the methods proposed above. Note that training the response ranking model is independent of template creation. We then test the resulting model and template pool using this platform. Instead of showing CSAs the standard chat box, the platform presents ten suggested responses chosen by the trained model from the pool generated by one of the clustering approaches. These 10 suggestions come from different clusters since we only send one template per cluster to the ranking model. They are based on the complete conversation history up to this point and are updated each time the customer or the agent sends a response. The CSA can pick any of the suggested templates as a response, or type their own text if none of the templates appears appropriate. An ideal template pool should minimize the chance that CSAs need to type their own text, and also have no overlapping templates in it.

We choose the following metrics for the human-in-the-loop evaluation, reported in Table 4[3]:

---

[3]For the human-in-the-loop experiment, we only include

	Rand-BL	Glove	GloVe-CS	BERT	ELMo	ELMo-CS	DSEC
NMI	0.22	0.43	0.54	0.31	0.30	0.54	**0.60**
ACC	0.10	0.24	0.33	0.16	0.16	0.31	**0.39**
ARI	0.00	0.11	**0.20**	0.04	0.03	0.18	0.12

Table 2: Results of Automatic Evaluation on CM Data

	Rand-BL	Glove	GloVe-CS	BERT	ELMo	ELMo-CS	DSEC
NMI	0.23	0.49	0.62	0.39	0.40	0.61	**0.63**
ACC	0.10	0.31	0.47	0.2	0.24	0.41	**0.51**
ARI	0.00	0.15	0.32	0.12	0.09	0.26	**0.34**

Table 3: Results of Automatic Evaluation on DNR Data

1. Top-10 acceptance rate: The percentage of utterances for which the CSA selects one of the suggested responses.
2. Top-1 acceptance rate: The percentage of utterances for which the CSA selects the first suggested response.
3. All suggestions accepted: The percentage of contacts that are handled using only suggested utterances.
4. Average depth of first rejection: The percentage of utterances in the conversation that occur before the agent rejects all suggestions and types their own text.
5. Unique rate: This measures the variation of the template pool, calculated as one minus the percentage of templates that can be removed without reducing the coverage. Ideally, this number would be 1.0.
6. Number of missing templates: The number of utterances that are reported missing from agents. Ideally, this number would be 0.

In this experiment, we compare the performance of (1) the end-to-end approach (DSEC), (2) the sequential setup that performs best in the automatic evaluation (GloVe-CS with weighted-mean pooling and Ward's clustering), and (3) a random baseline in which we randomly select 50 utterances from the dataset to be used as templates. Additionally, we include a human/gold baseline for which the template pool is manually created and refined by collecting feedback from agents over the course of one month.

The utterance acceptance rate indicates that DSEC outperforms both the random and the sequential baseline and performs only slightly worse than the human template pool. As expected, the "all suggestions accepted" rate is much lower for the CM dataset due to limited agent resources.

DSEC than for the gold/human pool, but better than for the other automated methods. We find that the sequential approach manages to minimize the length of the conversation (i.e. the number of CSA utterances). One possibility is that it results in a better coverage rate so that it can guide the agents to solve contacts more efficiently than the other methods.

We measure coverage by asking agents to report missing templates. Agents reported a few missing templates for all of the automatically generated pools. The variance in this metric is high because the experiment is only run for about 200 contacts for each experimental configuration. In this way, corner examples may not show up for all of the configurations, and a larger experiment is needed to determine exactly how many templates are missing.

Lastly, the sequential baseline results in a higher depth of first rejection than the manual approach. A possible cause is that this approach leads to a larger proportion of shorter contacts: The sequential approach has 4% more contacts that have less than 10 CSA utterances than the manual one. This could indicate that automatically generated templates can increase the efficiency of contact handling by steering CSAs away from utterances that could lead to longer conversations.

5 Conclusion & Future Work

We present DSEC, an end-to-end sentence encoding and clustering approach that can help automate template creation for template-based conversational models. The purpose is to avoid the human effort required to manually create a template pool when training a response generation model for a conversational system. We evaluate the proposed approach on two customer service datasets and find that it outperforms both a strong sequential baseline and a random baseline in most cases. In addition,

Metric	Rand	Gold	Scq	DSEC
Total contacts	187	250	211	209
Average number of CSA turns per contact	12.0	12.5	10.1	12.0
Top-10 acceptance rate (% utterances)	48.8	56.4	50.5	52.0
Top-1 acceptance rate (% utterances)	20.9	26.7	22	23.8
All suggestions accepted (% contacts)	2.7	10.3	4.2	6.3
All but 1 accepted (% contacts)	7.8	13.1	10.3	12.4
Average depth of 1st rejection (% contacts)	30.7	31.7	32.3	31.2
Unique rate	0.67	1.0	0.77	0.71
Number of missing templates	4	0	2	2

Table 4: Results of Human-in-the-Loop Experiment on CM Data

we use the resulting template pools in a human-in-the-loop experiment and observe that the template pool created using DSEC performs only slightly worse than a manually created template pool that takes over a month of human effort to develop. In future work, we plan on exploring building a pipeline that can automatically polish and update the generated template pool using feedback from agents.

Acknowledgements

We thank the three anonymous reviewers for their feedback and insights in improving the work.

References

Akiko Aizawa. 2003. An information-theoretic perspective of tf–idf measures. *Information Processing & Management*, 39(1):45–65.

Ashutosh Baheti, Alan Ritter, Jiwei Li, and Bill Dolan. 2018. Generating more interesting responses in neural conversation models with distributional constraints. In *Proceedings of the 2018 Conference on Empirical Methods in Natural Language Processing*.

Kyunghyun Cho, Bart Van Merriënboer, Caglar Gulcehre, Dzmitry Bahdanau, Fethi Bougares, Holger Schwenk, and Yoshua Bengio. 2014. Learning phrase representations using rnn encoder-decoder for statistical machine translation. *arXiv preprint arXiv:1406.1078*.

Jacob Devlin, Ming-Wei Chang, Kenton Lee, and Kristina Toutanova. 2018. Bert: Pre-training of deep bidirectional transformers for language understanding. *arXiv preprint arXiv:1810.04805*.

B. J. Frey and D. Dueck. 2007. Clustering by Passing Messages Between Data Points. *Science*, 315(5814):972–976.

Xifeng Guo, Xinwang Liu, En Zhu, and Jianping Yin. 2017. Deep clustering with convolutional autoencoders. In *International Conference on Neural Information Processing*, pages 373–382. Springer.

Sepp Hochreiter and Jürgen Schmidhuber. 1997. Long short-term memory. *Neural computation*, 9(8):1735–1780.

Lawrence Hubert and Phipps Arabie. 1985. Comparing partitions. *Journal of classification*, 2(1):193–218.

Anjuli Kannan, Karol Kurach, Sujith Ravi, Tobias Kaufmann, Andrew Tomkins, Balint Miklos, Greg Corrado, Laszlo Lukacs, Marina Ganea, Peter Young, et al. 2016. Smart reply: Automated response suggestion for email. In *Proceedings of the 22nd ACM SIGKDD International Conference on Knowledge Discovery and Data Mining*, pages 955–964. ACM.

Jiwei Li, Michel Galley, Chris Brockett, Jianfeng Gao, and Bill Dolan. 2016. A diversity-promoting objective function for neural conversation models. In *Proceedings of the 2016 Conference of the North American Chapter of the Association for Computational Linguistics: Human Language Technologies*, pages 110–119.

Bing Liu, Gokhan Tur, Dilek Hakkani-Tur, Pararth Shah, and Larry Heck. 2018. Dialogue learning with human teaching and feedback in end-to-end trainable task-oriented dialogue systems. In *Proceedings of the 2018 Conference of the North American Chapter of the Association for Computational Linguistics: Human Language Technologies, Volume 1 (Long Papers)*, volume 1, pages 2060–2069.

Yichao Lu, Manisha Srivastava, Jared Kramer, Heba Elfardy, Andrea Kahn, Song Wang, and Vikas Bhardwaj. 2019. Goal-oriented end-to-end conversational models with profile features in a real-world setting. In *Proceedings of the 2019 Conference of the North American Chapter of the Association for Computational Linguistics: Human Language Technologies, Volume 2 (Industry Papers)*, pages 48–55.

James MacQueen et al. 1967. Some methods for classification and analysis of multivariate observations. In *Proceedings of the fifth Berkeley symposium on mathematical statistics and probability*, volume 1, pages 281–297. Oakland, CA, USA.

Daniel Müllner. 2011. Modern hierarchical, agglomerative clustering algorithms. *arXiv:1109.2378 [cs, stat]*. ArXiv: 1109.2378.

Fionn Murtagh and Pierre Legendre. 2014. Wards Hierarchical Agglomerative Clustering Method: Which Algorithms Implement Wards Criterion? *Journal of Classification*, 31(3):274–295.

Jeff Pasternack, Nimesh Chakravarthi, Adam Leon, Nandeesh Rajashekar, Birjodh Tiwana, and Bing Zhao. 2017. Building smart replies for member messages.

Jeffrey Pennington, Richard Socher, and Christopher Manning. 2014. Glove: Global vectors for word representation. In *Proceedings of the 2014 conference on empirical methods in natural language processing (EMNLP)*, pages 1532–1543.

Matthew Peters, Mark Neumann, Luke Zettlemoyer, and Wen-tau Yih. 2018a. Dissecting contextual word embeddings: Architecture and representation. In *Proceedings of the 2018 Conference on Empirical Methods in Natural Language Processing*, pages 1499–1509.

Matthew E Peters, Mark Neumann, Mohit Iyyer, Matt Gardner, Christopher Clark, Kenton Lee, and Luke Zettlemoyer. 2018b. Deep contextualized word representations. In *Proceedings of NAACL-HLT*, pages 2227–2237.

Minghui Qiu, Feng-Lin Li, Siyu Wang, Xing Gao, Yan Chen, Weipeng Zhao, Haiqing Chen, Jun Huang, and Wei Chu. 2017. Alime chat: A sequence to sequence and rerank based chatbot engine. In *Proceedings of the 55th Annual Meeting of the Association for Computational Linguistics (Volume 2: Short Papers)*, pages 498–503.

Iulian Vlad Serban, Alessandro Sordoni, Yoshua Bengio, Aaron C Courville, and Joelle Pineau. 2016. Building end-to-end dialogue systems using generative hierarchical neural network models. In *AAAI*, volume 16, pages 3776–3784.

Yuanlong Shao, Stephan Gouws, Denny Britz, Anna Goldie, Brian Strope, and Ray Kurzweil. 2017. Generating high-quality and informative conversation responses with sequence-to-sequence models. In *Proceedings of the 2017 Conference on Empirical Methods in Natural Language Processing*.

Jianbo Shi and Jitendra Malik. 2000. Normalized Cuts and Image Segmentation. *IEEE Transactions on Pattern Analysis and Machine Intelligence*, 22(8):18.

Oriol Vinyals and Quoc Le. 2015. A neural conversational model. *arXiv preprint arXiv:1506.05869*.

Junyuan Xie, Ross Girshick, and Ali Farhadi. 2016. Unsupervised deep embedding for clustering analysis. In *International conference on machine learning*, pages 478–487.

Ruqing Zhang, Jiafeng Guo, Yixing Fan, Yanyan Lan, Jun Xu, and Xueqi Cheng. 2018. Learning to control the specificity in neural response generation. In *Proceedings of the 56th Annual Meeting of the Association for Computational Linguistics (Volume 1: Long Papers)*, volume 1.

Tian Zhang, Raghu Ramakrishnan, and Miron Livny. 1997. BIRCH: A New Data Clustering Algorithm and Its Applications. *Data Mining and Knowledge Discovery*, 1(2):141–182.

Xiangyang Zhou, Lu Li, Daxiang Dong, Yi Liu, Ying Chen, Wayne Xin Zhao, Dianhai Yu, and Hua Wu. 2018. Multi-turn response selection for chatbots with deep attention matching network. In *Proceedings of the 56th Annual Meeting of the Association for Computational Linguistics (Volume 1: Long Papers)*, volume 1.

From Machine Reading Comprehension to Dialogue State Tracking:
Bridging the Gap

Shuyang Gao[*,1]   **Sanchit Agarwal**[*,1]   **Tagyoung Chung**[1]   **Di Jin**[2]   **Dilek Hakkani-Tur**[1]

[1]Amazon Alexa AI, Sunnyvale, CA, USA

[2]Computer Science & Artificial Intelligence Laboratory, MIT, MA, USA

{shuyag, agsanchi, tagyoung, hakkanit}@amazon.com, jindi15@mit.edu

Abstract

Dialogue state tracking (DST) is at the heart of task-oriented dialogue systems. However, the scarcity of labeled data is an obstacle to building accurate and robust state tracking systems that work across a variety of domains. Existing approaches generally require some dialogue data with state information and their ability to generalize to unknown domains is limited. In this paper, we propose using machine reading comprehension (RC) in state tracking from two perspectives: model architectures and datasets. We divide the slot types in dialogue state into *categorical* or *extractive* to borrow the advantages from both *multiple-choice* and *span-based* reading comprehension models. Our method achieves near the current state-of-the-art in joint goal accuracy on MultiWOZ 2.1 given full training data. More importantly, by leveraging machine reading comprehension datasets, our method outperforms the existing approaches by many a large margin in few-shot scenarios when the availability of in-domain data is limited. Lastly, even *without* any state tracking data, i.e., zero-shot scenario, our proposed approach achieves greater than 90% average slot accuracy in 12 out of 30 slots in MultiWOZ 2.1.

1   Introduction

Building a task-oriented dialogue system that can comprehend users' requests and complete tasks on their behalf is a challenging but fascinating problem. Dialogue state tracking (DST) is at the heart of task-oriented dialogue systems. It tracks the *state* of a dialogue during the conversation between a user and a system. The *state* is typically defined as the *(slot_name, slot_value)* pair that represents, given a slot, the value that the user provides or system-provided value that the user accepts.

Despite the importance of DST in task-oriented dialogues systems, few large datasets are available. To address this issue, several methods have been proposed for data collection and bootstrapping the DST system. These approaches either utilize Wizard-of-Oz setup via crowd sourcing (Wen et al., 2017; Budzianowski et al., 2018) or Machines Talking To Machines (M2M) framework (Shah et al., 2018). Currently the most comprehensive dataset with state annotation is MultiWOZ (Budzianowski et al., 2018), which contains seven domains with around $10,000$ dialogues. However, compared to other NLP datasets, MultiWOZ is still relatively small, especially for training data-intensive neural models. In addition, it is also a non-trivial to get a large amount of clean labeled data given the nature of task-oriented dialogues (Eric et al., 2019).

Another thread of approaches have tried to utilize data in a more efficient manner. These approaches (Wu et al., 2019; Zhou and Small, 2019) usually train the models on several domains and perform zero-shot or few-shot learning on unseen domains. However, these methods require slot definitions to be similar between the training data and the unseen test data. If such systems are given a completely new slot type, the performance would degrade significantly. Therefore, these approaches still rely on considerable amount of DST data to cover a broad range of slot categories.

We find machine reading comprehension task (RC) (Rajpurkar et al., 2016; Chen, 2018) as a source of inspiration to tackle these challenges. The RC task aims to evaluate how well machine models can understand human language, whose goals are actually similar to DST. Ultimately, DST focuses on the contextual *understanding* of users' request and inferring the *state* from the conversation, whereas RC focuses on the general understanding of the text regardless of its format, which can be either passages or conversations. In addition,

---

*Authors contributed equally.

79

Proceedings of the 2nd Workshop on Natural Language Processing for Conversational AI, pages 79–89

July 9, 2020. ©2020 Association for Computational Linguistics

recent advances have shown tremendous success in RC tasks. Thus, if we could formulate the DST task as a RC task, it could benefit DST in two aspects: first, we could take advantage of the fast-growing RC research advances; second, we could make use of the abundant RC data to overcome the data scarcity issue in DST task.

Building upon this motivation, we formulate the DST task into an RC task by specially designing a question for each slot in the dialogue state, similar to Gao et al. (2019). Then, we divide the slots into two types: *categorical* and *extractive*, based on the number of slot values in the ontology. For instance, in MultiWOZ, slots such as *parking* take values of {*Yes, No, Don't Care*} and can thus be treated as *categorical*. In contrast, slots such as *hotel-name* may accept an unlimited number of possible values and these are treated as *extractive*. Accordingly, we propose two machine reading comprehension models for dialogue state tracking. For categorical slots, we use multiple-choice reading comprehension models where an answer has to be chosen from a limited number of options. And for the extractive dialogue state tracking, span-based reading comprehension are applied where the answer can be found in the form of a span in the conversation.

To summarize our approach and contributions:

- We divide the dialogue state slots into categorical and extractive types and use RC techniques for state tracking. Our approach can leverage the recent advances in the field of machine reading comprehension, including both multiple-choice and span-based reading comprehension models.

- We propose a two-stage training strategy. We first coarse-train the state tracking models on reading comprehension datasets, then fine-tune them on the target state tracking dataset.

- We show the effectiveness of our method under three scenarios: First, in full data setting, we show our method achieves close to the current state-of-the-art on MultiWoz 2.1 in terms of joint goal accuracy. Second, in few-shot setting, when only 1–10% of the training data is available, we show our methods significantly outperform the previous methods for 5 test domains in MultiWoz 2.0. In particular, we achieve 45.91% joint goal accuracy with just 1% (around 20–30 dialogues) of hotel domain data as compared to previous best result of 19.73% (Wu et al., 2019).

Thirdly, in zero-shot setting where no state tracking data is used for training, our models still achieve considerable average slot accuracy. More concretely, we show that 13 out of 30 slots in MultiWOZ 2.1 can achieve an average slot accuracy of greater than 90% without any training.

- We demonstrate the impact of canonicalization on extractive dialogue state tracking. We also categorize errors based on *None* and *Not None* slot values. We found the majority errors for our DST model come from distinguishing *None* or *Not None* for slots.

2 Related Works

Traditionally, dialogue state tracking methods (Liu and Lane, 2017; Mrkšić et al., 2016; Zhong et al., 2018; Nouri and Hosseini-Asl, 2018; Lee et al., 2019) assume a fully-known fixed ontology for all slots where the output space of a slot is constrained by the values in the ontology. However, such approaches cannot handle previously unseen values and do not scale well for slots such as *restaurant-name* that can take potentially unbounded set of values. To alleviate these issues, Rastogi et al. (2017); Goel et al. (2018) generate and score slot-value candidates from the ontology, dialogue context n-grams, slot tagger outputs, or a combination of them. However, these approaches suffer if a reliable slot tagger is not available or if the slot value is longer than the candidate n-grams. Xu and Hu (2018) proposed attention-based pointing mechanism to find the start and end of the slot value to better tackle the issue of unseen slot values. Gao et al. (2019) proposed using a RC framework for state tracking. They track slot values by answering the question "what is the value of the slot?" through attention-based pointing to the dialogue context. Chao and Lane (2019); Rastogi et al. (2019) utilize BERT to encode the dialogue context and then point to slot-value span in the encoded context. Although these approaches are more practical and scalable, they suffer when the exact slot value does not appear in the context as expected by the back-end database or if the value is not *pointable*. More recently, hybrid approaches have attempted to combine the benefits of both using predefined ontology (closed vocabulary) and dynamically generating candidate set or pointing (open vocabulary) approaches. Goel et al. (2019) select between the two approaches per slot based on dev set. Wu et al.

(2019) utilize pointer generator network to either copy from the context or generate from vocabulary.

Perhaps, the most similar to our work is by Zhang et al. (2019) and Zhou and Small (2019) where they divide slot types into span-based (extractive) slots and pick-list (categorical) slots and use QA framework to point or pick values for these slots. A major limitation of these works is that they utilize heuristics to determine which slots should be categorical and which non-categorical. Moreover, in these settings most of the slots are treated as categorical (21/30 and 25/30), even though some of them have very large number of possible values, e.g., *restaurant-name*. This is not scalable especially when the ontology is large, not comprehensive, or when new domains/slots can occur at test time as in DSTC8 dataset (Rastogi et al., 2019).

There are recent efforts into building or adapting dialog state tracking systems in low source data scenarios Wu et al. (2019); Zhou and Small (2019). The general idea in these approaches is to treat all but one domain as in-domain data and test on the remaining unseen domain either directly (zero shot) or after fine-tuning on small percentage (1%-10%) of the unseen domain data (few shot). A major drawback of these approaches is that they require several labeled in-domain examples in order perform well on the unseen domain. This limits these approaches to in-domain slots and slot definitions and they do not generalize very well to new slots or completely unseen target domain. This also requires large amount of labeled data in the source domain, which may not be available in real-world scenario. Our proposed approach, on the other hand, utilizes domain-agnostic QA datasets with zero or a small percentage of DST data and significantly outperforms these approaches in low-resource settings.

3 Methods

3.1 Dialogue State Tracking as Reading Comprehension

Dialogue as Paragraph For a given dialogue at turn t, let us denote the user utterance tokens and the agent utterance tokens as $\mathbf{u}_t$ and $\mathbf{a}_t$ respectively. We concatenate the user utterance tokens and the agent utterance tokens at each turn to construct a sequence of tokens as $\mathbf{D}_t = \{\mathbf{u}_1, \mathbf{a}_1, ..., \mathbf{u}_t\}$. $\mathbf{D}_t$ can be viewed as the paragraph that we are going to ask questions on at turn t.

Slot as Question We can formulate a natural language question $\mathbf{q}_i$, for each slot s_i in the dialogue state. Such a question describes the meaning of that slot in the dialogue state. Examples of (slot, question) pairs can be seen in Table 2 and 3. We formulate questions by considering characteristics of domain and slot. In this way, DST becomes finding answers $\mathbf{a}_i$ to the question $\mathbf{q}_i$ given the paragraph $\mathbf{D}_t$. Note that Gao et al. (2019) formulate dialogue state tracking problem in a similar way but their question formulation *"what is the value of a slot ?"* is more abstract, whereas our questions are more concrete and meaningful to the dialogue.

3.2 Span-based RC To Extractive DST

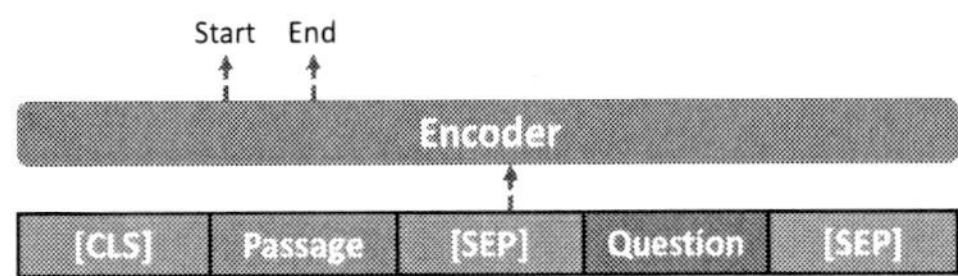

Figure 1: Model architecture for extractive state tracking. "Encoder" is a pre-trained sentence encoder such as BERT.

For many slots in the dialogue state such as names of attractions, restaurants, and departure times, one can often find their values in the dialogue context with exact matches. Slots with a wide range of values fits this description. Table 1 shows the exact match rate for each slot in Multi-WOZ 2.1 dataset (Budzianowski et al., 2018; Eric et al., 2019) where slots with large number of possible values tend to have higher exact match rate ($\geq 80\%$). We call tracking such slots as *extractive dialogue stack tracking (EDST)*.

This problem is similar to span-based RC where the goal is to find a span in the passage that best answers the question. Therefore, for EDST, we adopt the simple BERT-based question answering model used by Devlin et al. (2019), which has shown strong performance on multiple datasets (Rajpurkar et al., 2016, 2018; Reddy et al., 2019). In this model as shown in Figure 1, the slot question and the dialogue are represented as a single sequence. The probability of a dialogue token t_i being the start of the slot value span is computed as $p_i = \frac{e^{\mathbf{s} \cdot \mathbf{T}_i}}{\sum_j e^{\mathbf{s} \cdot \mathbf{T}_j}}$, where $\mathbf{T}_j$ is the embedding of each token t_j and $\mathbf{s}$ is a learnable vector. A similar formula is applied for finding the end of the span.

Handling *None* Values At any given turn in the conversation, there are typically, many slots that

Slot Name	# Possible Values	Exact Match Rate	Extractive	Categorical
hotel.semi.type	3	61.1%	×	✓
hotel.semi.internet	3	62.1%	×	✓
hotel.semi.parking	4	63.1%	×	✓
restaurant.semi.pricerange	4	97.8%	✓	✓
hotel.semi.pricerange	6	97.7%	✓	✓
hotel.semi.area	6	98.8%	✓	✓
attraction.semi.area	6	99.0%	✓	✓
restaurant.semi.area	6	99.2%	✓	✓
hotel.semi.stars	7	99.2%	✓	✓
hotel.book.people	8	98.2%	✓	✓
hotel.book.stay	8	98.9%	✓	✓
train.semi.day	8	99.3%	✓	✓
restaurant.book.day	8	98.7%	✓	✓
restaurant.book.people	8	99.1%	✓	✓
hotel.book.day	11	98.1%	✓	✓
train.book.people	12	94.7%	✓	×
train.semi.destination	27	98.2%	✓	×
attraction.semi.type	27	86.6%	✓	×
train.semi.departure	31	97.6%	✓	×
restaurant.book.time	67	97.2%	✓	×
hotel.semi.name	78	88.7%	✓	×
taxi.semi.arriveby	97	91.9%	✓	×
restaurant.semi.food	103	96.4%	✓	×
taxi.semi.leaveat	108	81.1%	✓	×
train.semi.arriveby	156	91.5%	✓	×
attraction.semi.name	158	84.3%	✓	×
restaurant.semi.name	182	93.9%	✓	×
train.semi.leaveat	201	87.4%	✓	×
taxi.semi.destination	251	87.9%	✓	×
taxi.semi.departure	253	84.6%	✓	×

Table 1: Slot statistics for MultiWOZ 2.1. We classify the slots into extractive or categorical based on their exact match rate in conversation as well as number of possible values. 3 slots are categorical only, 12 slots are both extractive and categorical, the remaining 15 slots are extractive only.

Dialogue
U: I'm so hungry. Can you find me a place to eat in the city centre?
A: I'm happy to help! There are a great deal of restaurants there. What type of food did you have in mind?
U: I do not care, it just needs to be expensive.
A: Fitzbillies restaurant serves British food would that be okay?
U: Yes, may I have the address?
restaurant.semi.food: What type of food does the user want to eat?
Answer: [52-53] *(I do not care, it just needs to be expensive)*
restaurant.semi.name: What is the name of the restaurant where the user wants to eat?
Answer: [53-55] *(Fitzbillies restaurant)*

Table 2: Sample dialogue from MultiWOZ dataset showing framing of extractive DST to span-based RC. The span text (or *don't care* user utterance) is also shown in italics.

have not been mentioned or accepted yet by the user. All these slots must be assigned a *None* value in the dialogue state. We can view such cases as *no answer exists* in reading comprehension formulation. Similar to Devlin et al. (2019) for SQuAD 2.0 task, we assign the answer span with start and end at the beginning token [CLS] for these slots.

Handling *Don't Care* Values To handle *don't care* value in EDST, a span is also assigned to *don't care* in the dialogue. We find the dialogue turn when the slot value first becomes *don't care* and set the start and end of *don't care* span to be the start and end of the user utterance of this turn. See Table 2 for an example.

3.3 Multiple-Choice Reading Comprehension to Categorical Dialogue State Tracking

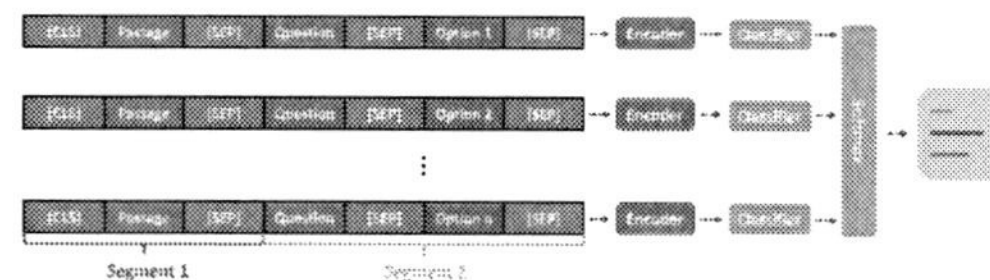

Figure 2: Model architecture for categorical dialog state tracking. "Encoder"is a pre-trained sentence encoder such as BERT. "Classifier" is a top-level fully connected layer.

The other type of slots in the dialogue state cannot be filled through exact match in the dialogue

	Dialogue

Dialogue
U: I am looking for a place to to stay that has cheap price range it should be in a type of hotel
A: Okay , Do you have a specific area you want to stay in?
U: No, I just need to make sure it's cheap. Oh, and I need parking.

hotel.semi.area: What is the area that the user wants to book a hotel in?
A. East   **B.** West   **C.** North   **D.** South   **E.** Centre   **F.** Don't Care ✓   **G.** Not Mentioned

hotel.semi.parking: Does the user want parking at the hotel?
A. Yes ✓   **B.** No   **C.** Don't Care   **D.** Not Mentioned

Table 3: Sample dialogue from MultiWOZ dataset showing framing of categorical DST to multiple-choice RC.

context in a large number of cases. For example, a user might express intent for hotel parking as *"oh! and make sure it has parking"* but the slot *hotel-parking* only accepts values from {*Yes, No, Don't Care*}. In this case, the state tracker needs to infer whether or not the user wants parking based on the user utterance and select the correct value from the list. These kind of slots may not have exact-match spans in the dialogue context but usually require a limited number of values to choose from.

Tracking these type of slots is surprisingly similar to multiple-choice reading comprehension (MCRC) tasks. In comparison to span-based RC tasks, the answers of MCRC datasets (Lai et al., 2017; Sun et al., 2019) are often in the form of open, natural language sentences and are not restricted to spans in text. Following the traditional models of MCRC (Devlin et al., 2019; Jin et al., 2019), we concatenate the slot question, the dialogue context and one of the answer choices into a long sequence. We then feed this sequence into a sentence encoder to obtain a logit vector. Given a question, we can get m logit vectors assuming there are m answer choices. We then transform these m logit vectors into a probability vector through a fully connected layer and a softmax layer, see Figure 2 for details.

Handling *None* and *Don't Care* Values For each question, we simply add two additional choices "not mentioned" and "do not care" in the answer options, representing *None* and *don't care*, as shown in Table 3. It is worth noting that certain slots not only accept a limited number of values but also their values can be found as an exact-match span in the dialogue context. For these slots, both extractive and categorical DST models can be applied as shown in Table 1.

4 Experiments

4.1 Datasets

	# of passages	# of examples
MRQA (span-based)	386,384	516,819
DREAM (multi-choice)	6,444	10,197
RACE (multi-choice)	27,933	97,687
MultiWOZ	8,420	298,978[*]

Table 4: Statistics of datasets used. (*: we only report the number of positive examples (a non-empty value) in Multi-WOZ for fair comparison.)

MultiWOZ We use the largest available multi-domain dialogue dataset with state annotation: MultiWOZ 2.0 (Budzianowski et al., 2018) and MultiWOZ 2.1 (Eric et al., 2019), an enhanced, less noisier version of MultiWOZ 2.0 dataset, which contains 7 distinct domains across 10K dialogues. We exclude *hospital* and *police* domain that have very few dialogues. This results in 5 remaining domains *attraction*, *restaurant*, *taxi*, *train*, *hotel* with a total of 30 (domain, slot) pairs in the dialog state following Wu et al. (2019); Zhang et al. (2019).

Reading Comprehension Datasets For span-based RC dataset, we use the dataset from Machine Reading for Question Answering (MRQA) 2019 shared task (Fisch et al., 2019) that was focused on extractive question answering. MRQA contains six distinct datasets across different domains: SQuAD, NewsQA, TriviaQA, SearchQA, HotpotQA, and NaturalQuestions. In this dataset, any answer to a question is a segment of text or span in a given document. For multiple-choice RC dataset, we leverage the current largest multiple-choice QA dataset, RACE (Lai et al., 2017) as well as a dialogue-based multiple-choice QA dataset, DREAM (Sun et al., 2019). Both of these datasets are collected from English language exams that are carefully designed by educational experts to assess the comprehension level of English learners. Table 4 summarizes the statistics of datasets. It is worth noting that for MultiWOZ, although the number of examples are significantly more than multiple-choice QA datasets, the number of distinct questions are only 30 due to limited number of slot types.

4.2 Canonicalization for Extractive Dialogue State Tracking

For extractive dialogue state tracking, it is common that the model will choose a span that is either a super-set of the correct reference or has a similar meaning as the correct value but with a different wording. Following this observation, we adopt a simple canonicalization procedure after our span-based model prediction. If the predicted value does not exist in the ontology of the slot, then we match the prediction with the value in the ontology that is closest to the predicted value in terms of edit distance[1]. Note that this procedure is only applied at model *inference* time. At training time for extractive dialogue state tracking, the ontology is not required.

4.3 Two-stage Training

A two-stage training procedure is used to train the extractive and categorical dialogue state tracking models with both types of reading comprehension datasets (DREAM, RACE, and MRQA) and the dialogue state tracking dataset (MultiWOZ).

Reading Comprehension Training Stage For categorical dialogue state tracking model, we coarse-tune the model on DREAM and RACE. For extractive dialogue state tracking model, we coarse-tune the model on MRQA dataset as a first step.

Dialog State Tracking Training Stage After being trained on the reading comprehension datasets, we expect our models to be capable of answering (passage, question) pairs. In this phase, we further fine-tune these models on the MultiWOZ dataset.

5 Results and Analyses

5.1 DST with Full Training Data

Joint Goal Accuracy	
SpanPtr (Xu and Hu, 2018)	29.09%
FJST (Eric et al., 2019)	38.00%
HyST (Goel et al., 2019)	39.10%
DSTreader (Gao et al., 2019)	36.40%
TRADE (Wu et al., 2019)	45.96%
DS-DST (Zhang et al., 2019)	**51.21%**
DSTQA w/span (Zhou and Small, 2019)	49.67%
DSTQA w/o span (Zhou and Small, 2019)	51.17%
STARC (this work)	49.48%

Table 5: Joint Goal Accuracy on MultiWOZ 2.1 test set.

We use the full data in MultiWOZ 2.1 to test our models. For the first 15 slots with lowest number of possible values (from *hotel.semi.type* to *ho-*

---

[1]we use the function *get_closest_matches* of *difflib* in Python for this implementation.

tel.book.day in Table 1, we use our proposed categorical dialogue state tracking model whereas for the remaining 15 slots, we use the extractive dialogue state tracking model. We use the pre-trained word embedding RoBERTa-Large (Liu et al., 2019) in our experiment.

Table 5 summarizes the results. We can see that our model, STARC (State Tracking As Reading Comprehension), achieves close to the state-of-the-art accuracy on MultiWOZ 2.1 in the full data setting. It is worth noting that the best performing approach DS-DST (Zhang et al., 2019), cherry-picks 9 slots as span-based slots whereas the remaining 21 slots are treated as categorical. Further, the second best result DSTQA w/o span (Zhou and Small, 2019) does not use span-based model for any slot. Unlike these state-of-the-art methods, our method simply categorizes the slots based on the number of values in the ontology. As a result, our approach uses less number of (15 as compared to 21 in DS-DST) and more reasonable (only those with few values in the ontology) categorical slots. Thus, our approach is more practical to be applied in a real-world scenario.

Ablation	Dev Accuracy
STARC (this work)	**53.95%**
– RC Coarse Tuning	52.35%
– Canonicalization	51.07%
– RC Coarse Tuning – Canonicalization	50.84%
– Categorical Model	47.86%
– Categorical Model – Canonicalization	41.86%
DS-DST Threshold-10	49.08%
DS-DST Span Only	40.39%

Table 6: Ablation study with different aspects of our model and other comparable approaches. The numbers reported are joint goal accuracy on MultiWOZ 2.1 development set.

Ablation Study We also run ablation study to understand which component of our model helps with accuracy. Table 6 summarizes the results. For fair comparison, we also report the numbers for DS-DST Threshold-10 (Zhang et al., 2019) where they also use the first 15 slots for categorical model and the remaining for extractive model. We observe that both two-stage training strategy using reading comprehension data and canonicalization play important role in higher accuracy. Without the categorical model (using extractive model for all slots), STARC is still able to achieve joint goal accuracy of 47.86%. More interestingly, if we remove the categorical model as well as the canonicalization, the performance drops drastically, but is still slight better than purely extractive model of DS-DST.

Error Type	Extractive	Categorical
ref not none, predicted none	43.7%	31.4%
ref none, predicted not none	25.6%	58.4%
ref not none, predicted not none	30.6%	10.0%

Table 7: Type of errors made by each model.

Handling *None* Value Through error analysis of our models, we have learned that models' performance on *None* value has a significant impact on the overall accuracy. Table 7 summarizes our findings. We found that plurality errors for extractive model comes from cases where ground-truth is not *None* but model predicted *None*. For categorical model, the opposite was true. The majority errors were from model predicting not *None* value but the ground-truth is actually *None*. We leave further investigation on this issue as a future work.

5.2 Few shot from RC to DST

In few-shot setting, our model (both extractive and categorical) is pre-trained on reading comprehension datasets and we randomly select limited amount of *target* domain data for fine-tuning. We do not use out-of-domain MultiWOZ data for training for few-shot experiments unlike previous works. We evaluate our model with 1%, 5% and 10% of training data in the target domain. Table 8 shows the results of our model under this setting for five domains in MultiWOZ 2.0[2]. We also report the few-shot results for other two models: TRADE (Wu et al., 2019) and DSTQA (Zhou and Small, 2019), where they perform the same few-shot experiments but pre-trained with a hold-out strategy, i.e., training on the other four domains in MultiWOZ and fine-tune on the held-out domain. We can see that under all three different data settings, our model outperforms the TRADE and DSTQA models (expect the attraction domain for DSTQA) by a large margin. Especially in 1% data setting for hotel domain, which contains the most number of slots (10) among all the five domains, the joint goal accuracy dropped to 19.73% for TRADE while our model can still achieve relatively high joint goal accuracy of 45.91%. This significant performance difference can be attributed to pre-training our models on reading comprehension datasets, which gives our model ability to comprehend passages or dialogues (which we have empiri-

---

[2]We are showing results on MultiWOZ 2.0 rather than 2.1 for the purpose of comparison to previous works.

cally verified in next section). The formulation of dialogue state tracking as a reading comprehension task helps the model to transfer comprehension capability. We also tried to repeat these experiments with vanilla pre-trained Roberta-Large model (without pretraining on RC dataset), but we could not even get these models to converge in such low-resource data settings. This further highlights the importance of RC pretraining for low resource dialogue state tracking.

5.3 Zero shot from RC to DST

In zero-shot experiments, we want to investigate how would the reading comprehension models behave on MultiWOZ dataset *without* any training on state tracking data. To do so, we train our models on reading comprehension datasets and test on MultiWOZ 2.1. Note that, in this setting, we only take labels in MultiWOZ 2.1 that are not missing, ignoring the data that is "None" in the dialogue state. For zero-shot experiments from multiple-choice RC to DST, we take the first fifteen slots in Table 1 that are classified as categorical. For zero shot from span-based RC to DST, we take twenty-seven slots which are extractive expect the first three slots in Table 1.

Figure 3 summarizes the results for hotel, restaurant, taxi and train domain in MultiWOZ 2.1. For attraction domain, please refer to the supplementary section A. We can see that most of the slots have an average accuracy of at least 50% or above in both multiple-choice RC and span-based RC approaches, indicating the effectiveness of RC data. For some slots such as *hotel.stay*, *hotel.people*, *hotel.day*, *restaurant.people*, *restaurant.day*, and *train.day*, we are able to achieve very high zero-shot accuracy (greater than 90%). The zero-shot setting in TRADE (Wu et al., 2019), where the transfer is from the four source domains to the held-out target domain, fails completely on certain slot types like *hotel.name*. In contrast, our zero-shot experiments from RC to DST are able to transfer almost all the slots.

Table 9 illustrates the zero shot examples for span-based RC model. We can see that although the span-based RC model does not directly point to the state value itself, it usually points to a span that *contains* the ground truth state value and the canonicalization procedure then turns the span into the actual slot value. Such predicted spans can be viewed as *evidence* for getting the ground-truth

	Hotel			Restaurant			Attraction			Train			Taxi		
	1%	*5%*	*10%*	*1%*	*5%*	*10%*	*1%*	*5%*	*10%*	*1%*	*5%*	*10%*	*1%*	*5%*	*10%*
TRADE	19.73	37.45	41.42	42.42	55.70	60.94	35.88	57.55	63.12	59.83	69.27	71.11	63.81	66.58	70.19
DSTQA	N/A	50.18	53.68	N/A	58.95	64.51	N/A	**70.47**	**71.60**	N/A	70.35	74.50	N/A	70.90	74.19
STARC	**45.91**	**52.59**	**57.37**	**51.65**	**60.49**	**64.66**	**40.39**	65.34	66.27	**65.67**	**74.11**	**75.08**	**72.58**	**75.35**	**79.61**

Table 8: Joint goal accuracy for few-shot experiments. Best numbers reported by TRADE and DSTQA are also shown.

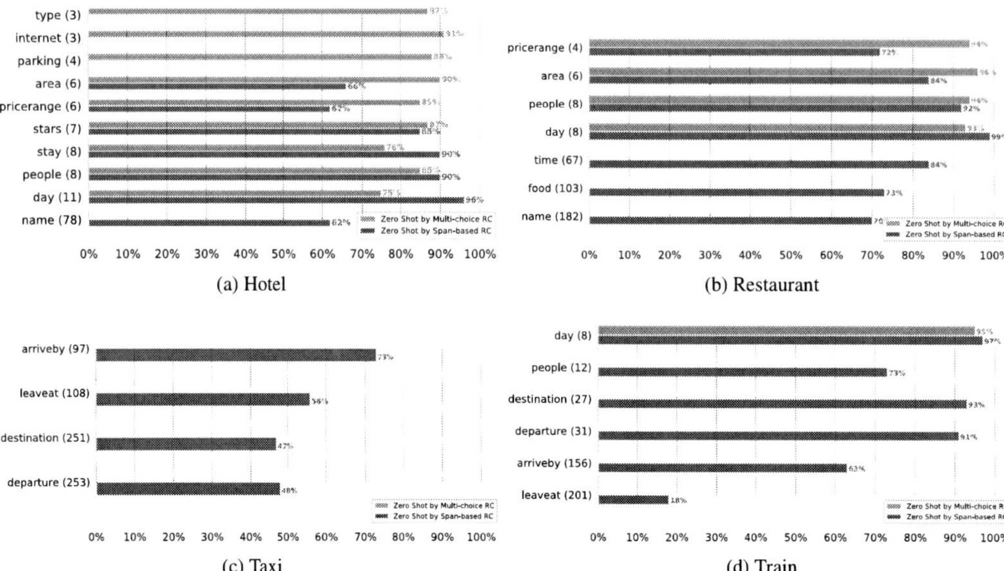

(a) Hotel

(b) Restaurant

(c) Taxi

(d) Train

Figure 3: Zero-shot average slot accuracy using multi-choice and span-based RC to DST in hotel, restaurant, taxi, and train domain of MultiWOZ 2.1. The number in parentheses indicates the number of possible values that a slot can take.

Example (Span-based RC model prediction is bolded)	Ground Truth State Value
Dialogue: "….A: sure , what area are you thinking of staying, U: *i do not have an area* *preference* but it needs to have free wifi and parking at a moderate price…." Question: "which area is the hotel at?" (hotel.semi.area)	don't care
Dialogue: "U: i am looking for something fun to do on the ***east side of town*** . funky fun house is my favorite place on the east side... Question: "which area is the restaurant at?" (restaurant.semi.area)	east
Dialogue: "U: I need 1 that leaves after 13:30 for bishops stortford how about the tr8017 ? A: ***it leaves at 15:29*** and arrives at 16:07 in bishops stortford …." Question: "what time will the train leave from the departure location?" (train.semi.leaveat)	15:29
Dialogue: "U: hello i want to see some ***authentic architectures*** in cambridge!..." Question: "what is the type of the attraction?" (attraction.semi.type)	architecture
Dialogue: "...A: can i help you with anything else ? U: i would like to book a taxi ***from the*** ***hong house*** to the hotel leaving by 10:15..." Question: "where does the taxi leave from?" (taxi.semi.departure)	lan hong house

Table 9: Zero-shot examples to MultiWOZ 2.1 by span-based reading comprehension model trained on MRQA dataset. The predicted span by the span-based RC model are bolded.

dialogue state, which makes dialogue state tracking more explainable.

6 Conclusion

Task-oriented dialogue systems aim to help users to achieve a variety of tasks. It is not unusual to have hundreds of different domains in modern task-oriented virtual assistants. How can we ensure the dialogue system is robust enough to scale to different tasks given limited amount of data? Some approaches focus on domain expansion by training on several source domains and then adapting to the target domain. While such methods can be successful in certain cases, it is hard for them to generalize to other completely different out-of-domain tasks.

Machine reading comprehension provides us a clear and general basis for understanding the context given a wide variety of questions. By formulating the dialogue state tracking as reading comprehension, we can utilize the recent advances in reading comprehension models. More importantly, we can utilize reading comprehension datasets to mitigate some of the resource issues in task-oriented dialogue systems. As a result, we achieve much higher accuracy in dialogue state tracking across different domains given limited amount of data compared to the existing methods. As the variety of tasks and functionalities in a dialogue system continues to grow, general methods for tracking dialogue state across all tasks will become increasingly necessary. We hope that the developments suggested here will help to address this need.

Acknowledgments

We thank the anonymous reviewers for their insightful feedback that helped improve the paper.

References

Paweł Budzianowski, Tsung-Hsien Wen, Bo-Hsiang Tseng, Iñigo Casanueva, Ultes Stefan, Ramadan Osman, and Milica Gašić. 2018. Multiwoz - a large-scale multi-domain wizard-of-oz dataset for task-oriented dialogue modelling. In *Proceedings of the 2018 Conference on Empirical Methods in Natural Language Processing (EMNLP)*.

Guan-Lin Chao and Ian Lane. 2019. Bert-dst: Scalable end-to-end dialogue state tracking with bidirectional encoder representations from transformer. *Proc. Interspeech 2019*, pages 1468–1472.

Danqi Chen. 2018. *Neural Reading Comprehension and Beyond*. Ph.D. thesis, Stanford University.

Jacob Devlin, Ming-Wei Chang, Kenton Lee, and Kristina Toutanova. 2019. Bert: Pre-training of deep bidirectional transformers for language understanding. In *Proceedings of the 2019 Conference of the North American Chapter of the Association for Computational Linguistics: Human Language Technologies, Volume 1 (Long and Short Papers)*, pages 4171–4186.

Mihail Eric, Rahul Goel, Shachi Paul, Abhishek Sethi, Sanchit Agarwal, Shuyang Gao, and Dilek Hakkani-Tur. 2019. Multiwoz 2.1: Multi-domain dialogue state corrections and state tracking baselines. *arXiv preprint arXiv:1907.01669*.

Adam Fisch, Alon Talmor, Robin Jia, Minjoon Seo, Eunsol Choi, and Danqi Chen. 2019. Mrqa 2019 shared task: Evaluating generalization in reading comprehension. *arXiv preprint arXiv:1910.09753*.

Shuyang Gao, Abhishek Sethi, Sanchit Agarwal, Tagyoung Chung, and Dilek Hakkani-Tur. 2019. Dialog state tracking: A neural reading comprehension approach. *arXiv preprint arXiv:1908.01946*.

Rahul Goel, Shachi Paul, Tagyoung Chung, Jeremie Lecomte, Arindam Mandal, and Dilek Hakkani-Tur. 2018. Flexible and scalable state tracking framework for goal-oriented dialogue systems. *arXiv preprint arXiv:1811.12891*.

Rahul Goel, Shachi Paul, and Dilek Hakkani-Tür. 2019. Hyst: A hybrid approach for flexible and accurate dialogue state tracking. *arXiv preprint arXiv:1907.00883*.

Di Jin, Shuyang Gao, Jiun-Yu Kao, Tagyoung Chung, and Dilek Hakkani-tur. 2019. Mmm: Multi-stage multi-task learning for multi-choice reading comprehension. *arXiv preprint arXiv:1910.00458*.

Guokun Lai, Qizhe Xie, Hanxiao Liu, Yiming Yang, and Eduard Hovy. 2017. Race: Large-scale reading comprehension dataset from examinations. In *Proceedings of the 2017 Conference on Empirical Methods in Natural Language Processing*, pages 785–794.

Hwaran Lee, Jinsik Lee, and Tae-Yoon Kim. 2019. Sumbt: Slot-utterance matching for universal and scalable belief tracking. *arXiv preprint arXiv:1907.07421*.

Bing Liu and Ian Lane. 2017. An end-to-end trainable neural network model with belief tracking for task-oriented dialog. *arXiv preprint arXiv:1708.05956*.

Yinhan Liu, Myle Ott, Naman Goyal, Jingfei Du, Mandar Joshi, Danqi Chen, Omer Levy, Mike Lewis, Luke Zettlemoyer, and Veselin Stoyanov. 2019. RoBERTa: A robustly optimized BERT pretraining approach. *arXiv preprint arXiv:1907.11692*.

Nikola Mrkšić, Diarmuid O Séaghdha, Tsung-Hsien Wen, Blaise Thomson, and Steve Young. 2016. Neural belief tracker: Data-driven dialogue state tracking. *arXiv preprint arXiv:1606.03777*.

Elnaz Nouri and Ehsan Hosseini-Asl. 2018. Toward scalable neural dialogue state tracking model. *arXiv preprint arXiv:1812.00899*.

Pranav Rajpurkar, Robin Jia, and Percy Liang. 2018. Know what you don't know: Unanswerable questions for squad. In *Proceedings of the 56th Annual*

Meeting of the Association for Computational Linguistics (Volume 2: Short Papers), pages 784–789.

Pranav Rajpurkar, Jian Zhang, Konstantin Lopyrev, and Percy Liang. 2016. Squad: 100,000+ questions for machine comprehension of text. In *Proceedings of the 2016 Conference on Empirical Methods in Natural Language Processing*, pages 2383–2392.

Abhinav Rastogi, Dilek Hakkani-Tür, and Larry Heck. 2017. Scalable multi-domain dialogue state tracking. In *2017 IEEE Automatic Speech Recognition and Understanding Workshop (ASRU)*, pages 561–568. IEEE.

Abhinav Rastogi, Xiaoxue Zang, Srinivas Sunkara, Raghav Gupta, and Pranav Khaitan. 2019. Towards scalable multi-domain conversational agents: The schema-guided dialogue dataset. *arXiv preprint arXiv:1909.05855*.

Siva Reddy, Danqi Chen, and Christopher D Manning. 2019. Coqa: A conversational question answering challenge. *Transactions of the Association for Computational Linguistics*, 7:249–266.

Pararth Shah, Dilek Hakkani-Tur, Bing Liu, and Gokhan Tur. 2018. Bootstrapping a neural conversational agent with dialogue self-play, crowdsourcing and on-line reinforcement learning. In *Proceedings of the 2018 Conference of the North American Chapter of the Association for Computational Linguistics: Human Language Technologies, Volume 3 (Industry Papers)*, pages 41–51.

Kai Sun, Dian Yu, Jianshu Chen, Dong Yu, Yejin Choi, and Claire Cardie. 2019. Dream: A challenge data set and models for dialogue-based reading comprehension. *Transactions of the Association for Computational Linguistics*, 7:217–231.

TH Wen, D Vandyke, N Mrkšíc, M Gašíc, LM Rojas-Barahona, PH Su, S Ultes, and S Young. 2017. A network-based end-to-end trainable task-oriented dialogue system. In *15th Conference of the European Chapter of the Association for Computational Linguistics, EACL 2017-Proceedings of Conference*, volume 1, pages 438–449.

Chien-Sheng Wu, Andrea Madotto, Ehsan Hosseini-Asl, Caiming Xiong, Richard Socher, and Pascale Fung. 2019. Transferable multi-domain state generator for task-oriented dialogue systems. *arXiv preprint arXiv:1905.08743*.

Puyang Xu and Qi Hu. 2018. An end-to-end approach for handling unknown slot values in dialogue state tracking. *arXiv preprint arXiv:1805.01555*.

Jian-Guo Zhang, Kazuma Hashimoto, Chien-Sheng Wu, Yao Wan, Philip S Yu, Richard Socher, and Caiming Xiong. 2019. Find or classify? dual strategy for slot-value predictions on multi-domain dialog state tracking. *arXiv preprint arXiv:1910.03544*.

Victor Zhong, Caiming Xiong, and Richard Socher. 2018. Global-locally self-attentive dialogue state tracker. *arXiv preprint arXiv:1805.09655*.

Li Zhou and Kevin Small. 2019. Multi-domain dialogue state tracking as dynamic knowledge graph enhanced question answering. *arXiv preprint arXiv:1911.06192*.

A Zero shot experiments for Attraction domain in MultiWOZ 2.1

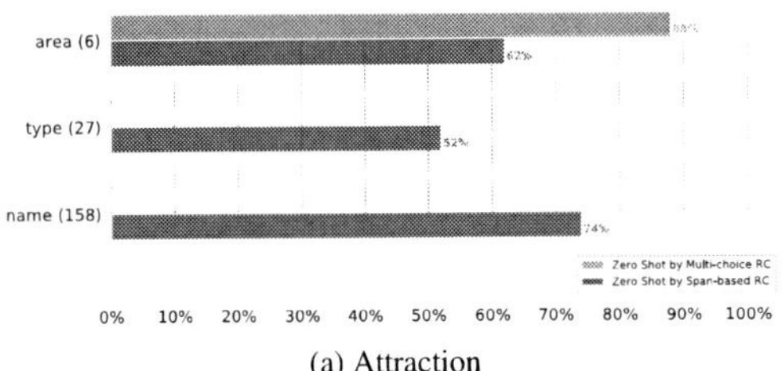

(a) Attraction

Figure 1: Zero shot average slot accuracy from RC to DST in attraction domain of MultiWOZ 2.1. The number within the brackets associated with each slot name in y-axis indicates the number of possible values that a slot can take.

B Question Formation for Reading Comprehension

The structural construct and the surface form of the question can have an impact on the performance of RC models. In this work, we handcrafted a question for each slot that needs to be tracked. Each question roughly asks *What is the value of the slot that the user in interested in?*. The exact question was tailored to each specific slot also taking domains into account. We experimented with two sets of handcrafted questions. The first set was created in a procedural manner largely following a template. The other was created in a more free-form manner and was more natural. We did not notice any significant model performance difference between the two sets. However, we did not explore this dimension any further and leave it to future work. An interesting future direction could be to use a decoder to generate questions given slot description as the input.

Improving Slot Filling by Utilizing Contextual Information

Amir Pouran Ben Veyseh[*1]**, Franck Dernoncourt**[2]**,
and Thien Huu Nguyen**[1]
[1]Department of Computer and Information Science,
University of Oregon, Eugene, Oregon, USA
[2]Adobe Research, San Jose, CA, USA
{apouranb, thien}@cs.uoregon.edu
franck.dernoncourt@adobe.com

Abstract

Slot Filling (SF) is one of the sub-tasks of Spoken Language Understanding (SLU) which aims to extract semantic constituents from a given natural language utterance. It is formulated as a sequence labeling task. Recently, it has been shown that contextual information is vital for this task. However, existing models employ contextual information in a restricted manner, e.g., using self-attention. Such methods fail to distinguish the effects of the context on the word representation and the word label. To address this issue, in this paper, we propose a novel method to incorporate the contextual information in two different levels, i.e., representation level and task-specific (i.e., label) level. Our extensive experiments on three benchmark datasets on SF show the effectiveness of our model leading to new state-of-the-art results on all three benchmark datasets for the task of SF.

1 Introduction

Slot Filling (SF) is the task of identifying the semantic constituents expressed in a natural language utterance. It is one of the sub-tasks of spoken language understanding (SLU) and plays a vital role in personal assistant tools such as Siri, Alexa, and Google Assistant. This task is formulated as a sequence labeling problem. For instance, in the given sentence "*Play Signe Anderson chant music that is newest.*", the goal is to identify "*Signe Anderson*" as "*artist*", "*chant music*" as "*music-item*" and "*newest*" as "*sort*".

Early work on SF has employed feature engineering methods to train statistical models, e.g., Conditional Random Field (Raymond and Riccardi, 2007). Later, deep learning emerged as a promising approach for SF (Yao et al., 2014; Peng et al., 2015;

Liu and Lane, 2016). The success of deep models could be attributed to pre-trained word embeddings to generalize words and deep learning architectures to compose the word embeddings to induce effective representations. In addition to improving word representation using deep models, Liu and Lane (2016) showed that incorporating the context of each word into its representation could improve the results. Concretely, the effect of using context in word representation is two-fold: (1) **Representation Level**: As the meaning of the word is dependent on its context, incorporating the contextual information is vital to represent the true meaning of the word in the sentence (2) **Task Level**: For SF, the label of the word is related to the other words in the sentence and providing information about the other words, in prediction layer, could improve the performance. Unfortunately, the existing work employs the context in a restricted manner, e.g., via attention mechanism, which obfuscates the model about the two aforementioned effects of the contextual information.

In order to address the limitations of the prior work to exploit the context for SF, in this paper, we propose a multi-task setting to train the model. More specifically, our model is encouraged to explicitly ensure the two aforementioned effects of the contextual information for the task of SF. In particular, in addition to the main sequence labeling task, we introduce new sub-tasks to ensure each effect. Firstly, in the representation level, we enforce the consistency between the word representations and their context. This enforcement is achieved via increasing the Mutual Information (MI) between these two representations. Secondly, in the task level, we propose two new sub-tasks: (1) To predict the label of the word solely from its context and (2) To predict which labels exist in the given sentence in a multi-label classification setting. By doing so, we encourage the model to encode task-

---

* This work was done when the first author was an intern at Adobe Research.

90

Proceedings of the 2nd Workshop on Natural Language Processing for Conversational AI, pages 90–95
July 9, 2020. ©2020 Association for Computational Linguistics

specific features in the context of each word. Our extensive experiments on three benchmark datasets, empirically prove the effectiveness of the proposed model leading to new the state-of-the-art results on all three datasets.

2 Related Work

In the literature, Slot Filling (SF), is categorized as one of the sub-tasks of spoken language understanding (SLU). Early work employed feature engineering for statistical models, e.g., Conditional Random Field (Raymond and Riccardi, 2007). Due to the lack of generalisation ability of feature based models, deep learning based models superseded them (Yao et al., 2014; Peng et al., 2015; Kurata et al., 2016; Hakkani-Tür et al., 2016). Also, joint models to simultaneously predict the intent of the utterance and to extract the semantic slots has also gained a lot of attention (Guo et al., 2014; Liu and Lane, 2016; Zhang and Wang, 2016; Wang et al., 2018; Goo et al., 2018; Qin et al., 2019; E et al., 2019). In addition to the supervised settings, recently other setting such as progressive learning (Shen et al., 2019) or zero-shot learning has also been studied (Shah et al., 2019). To the best of our knowledge, none of the existing work introduces a multi-task learning solely for the SF to incorporate the contextual information in both representation and task levels.

3 Model

Our model is trained in a multi-task setting in which the main task is slot filling to identify the best possible sequence of labels for the given sentence. In the first auxiliary task we aim to increase consistency between the word representation and its context. The second auxiliary task is to enhance task specific information in contextual information. In this section, we explain each of these tasks in more details.

3.1 Slot Filling

Formally, the input to a SF model is a sequence of words $X = [x_1, x_2, \ldots, x_n]$ and our goal is to predict the sequence of labels $Y = [y_1, y_2, \ldots, y_n]$. In our model, the word x_i is represented by vector e_i which is the concatenation of the pre-trained word embedding and POS tag embedding of the word x_i. In order to obtain a more abstract representation of the words, we employ a Bi-directional Long Short-Term Memory (BiLSTM) over the word rep-

resentations $E = [e_1, e_2, \ldots, e_n]$ to generate the abstract vectors $H = [h_1, h_2, \ldots, h_n]$. The vector h_i is the final representation of the word x_i and is fed into a two-layer feed forward neural net to compute the label scores s_i for the given word, $s_i = FF(h_i)$. As the task of SF is formulated as a sequence labeling task, we exploit a conditional random field (CRF) layer as the final layer of SF prediction. More specifically, the predicted label scores $S = [s_1, s_2, \ldots, s_n]$ are provided as emission score to the CRF layer to predict the label sequence $\hat{Y} = [\hat{y}_1, \hat{y}_2, \ldots, \hat{y}_n]$. To train the model, the negative log-likelihood is used as the loss function for SF prediction, i.e., $\mathcal{L}_{pred}$.

3.2 Consistency between Word and Context

In this sub-task we aim to increase the consistency between the word representation and its context. To obtain the context of each word, we use max pooling over the outputs of the BiLSTM for all words of the sentence excluding the word itself, $h_i^c = MaxPooling(h_1, h_2, ..., h_n/h_i)$. We aim to increase the consistency between vectors h_i and h_i^c. To this end, we propose to maximize the Mutual Information (MI) between the word representation and its context. In information theory, MI evaluates how much information we know about one random variable if the value of another variable is revealed. Formally, the mutual information between two random variable X_1 and X_2 is obtained by:

$$
\begin{aligned}
MI(X_1, X_2) = \int_{X_1} \int_{X_2} & P(X_1, X_2) \cdot \\
log \frac{P(X_1, X_2)}{P(X_1)P(X_2)} & dX_1 dX_2
\end{aligned}
\tag{1}
$$

Using this definition of MI, we can reformulate the MI equation as KL-Divergence between the joint distribution $P_{X_1 X_2} = P(X_1, X_2)$ and the product of marginal distributions $P_{X_1 \otimes X_2} = P(X_1)P(X_2)$:

$$
MI(X_1, X_2) = D_{KL}(P_{X_1 X_2} || P_{X_1 \otimes X_2})
\tag{2}
$$

Based on this understanding of MI, if the two random variables are dependent then the mutual information between them (i.e. the KL-Divergence in Equation 2) would be the highest. Consequently, if the representations h_i and h_i^c are encouraged to have large mutual information, we expect them to share more information.

Computing the KL-Divergence in equation 2 could be prohibitively expensive (Belghazi et al., 2018), so we need to estimate it. To this end, we exploit the adversarial method introduced in (Hjelm et al., 2019). In this method, a discriminator is employed to distinguish between samples from the joint distribution and the product of the marginal distributions to estimate the KL-Divergence in Equation 2. In our case, the sample from joint distribution is the concatenation $[h_i : h_i^c]$ and the sample from the product of the marginal distribution is the concatenation $[h_i : h_j^c]$ where h_j^c is a context vector randomly chosen from the words in the mini-batch. Formally:

$$\mathcal{L}_{disc} = \frac{1}{n}\Sigma_{i=1}^n - (\log(D[h_i, h_i^c]) + \log(1 - D([h_i, h_j^c]))) \quad (3)$$

Where D is the discriminator. This loss is added to the final loss function of the model.

3.3 Prediction by Contextual Information

In addition to increasing consistency between the word representation and its context representation, we aim to increase the task-specific information in contextual representations. To this end, we train the model on two auxiliary tasks. The first one aims to use the context of each word to predict the label of that word. The goal of the second auxiliary task is to use the global context information to predict sentence level labels. We describe each of these tasks in more details in the following subsections.

Predicting Word Label

In this sub-task, we use the context representations of each word to predict its label. It will increase the information encoded in the context of the word about the label of the word. We use the same context vector h_i^c for the i-th word as described in the previous section. This vector is fed into a two-layer feed forward neural network with a softmax layer at the end to output the probabilities for each class, $P_i(.|\{x_1, x_2, ..., x_n\}/x_i) = softmax(FF(h_i^c))$. Finally, we use the following negative log-likelihood as the loss function to be optimized during training:

$$\mathcal{L}_{wp} = \frac{1}{n}\Sigma_{i=1}^n - \log(P_i(y_i|\{x_1, x_2, ..., x_n\}/x_i)) \quad (4)$$

Predicting Sentence Labels

The word label prediction enforces the context of each word to contain information about its label but it lacks a global view about the entire sentence. In order to increase the global information about the sentence in the representation of the words, we aim to predict the labels existing in a sentence from the representations of its words. More specifically, we introduce a new sub-task to predict which labels exists in the given sentence. We formulate this task as a multi-label classification problem. Formally, for each sentence, we predict the binary vector $Y^s = [y_1^s, y_2^s, ..., y_{|L|}^s]$ where L is the set of all possible word labels. In the vector Y^s, y_i^s is 1 if the sentence X contains i-th label from the label set L otherwise it is 0.

To predict vector Y^s, we first compute the representation of the sentence. This representation is obtained by max pooling over the outputs of the BiLSTM, $H = MaxPooling(h_1, h_2, ..., h_n)$. Afterwards, the vector H is fed into a two-layer feed forward neural net with a sigmoid activation function at the end to compute the probability distribution of Y^s (i.e., $P_k(.|x_1, x_2, ..., x_n) = \sigma_k(FF(H))$ for k-th label in L). Note that since this task is a multi-label classification, the number of neurons at the final layer is equal to $|L|$. We optimize the following binary cross-entropy loss:

$$\mathcal{L}_{sp} = \frac{1}{|L|}\Sigma_{k=1}^{|L|} - (y_k^s \cdot \log(P_k(y_k^s|x_1, x_2, ..., x_n)) + (1 - y_k^s) \cdot \log(1 - P_k(y_k^s|x_1, x_2, ..., x_n))) \quad (5)$$

Finally, to train the entire model we optimize the following combined loss:

$$\mathcal{L} = \mathcal{L}_{pred} + \alpha\mathcal{L}_{discr} + \beta\mathcal{L}_{wp} + \gamma\mathcal{L}_{sp} \quad (6)$$

where α, β and γ are the trade-off parameters to be tuned based on the development set performance.

4 Experiments

4.1 Dataset and Parameters

We evaluate our model on three SF datasets. Namely, we employ ATIS (Hemphill et al., 1990), SNIPS (Coucke et al., 2018) and EditMe (Manuvinakurike et al., 2018). ATIS and SNIPS are two widely adopted SF dataset and EditMe is a SF dataset for editing images with four slot labels (i.e., *Action*, *Object*, *Attribute* and *Value*). The statistics of the datasets are presented in the Appendix A. Based on the experiments on EditMe development set, the following parameters are selected: GloVe embedding with 300 dimensions to initialize word embedding ; 200 dimensions for the all hidden layers in LSTM and feed forward neural net; 0.1 for trade-off parameters α, β and γ; and Adam optimizer with learning rate 0.001. Following previous work, we use F1-score to evaluate the model.

4.2 Baselines

We compare our model with other deep learning based models for SF. Namely, we compare the proposed model with Joint Seq (Hakkani-Tür et al., 2016), Attention-Based (Liu and Lane, 2016), Sloted-Gated (Goo et al., 2018), SF-ID (E et al., 2019), CAPSULE-NLU (Zhang et al., 2019), and SPTID (Qin et al., 2019). Note that we compare our model with the single-task version of these baselines. We also compare our model with other sequence labeling models which are not specifically proposed for SF. Namely, we compare the model with CVT (Clark et al., 2018) and GCDT (Liu et al., 2019). CVT aims to improve input representation using improving partial views and GCDT exploits contextual information to enhance word representations via concatenation of context and word representation.

4.3 Results

Table 1 reports the performance of the model and baselines. The proposed model outperforms all baselines in all datasets. Among all baselines, GCDT achieves best results on two out of three datasets. This superiority shows the importance of explicitly incorporating the contextual information into word representation for SF. However, the proposed model improves the performance substantially on all datasets by explicitly encouraging the consistency between a word and its context in representation level and task-specific (i.e., label) level. Also, Table 1 shows that EditMe dataset is more challenging than the other datasets, despite having fewer slot types. This difficulty could be explained by the limited number of training examples and more diversity in sentence structures in this dataset.

4.4 Ablation Study

Our model consists of three major components: (1) **MI**: Increasing mutual information between word

Model	SNIPS	ATIS	EditMe
Joint Seq(2016)	87.3	94.3	-
Attention-Based(2016)	87.8	94.2	-
Sloted-Gated(2018)	89.2	95.4	84.9
SF-ID(2019)	90.9	95.5	85.2
CAPSULE-NLU(2019)	91.8	95.2	84.6
SPTID(2019)	90.8	95.1	85.3
CVT(2018)	91.4	94.8	85.4
GCDT(2019)	92.0	95.1	85.6
Ours	**93.6**	**95.8**	**87.2**

Table 1: Performance of the model and baselines on the Test sets.

Model	SNIPS	ATIS	EditMe
Full	**93.6**	**95.8**	**87.2**
Full - MI	92.9	95.3	84.2
Full - WP	91.7	94.9	83.2
Full - SP	92.5	95.2	84.1

Table 2: Test F1-score for the ablated models

and its context representations (2) **WP**: Predicting the label of the word using its context to increase word level task-specific information in the word context (3) **SP**: Predicting which labels exist in the given sentence in a multi-label classification to increase sentence level task-specific information in word representations. In order to analyze the contribution of each of these components, we also evaluate the model performance when we remove one of the components and retrain the model. The results are reported in Table 2. This Table shows that all components are required for the model to have its best performance. Among all components, the word level prediction using the contextual information has the major contribution to the model performance. This fact shows that contextual information trained to be informative about the final task is necessary to obtain the representations which could boost the performance.

5 Conclusion

In this work, we introduced a new deep model for the task of Slot Filling (SF). In a multi-task setting, our model increases the mutual information between the word representation and its context, improves label information in the context and predicts which concepts are expressed in the given sentence. Our experiments on three benchmark datasets show the effectiveness of our model by achieving the state-of-the-art results on all datasets for the SF task.

References

Mohamed Ishmael Belghazi, Aristide Baratin, Sai Rajeswar, Sherjil Ozair, Yoshua Bengio, R. Devon Hjelm, and Aaron C. Courville. 2018. Mutual information neural estimation. In *ICML*.

Kevin Clark, Minh-Thang Luong, Christopher D Manning, and Quoc V Le. 2018. Semi-supervised sequence modeling with cross-view training. In *EMNLP*.

Alice Coucke, Alaa Saade, Adrien Ball, Théodore Bluche, Alexandre Caulier, David Leroy, Clément Doumouro, Thibault Gisselbrecht, Francesco Caltagirone, Thibaut Lavril, and et al. 2018. Snips voice platform: an embedded spoken language understanding system for private-by-design voice interfaces. In *arXiv*.

Haihong E, Peiqing Niu, Zhongfu Chen, and Meina Song. 2019. A novel bi-directional interrelated model for joint intent detection and slot filling. In *ACL*.

Chih-Wen Goo, Guang Gao, Yun-Kai Hsu, Chih-Li Huo, Tsung-Chieh Chen, Keng-Wei Hsu, and Yun-Nung Chen. 2018. Slot-gated modeling for joint slot filling and intent prediction. In *NAACL-HLT*.

Daniel Guo, Gokhan Tur, Wen-tau Yih, and Geoffrey Zweig. 2014. Joint semantic utterance classification and slot filling with recursive neural networks. In *SLT*.

Dilek Hakkani-Tür, Gökhan Tür, Asli Celikyilmaz, Yun-Nung Chen, Jianfeng Gao, Li Deng, and Ye-Yi Wang. 2016. Multi-domain joint semantic frame parsing using bi-directional rnn-lstm. In *Interspeech*.

Charles T. Hemphill, John J. Godfrey, and George R. Doddington. 1990. The ATIS spoken language systems pilot corpus. In *Speech and Natural Language: Proceedings of a Workshop Held at Hidden Valley, Pennsylvania, June 24-27,1990*.

R Devon Hjelm, Alex Fedorov, Samuel Lavoie-Marchildon, Karan Grewal, Phil Bachman, Adam Trischler, and Yoshua Bengio. 2019. Learning deep representations by mutual information estimation and maximization. In *ICLR*.

Gakuto Kurata, Bing Xiang, Bowen Zhou, and Mo Yu. 2016. Leveraging sentence-level information with encoder LSTM for semantic slot filling. In *EMNLP*.

Bing Liu and Ian Lane. 2016. Attention-based recurrent neural network models for joint intent detection and slot filling. In *arXiv*.

Yijin Liu, Fandong Meng, Jinchao Zhang, Jinan Xu, Yufeng Chen, and Jie Zhou. 2019. GCDT: A global context enhanced deep transition architecture for sequence labeling. In *ACL*.

Ramesh Manuvinakurike, Jacqueline Brixey, Trung Bui, Walter Chang, Doo Soon Kim, Ron Artstein, and Kalliroi Georgila. 2018. Edit me: A corpus and a framework for understanding natural language image editing. In *Proceedings of the Eleventh International Conference on Language Resources and Evaluation (LREC 2018)*, Miyazaki, Japan. European Language Resources Association (ELRA).

Baolin Peng, Kaisheng Yao, Li Jing, and Kam-Fai Wong. 2015. Recurrent neural networks with external memory for spoken language understanding. In *NLPCC*.

Libo Qin, Wanxiang Che, Yangming Li, Haoyang Wen, and Ting Liu. 2019. A stack-propagation framework with token-level intent detection for spoken language understanding. In *EMNLP*.

Christian Raymond and Giuseppe Riccardi. 2007. Generative and discriminative algorithms for spoken language understanding. In *ISCA*.

Darsh J Shah, Raghav Gupta, Amir A Fayazi, and Dilek Hakkani-Tur. 2019. Robust zero-shot cross-domain slot filling with example values. *arXiv*.

Yilin Shen, Xiangyu Zeng, and Hongxia Jin. 2019. A progressive model to enable continual learning for semantic slot filling. In *EMNLP*.

Yu Wang, Yilin Shen, and Hongxia Jin. 2018. A bi-model based RNN semantic frame parsing model for intent detection and slot filling. In *NAANCL-HLT*.

Kaisheng Yao, Baolin Peng, Yu Zhang, Dong Yu, Geoffrey Zweig, and Yangyang Shi. 2014. Spoken language understanding using long short-term memory neural networks. In *SLT*.

Chenwei Zhang, Yaliang Li, Nan Du, Wei Fan, and Philip Yu. 2019. Joint slot filling and intent detection via capsule neural networks. In *ACL*.

Xiaodong Zhang and Houfeng Wang. 2016. A joint model of intent determination and slot filling for spoken language understanding. In *IJCAI*.

A   Dataset Statistics

In our experiments, we employ three benchmark datasets, ATIS, SNIPS and EditMe. Table 3 presents the statistics of these three datasets. Moreover, in order to provide more insight into the EditMe dataset, we report the labels statistics of this dataset in Table 4.

Dataset	Train	Dev	Test
SNIPS	13,084	700	700
ATIS	4,478	500	893
EditMe	1,737	497	559

Table 3: Total number of examples in test/dev/train splits of the datasets

Label	Train	Dev	Test
Action	1,562	448	479
Object	4,676	1,447	1,501
Attribute	1,437	403	462
Value	507	207	155

Table 4: Label Statistics of EditMe dataset

Learning to Classify Intents and Slot Labels Given a Handful of Examples

Jason Krone
Amazon AI
Palo Alto, CA
kronej@amazon.com

Yi Zhang
Amazon AI
Seattle, WA
yizhngn@amazon.com

Mona Diab[*]
The George Washington University
Washington, DC
mtdiab@gwu.edu

Abstract

Intent classification (IC) and slot filling (SF) are core components in most goal-oriented dialogue systems. Current IC/SF models perform poorly when the number of training examples per class is small. We propose a new few-shot learning task, *few-shot IC/SF*, to study and improve the performance of IC and SF models on classes not seen at training time in ultra low resource scenarios. We establish a *few-shot IC/SF* benchmark by defining few-shot splits for three public IC/SF datasets, ATIS, TOP, and SNIPS. We show that two popular few-shot learning algorithms, model agnostic meta learning (MAML) and prototypical networks, outperform a fine-tuning baseline on this benchmark. Prototypical networks achieves substantial gains in IC performance on the ATIS and TOP datasets, while both prototypical networks and MAML outperform the baseline with respect to SF on all three datasets. In addition, we demonstrate that joint training as well as the use of pre-trained language models, ELMo and BERT in our case, are complementary to these few-shot learning methods and yield further gains.

1 Introduction

In the context of goal-oriented dialogue systems, intent classification (IC) is the process of classifying a user's utterance into an intent, such as *Book-Flight* or *AddToPlaylist*, referring to the user's goal. While slot filling (SF) is the process of identifying and classifying certain tokens in the utterance into their corresponding labels, in a manner akin to named entity recognition (NER). However, in contrast to NER, typical slots are particular to the domain of the dialogue, such as music or travel. As a reference point, we list intent and slot label annotations for an example utterance from the SNIPS dataset with the *AddToPlaylist* IC in Figure 1.

Token	Slot Label
Please	O
add	O
some	O
Pete	AddToPlaylist:artist
Townshend	AddToPlaylist:artist
to	O
my	AddToPlaylist:playlist_owner
playlist	O
Fiesta	AddToPlaylist:playlist
Hits	AddToPlaylist:playlist
con	AddToPlaylist:playlist
Lali	AddToPlaylist:playlist

Figure 1: Tokens and corresponding slot labels for an utterance from the AddToPlaylist intent class in the SNIPS dataset prefixed by intent class name.

As of late, most state-of-the-art IC/SF models are based on feed-forward, convolutional, or recurrent neural networks (Hakkani-Tür et al., 2016; Goo et al., 2018; Gupta et al., 2019). These neural models offer substantial gains in performance, but they often require a large number of labeled examples (on the order of hundreds) per intent class and slot-label to achieve these gains. The relative scarcity of large-scale datasets annotated with intents and slots prohibits the use of neural IC/SF models in many promising domains, such as medical consultation, where it is difficult to obtain large quantities of annotated dialogues.

Accordingly, we propose the task of *few-shot IC/SF*, catering to domain adaptation in low resource scenarios, where there are only a handful of annotated examples available per intent and slot in the target domain. To the best of our knowledge, this work is the first to apply the few-shot learning framework to a joint sentence classification and sequence labeling task. In the NLP literature, few-shot learning often refers to a low resource, cross lingual setting where there is limited data available in the target language. We emphasize that our definition of *few-shot IC/SF* is distinct in that we limit

---

[*]Work performed while at Amazon AI

Proceedings of the 2nd Workshop on Natural Language Processing for Conversational AI, pages 96–108
July 9, 2020. ©2020 Association for Computational Linguistics

the amount of data available per target class rather than target language.

Few-shot IC/SF builds on a large body of existing few-shot classification work. Drawing inspiration from computer vision, we experiment with two prominent few shot image classification approaches, *prototypical networks* and *model agnostic meta learning* (MAML). Both these methods seek to decrease over-fitting and improve generalization on small datasets, albeit via different mechanisms. *Prototypical networks* learns class specific representations, called *prototypes*, and performs inference by assigning the class label associated with the prototype closest to an input embedding. Whereas MAML modifies the learning objective to optimize for pre-training representations that transfer well when fine-tuned on a small number of labeled examples.

For benchmarking purposes, we establish few-shot splits for three publicly available IC/SF datasets: ATIS (Hemphill et al., 1990), SNIPS (Coucke et al., 2018), and TOP (Gupta et al., 2018). Empirically, prototypical networks yields substantial improvements on this benchmark over the popular *"fine-tuning"* approach (Goyal et al., 2018; Schuster et al., 2018), where representations are pre-trained on a large, *"source"* dataset and then fine-tuned on a smaller, *"target"* dataset. Despite performing worse on intent classification, MAML also achieves gains over *"fine-tuning"* on the slot filling task. Orthogonally, we experiment with the use of two pre-trained language models, BERT and ELMO, as well as joint training on multiple datasets. These experiments show that the use of pre-trained, contextual representations is complementary to both methods. While prototypical networks is uniquely able to leverage joint training to consistently boost slot filling performance.

In summary, our primary contributions are four-fold:

1. Formulating IC/SF as a few-shot learning task;

2. Establishing few-shot splits[1] for the ATIS, SNIPS, and TOP datasets;

3. Showing that MAML and prototypical networks can outperform the popular "fine-tuning" domain adaptation framework;

---

[1] Few-shot split intent assignments given in section A.1

4. Evaluating the complementary of contextual embeddings and joint training with MAML and prototypical networks.

2 Related Work

2.1 Few-shot Learning

Early adoption of few-shot learning in the field of computer vision has yielded promising results. Neural approaches to few-shot learning in computer vision fall mainly into three categories: *optimization-*, *metric-*, or *memory-based*. *Optimization-based* methods typically learn an initialization or fine-tuning procedure for a neural network. For instance, MAML (Finn et al., 2017) directly optimizes for representations that generalize well to unseen classes given a few labeled examples. Using an LSTM based meta-learner, Ravi and Larochelle (2016) learn both the initialization and the fine-tuning procedure. In contrast, *metric-based* approaches learn an embedding space or distance metric under which examples belonging to the same class have high similarity. Prototypical networks (Snell et al., 2017), siamese neural networks (Koch, 2015), and matching networks (Vinyals et al., 2016) all belong to this category. Alternatively, memory based approaches apply memory modules or recurrent networks with memory, such as a LSTM, to few-shot learning. These approaches include differentiable extensions to k-nearest-neighbors (Kaiser et al., 2017) and applications of the Neural Turing Machines (Graves et al., 2014; Santoro et al., 2016).

2.2 Few-shot Learning for Text Classification

To date, applications of few-shot learning to natural language processing focus primarily on text classification tasks. Yu et al. (2018) identify *"clusters"* of source classification tasks that transfer well to a given target task, and meta learn a linear combination of similarity metrics across *"clusters"*. The source tasks with the highest likelihood of transfer are used to pre-train a convolutional network that is subsequently fine-tuned on the target task. Han et al. (2018) propose *FewRel*, a few-shot relation classification dataset, and use this data to benchmark the performance of few-shot models, such as *prototypical networks* and *SNAIL* (Mishra et al., 2017). *ATAML* (Jiang et al., 2018), one of the few optimization based approaches to few-shot sentence classification, extends MAML to learn task-specific as well as task agnostic representations using feed-forward attention mechanisms. (Dou et al., 2019) show that further pre-training of contextual representations using *optimization-based* methods benefits downstream performance.

2.3 Few-shot Learning for Sequence Labeling

In one of the first works on few-shot sequence labeling, Fritzler et al. (2019) apply prototypical networks to few-shot named entity recognition by training a separate prototypical network for each named entity type. This design choice makes their extension of prototypical networks more restrictive than ours, which trains a single model to classify all sequence tags. (Hou et al., 2019) apply a CRF based approach that learns emission scores using pre-trained, contextualized embeddings to few-shot SF (on SNIPS) and few-shot NER.

3 Task Formulation

3.1 Few-shot Classification

The goal of *few-shot classification* is to adapt a classifier f_ϕ to a set of new classes L not seen at training time, given a *few* labeled examples per class $l \in L$. In this setting, train and test splits are defined by disjoint class label sets L_{train} and L_{test}, respectively. The classes in L_{train} are made available for pre-training and those in L_{test} are held out for low resource adaptation at test time. Few-shot evaluation is done episodically, i.e. over a number of mini adaptation datasets, called episodes. Each episode consists of a *support set* S and a *query set* Q. The *support set* contains k_l labeled examples $S_l = \{(x_l^i, y_l)|i \in (1 \ldots k_l)\}$ per held out class $l \in L$; we define $S = \bigcup_{l \in L} S_l$. Similarly, the *query set* contains k_q labeled instances $Q_l = \{(x_l^j, y_l)|j \in (1 \ldots k_q)\}$ for each class $l \in L$ s.t. $Q_l \cap S_l = \{\}$; we define $Q = \bigcup_{l \in L} Q_l$. The support set provides a few labeled examples of new classes not seen at training time that f_ϕ must adapt to i.e. learn to classify, whereas the query set is used for evaluation. The definition of few-shot classification requires that evaluation is done on episodes; however, most few-shot learning methods train as well as evaluate on episodes. Consistent with prior work, we train both MAML and prototypical networks methods on episodes, as opposed to mini-batches.

3.2 Few-shot IC/SF

Few-shot IC/SF extends the prior definition of *few-shot classification* to include both IC and SF tasks.

As Geng et al. (2019) showed, it is straightforward to formulate IC as a *few-shot classification* task. Simply let the class labels y_l in section 3.1 correspond to IC labels and partition the set of ICs into the train and test splits, L_{train} and L_{test}. Building on this few-shot IC formulation, we re-define the *support* and *query* sets to include the slots t_l, in addition the intent y_l, assigned to each example x_l. Thus, the set of *support* and *query* instances for class $l \in L$ become $S_l = \{(x_l^i, t_l^i, y_l)|i \in (1 \ldots k_l)\}$ and $Q_l = \{(x_l^j, t_l^j, y_l)|j \in (1 \ldots k_q)\}$, respectively. To construct an episode, we sample a total of $k_l + k_q$ labeled examples per IC $l \in L$ to form the support and query sets. Since utterances can exhibit many unique slot-label combinations, it is possible to sample an episode such that a slot-label appears in only the query or support set. Therefore, to ensure fair evaluation, we *"mask"* any slot-label that appears in only the query or support set by replacing it with the *Other* slot label, which is ignored by our SF evaluation metric.

4 Approach

4.1 Prototypical Networks for Joint Intent Classification and Slot Filling

The original formulation of prototypical networks (Snell et al., 2017) is not directly applicable to sequence labeling. Accordingly, we extend prototypical networks to perform joint sentence classification and sequence labeling. Our extension computes "prototypes" c_l and c_a for each intent class l and slot-label a, respectively. Each prototype $c \in \mathbb{R}^D$ is the mean vector of the embeddings belonging to a given intent class or slot-label class. These embeddings are output by a sequence encoder $f_\phi(x) :\to \mathbb{R}^D$, which takes a variable length utterance of m tokens $x^i = (x_1^i, x_2^i, \ldots, x_m^i)$ as input, and outputs the final hidden state $h \in \mathbb{R}^D$ of the encoder. For ease of notation, let $S_l = \{(x_l^i, t_l^i, y_l)\}$ be the support set instances with intent class y_l. And let $S_a = \{(x_{[1:j]}^i, t_{[1:j]}^i, y^i)|t_j^i = a\}$ be the support set sub-sequences with slot-label a for the token x_j^i in x^i. Using this notation, we calculate slot-label and intent class prototypes as follows:

$$c_l = \frac{1}{|S_l|} \sum_{(x^i, t^i, y_l) \in S_l} f_\phi(x^i) \tag{1}$$

$$c_a = \frac{1}{|S_a|} \sum_{(x_{[1:j]}^i, t_{[1:j]}^i, y^i)} f_\phi(x_{[1:j]}^i) \tag{2}$$

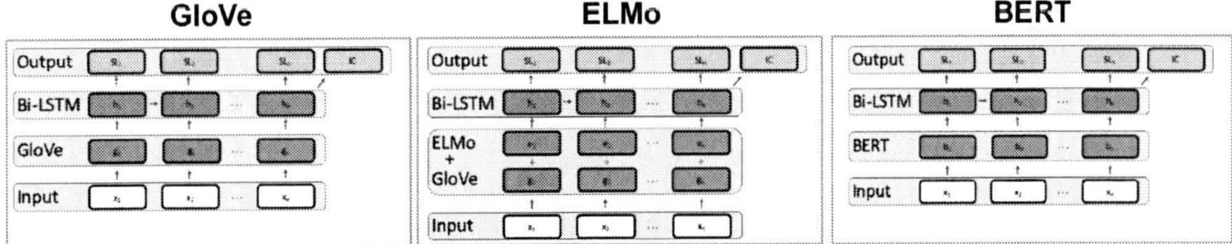

Figure 2: Three model architectures, each consisting of an embedding layer, comprised of either GloVe word embeddings (GloVe), GloVe word embeddings concatenated with ELMo embeddings (ELMo), or BERT embeddings (BERT), that feed into a bi-directional LSTM, which is followed by fully connected intent and slot output layers.

Given an example $(x^*, t^*, y^*) \in Q$, we compute the conditional probability $p(y = l \mid x^*, S)$ that the utterance x^* has intent class l as the normalized Euclidean distance between $f_\phi(x^*)$ and the prototype c_l,

$$p(y = l \mid x^*, S) = \frac{\exp(- \|f_\phi(x^*) - c_l\|_2^2)}{\sum_{l'} \exp(- \|f_\phi(x^*) - c_{l'}\|_2^2)}$$

Similarly, we compute the conditional probability $p(t_j^* = a \mid x^*, S)$ that the j-th token x_j^* in the utterance x^* has slot-label $t_j^* = a$ as the normalized Euclidean distance between $f_\phi(x_{[1:j]}^*)$ and the prototype c_a,

$$p(t_j^* = a \mid x^*, S) = \frac{\exp(- \left\|f_\phi(x_{[1:j]}^*) - c_a\right\|_2^2)}{\sum_{a'} \exp(- \left\|f_\phi(x_{[1:j]}^*) - c_{a'}\right\|_2^2)}$$

We define the joint IC and SF prototypical loss function $\mathcal{L}_{proto}$ as the sum of the IC and SF negative log-likelihoods averaged over the query set instances given the support set:

$$\mathcal{L}_{proto} = \frac{1}{|Q|} \sum_{(x^*, t^*, y^*) \in Q} \mathcal{L}_{protoIC} + \mathcal{L}_{protoSF}$$

$$\mathcal{L}_{protoIC} = - \log p(y = y^* \mid x^*, S)$$

$$\mathcal{L}_{protoSF} = - \sum_{t_j^* \in t^*} \log p(t_j^* = a \mid x^*, S)$$

4.2 Model Agnostic Meta Learning (MAML)

MAML optimizes the parameters ϕ of the encoder f_ϕ such that when ϕ is fine-tuned on the support set S for d steps, $\phi' \leftarrow \text{Finetune}(\phi, d \mid S)$, the fine-tuned model $f_{\phi'}$ generalizes well to new class instances in the query set Q. This is achieved by updating ϕ to minimize the loss of the fine-tuned model $\mathcal{L}(f_{\phi'}, Q)$ on the query set Q. The update

to ϕ takes the form $\phi \leftarrow \phi - \nabla_\phi \mathcal{L}(f_{\phi'}, Q)$, where $\mathcal{L}$ is the sum of IC and SF softmax cross entropy loss functions. Concretely, given a support and query set (S, Q), MAML performs the following two step optimization procedure:

1. $\phi' \leftarrow \text{Finetune}(\phi, d \mid S)$

2. $\phi \leftarrow \phi - \nabla_\phi \mathcal{L}(f_{\phi'}, Q)$

Although, the initial formulation of MAML, which we outline here, utilizes stochastic gradient descent (SGD) to update the initial parameters ϕ, in practice, an alternate gradient based update rule can be used in place of SGD. Empirically, we find it beneficial to use Adam in place of SGD.

A drawback to MAML is that computing the "meta-gradient" $\nabla_\phi \mathcal{L}(f_{\phi'}, Q)$ requires calculating a second derivative, since the gradient must backpropagate through the sequence of updates made by $\text{Finetune}(\phi, d \mid S)$. Fortunately, in the same work where (Finn et al., 2017) introduce MAML, they propose a first order approximation of MAML, foMAML, which ignores these second derivative terms and performs nearly as well as the original method. We utilize foMAML in our experiments to avoid memory issues associated with MAML.

5   Few-shot IC/SF Benchmark

As there is no existing benchmark for *few-shot IC/SF*, we propose few-shot splits for the Air Travel Information System (ATIS, Hemphill et al. (1990)), SNIPS (Coucke et al., 2018), and Task Oriented Parsing (TOP, (Gupta et al., 2018)) datasets. A *few-shot IC/SF* benchmark is beneficial for two reasons. Firstly, the benchmark evaluates generalization across multiple domains. Secondly, researchers can combine these datasets in the future to experiment with larger settings of n-way during training and evaluation.

Split	ATIS				SNIPS				TOP			
	#Utt	#IC	#SL	#SV	#Utt	#IC	#SL	#SV	#Utt	#IC	#SL	#SV
Train	4,373	5	116	461	8,230	4	33	8,549	20,345	7	38	5,574
Dev	662	7	122	260	-	-	-	-	4,333	5	33	2,228
Test	829	7	128	258	6,254	3	20	7,567	4,426	6	39	1,341
Total	5,864	19	366	583	14,484	7	53	13,599	29,104	18	110	6821

Table 1: Statistics on utterance (Utt), intent (IC), slot label (SL), and slot value (SV) counts for ATIS, TOP, and SNIPS few-shot train, development, and test splits as well as the full dataset, provided under the heading total.

5.1 Datasets

ATIS is a well-known dataset for dialog system research, which comprises conversations from the *airline* domain. SNIPS, on the other hand, is a public benchmark dataset developed by the Snips corporation to evaluate the quality of IC and SF services. The SNIPS dataset comprises multiple domains including music, media, and weather. TOP, which pertains to navigation and event search, is unique in that 35% of the utterances contain multiple, nested intent labels. These hierarchical intents require the use of specialized models. Therefore, we utilize only the remaining, non-hierarchical 65% of utterances in TOP. To put the size and diversity of these datasets in context, we provide utterance, intent, slot-label, and slot value counts for each dataset in table 1.

5.2 Few-shot Splits

We target train, development, and test split sizes of 70%, 15%, and 15%, respectively. However, the ICs in these datasets are highly imbalanced, which prevents us from hitting these targets exactly. Thereby, we manually select the ICs to include in each split. For the SNIPS dataset, we choose not to form a development split because there are only 7 ICs in the SNIPS dataset, and we require a minimum of 3 ICs per split. During preprocessing we modify slot label names by adding the associated IC as a prefix to each slot. This preprocessing step ensures that the slot labels are no longer pure named entities, but specific semantic roles in the context of particular intents. In table 1, we provide statistics on the few-shot splits for each dataset.

6 Experiments

6.1 Episode Construction

For train and test episodes, we sample both the the number of classes in each episode, the "way" n, and the number of examples to include for each sampled class l, the class "shot" k_l, using the procedure put forward in (Triantafillou et al., 2019). By sampling the shot and way, we allow for unbalanced support sets and a variable number of classes per episode. These allowances are compatible with the large degree of class imbalances present in our benchmark, which would make it difficult to apply a fixed shot and way for all intents.

To construct an episode given a few-shot class split L_{split}, we first sample the way n uniformly from the range $[3, |L_{split}|]$. We then sample n intent classes uniformly at random from L_{split} to form L. Next, we sample the query shot k_q for the episodes as follows:

$$k_q = \min(10, (\min_{l \in L} [0.5 * |X_l|]))$$

where X_l is the set of examples with class label l. Given the query shot k_q, we compute the target support set size for the episode as:

$$|S| = \min(K_{\max}, \sum_{l \in L} \lceil \beta \min(20, |X_l| - q) \rceil)$$

where β is sampled uniformly from the range $(0, 1]$ and $K_{\max}$ is the maximum episode size. Lastly, we sample the support shot k_l for each class as:

$$k_l = \min(\lfloor R_l * (|S| - |L|) \rfloor + 1, |X_l| - q)$$

where R_l is a noisy estimate of the normalized proportion of the dataset made up by class l, which we compute as follows:

$$R_l = \frac{\exp(\alpha_l) * |X_l|}{\sum_{l' \in L} \exp(\alpha_{l'}) * |X_{l'}|)}$$

The noise in our estimate of the proportion R_l is introduced by sampling the value of α_l uniformly from the interval $[\log(0.5), \log(2))$.

6.2 Episode Sizes

We present IC/SF results for two settings of maximum episode size, $K_{\max} = 20$ and $K_{\max} = 100$, in tables 2/4 and 3/5, respectively. When the maximum episode size $K_{\max} = 20$, the average support set shot k_l is 3.58 for ATIS, 3.78 for TOP, and 5.22 for SNIPS. In contrast, setting the maximum episode size to $K_{\max} = 100$ increases the average support set shot k_l to 9.15 for ATIS, 9.81 for TOP, and 10.83 for SNIPS.

6.3 Training Settings

In our experiments, we consider two training settings. One in which we train on episodes, or batches in the case of our baseline, from a single dataset. And another, *joint* training approach that randomly selects the dataset from which to sample a given episode/batch. After sampling an episode, we remove its contents from a buffer of available examples. If there are no longer enough examples in the buffer to create an episode, we refresh the buffer to contain all examples.

6.4 Network Architecture

We evaluate the network architectures depicted in Figure 2. These networks consist of an embedding layer, a sequence encoder, and two output layers for slots and intents, respectively. We greedily predict the slot-label for each token in the input sequence, according to the maximum output logit at each position. We plan to explore alternate search algorithms (e.g., beam search) in future work.

Each architecture uses a different pre-trained embedding layer type, which are either non-contextual or contextual. We experiment with one non-contextual embedding, GLOVE word vectors (Pennington et al., 2014), as well as two contextual embeddings, GLOVE concatenated with ELMO embeddings (Peters et al., 2018), and BERT embeddings (Devlin et al., 2018). The sequence encoder is a bi-directional LSTM (Hochreiter and Schmidhuber, 1997) with a 512-dimensional hidden state. Output layers are fully connected and take concatenated forward and backward LSTM hidden states as input. Pre-trained embeddings are kept frozen for training and adaptation. Attempts to fine-tune BERT led to inferior results. We refer to each architecture by its embedding type, namely GLOVE, ELMO, or BERT.

6.5 Baseline

We compare the performance of our approach against a FINE-TUNE baseline, which implements the domain adaptation framework commonly applied to low resource IC/SF (Goyal et al., 2018). We pre-train the FINE-TUNE baseline, either jointly or individually, on the classes in our training split(s). Then at evaluation time, we freeze the pre-trained encoder and "fine-tune" new output layers for the slots and intents included in the support set. This fine-tuned model is then used to predict the intent and slots for each held out example in the query set.

6.6 Hyper-parameters

We train all models using the Adam optimizer (Kingma and Ba, 2014). We use the default learning rate of 0.001 for the baseline and prototypical networks. For foMAML we set the outer learning rate to 0.0029 and finetune for $d = 8$ steps with an inner learning rate of 0.01. We pre-train the FINE-TUNE baseline with a batch size of 512. At test time, we fine-tune the baseline for 10 steps on the support set. We train the models without contextual embeddings (GloVe alone) for 50 epochs and those with contextual ELMo or BERT embeddings for 30 epochs because they exhibit faster convergence.

6.7 Evaluation Metrics

To assess the performance of our models, we report the average IC accuracy and slot F1 score over 100 episodes sampled from the test split of an individual dataset. We use the AllenNLP (Gardner et al., 2017) CategoricalAccuracy implementation to compute IC Accuracy. And to compute slot F1 score, we use the seqeval library's span based F1 score implementation.[2] The span based F1 score is a relatively harsh metric in the sense that a slot label prediction is only considered correct if the slot label and span exactly match the ground truth annotation.

7 Results

7.1 Few-shot Learning Algorithms

Prototypical networks Considering both IC and SF tasks, prototypical networks is the best performing algorithm. The most successful variant of prototypical networks, Proto ELMO + *joint* training, obtains absolute improvements over the FINE-TUNE

---

[2] https://github.com/chakki-works/seqeval

Embed.	Algorithm	IC Accuracy					
		SNIPS	SNIPS (joint)	ATIS	ATIS (joint)	TOP	TOP (joint)
GloVe	Fine-tune	69.52 ± 2.88	70.25 ± 1.85	49.50 ± 0.65	58.26 ± 1.12	37.58 ± 0.54	40.93 ± 2.77
GloVe	foMAML	61.08 ± 1.50	59.67 ± 2.12	54.66 ± 1.82	45.20 ± 1.47	33.75 ± 1.30	31.48 ± 0.50
GloVe	Proto	68.19 ± 1.76	68.77 ± 1.60	65.46 ± 0.81	63.91 ± 1.27	43.20 ± 0.85	38.65 ± 1.35
ELMo	Fine-tune	$\mathbf{85.53 \pm 0.35}$	$\mathbf{87.64 \pm 0.73}$	49.25 ± 0.74	58.69 ± 1.56	45.49 ± 0.61	47.63 ± 2.75
ELMo	foMAML	78.90 ± 0.77	78.86 ± 1.31	53.90 ± 0.96	52.47 ± 2.86	38.67 ± 1.02	36.49 ± 0.99
ELMo	Proto	83.54 ± 0.40	85.75 ± 1.57	$\mathbf{65.95 \pm 2.29}$	$\mathbf{65.19 \pm 1.29}$	50.57 ± 2.81	50.64 ± 2.72
BERT	Fine-tune	76.04 ± 8.84	77.53 ± 5.69	43.76 ± 4.61	50.73 ± 3.86	39.21 ± 3.09	40.86 ± 3.75
BERT	foMAML	67.36 ± 1.03	68.37 ± 0.48	50.27 ± 0.69	48.80 ± 2.82	38.50 ± 0.43	36.20 ± 1.21
BERT	Proto	81.39 ± 1.85	81.44 ± 2.91	58.84 ± 1.33	58.82 ± 1.55	$\mathbf{52.76 \pm 2.26}$	$\mathbf{52.64 \pm 2.58}$

Table 2: $K_{\max} = 20$ average IC accuracy on 100 test episodes from the ATIS, SNIPS, or TOP datasets in the form mean $\pm$ standard deviation, computed over 3 random seeds, comparing GloVe, ELMo, and BERT model variants for both individual and *joint* training, where we train on all training sets and test on a specific test set.

Embed.	Algorithm	IC Accuracy					
		SNIPS	SNIPS (joint)	ATIS	ATIS (joint)	TOP	TOP (joint)
GloVe	Fine-tune	72.24 ± 2.58	73.00 ± 1.84	49.91 ± 1.90	56.07 ± 2.94	39.66 ± 1.34	41.10 ± 0.65
GloVe	foMAML	66.75 ± 1.28	67.34 ± 2.62	54.92 ± 0.87	58.46 ± 1.91	33.62 ± 1.53	35.68 ± 0.62
GloVe	Proto	70.45 ± 0.49	72.66 ± 1.96	$\mathbf{70.25 \pm 0.39}$	69.58 ± 0.41	48.84 ± 1.59	46.85 ± 0.86
ELMo	Fine-tune	$\mathbf{87.69 \pm 1.05}$	$\mathbf{88.90 \pm 0.18}$	49.42 ± 0.79	56.99 ± 2.12	47.44 ± 1.61	48.87 ± 0.54
ELMo	foMAML	80.80 ± 0.47	81.62 ± 1.07	59.10 ± 2.52	56.16 ± 1.34	41.80 ± 1.49	36.24 ± 0.79
ELMo	Proto	86.76 ± 1.62	87.74 ± 1.08	70.10 ± 1.26	$\mathbf{71.89 \pm 1.45}$	58.60 ± 1.91	56.87 ± 0.39
BERT	Fine-tune	76.66 ± 8.68	79.53 ± 4.25	44.08 ± 6.05	49.71 ± 3.84	40.05 ± 2.35	40.46 ± 1.74
BERT	foMAML	70.43 ± 1.56	72.79 ± 1.11	51.36 ± 3.74	50.25 ± 0.88	36.15 ± 2.17	35.24 ± 0.35
BERT	Proto	83.51 ± 0.88	86.29 ± 1.09	66.89 ± 2.31	65.70 ± 2.31	$\mathbf{61.30 \pm 0.32}$	$\mathbf{62.51 \pm 1.79}$

Table 3: $K_{\max} = 100$ average IC accuracy on 100 test episodes from the ATIS, SNIPS, or TOP datasets in the form mean $\pm$ standard deviation, computed over 3 random seeds, comparing GloVe, ELMo, and BERT model variants for both individual and *joint* training, where we train on all training sets and test on a specific test set.

Embed.	Algorithm	Slot F1 Measure					
		SNIPS	SNIPS (joint)	ATIS	ATIS (joint)	TOP	TOP (joint)
GloVe	Fine-tune	6.72 ± 1.24	6.68 ± 0.40	2.57 ± 1.21	13.22 ± 1.07	0.90 ± 0.51	0.76 ± 0.21
GloVe	foMAML	14.07 ± 1.01	12.91 ± 0.43	18.44 ± 0.91	16.91 ± 0.32	5.34 ± 0.43	9.22 ± 1.03
GloVe	Proto	29.63 ± 0.75	27.75 ± 2.52	31.19 ± 1.15	38.45 ± 0.97	10.65 ± 0.83	18.55 ± 0.35
ELMo	Fine-tune	22.02 ± 1.13	16.00 ± 2.07	7.47 ± 2.60	7.19 ± 1.71	1.26 ± 0.46	1.17 ± 0.32
ELMo	foMAML	33.81 ± 0.33	32.82 ± 0.84	27.58 ± 1.25	24.45 ± 1.20	$\mathbf{22.35 \pm 1.23}$	15.53 ± 0.64
ELMo	Proto	$\mathbf{59.88 \pm 0.53}$	$\mathbf{59.73 \pm 1.72}$	33.97 ± 0.38	$\mathbf{40.90 \pm 2.21}$	20.12 ± 0.25	$\mathbf{28.97 \pm 0.82}$
BERT	Fine-tune	12.47 ± 0.31	8.75 ± 0.28	9.24 ± 1.67	15.93 ± 3.10	3.15 ± 0.28	1.08 ± 0.30
BERT	foMAML	12.72 ± 0.12	13.28 ± 0.53	18.91 ± 1.01	16.05 ± 0.32	5.93 ± 0.43	8.23 ± 0.81
BERT	Proto	42.09 ± 1.11	43.77 ± 0.54	$\mathbf{37.61 \pm 0.82}$	39.27 ± 1.84	20.81 ± 0.40	28.24 ± 0.53

Table 4: $K_{\max} = 20$ average Slot F1 score on 100 test episodes from the ATIS, SNIPS, or TOP datasets in the form mean $\pm$ standard deviation, computed over 3 random seeds, comparing GloVe, ELMo, and BERT model variants for both individual and *joint* training, where we train on all training sets and test on a specific test set.

Embed.	Algorithm	Slot F1 Measure					
		SNIPS	SNIPS (joint)	ATIS	ATIS (joint)	TOP	TOP (joint)
GloVe	Fine-tune	7.06 ± 1.87	7.76 ± 0.91	2.72 ± 1.65	17.20 ± 3.03	1.26 ± 0.44	0.67 ± 0.33
GloVe	foMAML	16.77 ± 0.67	16.53 ± 0.32	17.80 ± 0.42	23.33 ± 2.89	4.11 ± 0.81	9.89 ± 1.13
GloVe	Proto	31.57 ± 1.28	31.17 ± 1.31	31.32 ± 2.79	41.07 ± 1.14	9.99 ± 1.08	18.93 ± 0.77
ELMo	Fine-tune	22.37 ± 0.91	17.09 ± 2.57	8.93 ± 2.86	11.09 ± 2.00	2.04 ± 0.41	1.03 ± 0.24
ELMo	foMAML	36.10 ± 1.49	37.33 ± 0.24	26.91 ± 2.64	26.37 ± 0.15	18.32 ± 0.52	16.55 ± 0.79
ELMo	Proto	$\mathbf{62.71 \pm 0.40}$	$\mathbf{62.14 \pm 0.75}$	35.20 ± 2.46	41.28 ± 2.73	18.44 ± 2.41	28.33 ± 1.33
BERT	Fine-tune	14.71 ± 0.43	10.50 ± 0.90	11.53 ± 1.46	20.41 ± 1.85	4.98 ± 0.66	1.48 ± 0.85
BERT	foMAML	14.99 ± 1.29	15.83 ± 0.94	17.68 ± 2.42	17.11 ± 1.31	3.37 ± 0.36	10.58 ± 0.45
BERT	Proto	46.50 ± 0.75	48.77 ± 0.71	$\mathbf{40.63 \pm 3.37}$	$\mathbf{43.10 \pm 1.76}$	20.58 ± 2.27	$\mathbf{28.92 \pm 1.09}$

Table 5: $K_{\max} = 100$ average Slot F1 score on 100 test episodes from the ATIS, SNIPS, or TOP datasets in the form mean $\pm$ standard deviation, computed over 3 random seeds, comparing GloVe, ELMo, and BERT model variants for both individual and *joint* training, where we train on all training sets and test on a specific test set.

ELMO + *joint* training baseline of up to 6% IC accuracy and 43 slot F1 points for $K_{max} = 20$, and 14% IC accuracy and 45 slot F1 points for $K_{max} = 100$. The one case in which Proto ELMO + *joint* training does worse than the baseline is on SNIPS IC, but these losses are all under 2%. Over the 36 possible combinations of dataset, embedding type, and setting of K_{max}, Prototypical networks performs best in 27/36 instances for IC and 35/36 instances for SL. In comparison, FINE-TUNE performs best in 9/36 instances for IC and is never the best algorithm for SL. Conversely, foMAML is never the best algorithm for IC and is the best algorithm in 1/36 cases for SL.

foMAML The results for foMAML are more mixed in terms of IC and SF performance relative to the baseline. The best foMAML variant, foMAML ELMO, underperforms FINE-TUNE ELMO on SNIPS and TOP IC by up to 6%. Yet foMAML improves IC accuracy by 4% ($K_{max} = 20$) to 9% ($K_{max} = 100$) on ATIS. foMAML ELMO consistently outperforms FINE-TUNE ELMO on SF for all datasets, generating gains of 11~21 F1 points for $K_{max} = 20$ and 13~17 F1 points for $K_{max} = 100$. Notably, BERT and foMAML do not work well in combination. Specifically, the SF performance of foMAML BERT is comparable to, or worse than, foMAML GLOVE on all datasets for both $K_{max} = 20$ and $K_{max} = 100$.

7.2 Model Variants

Non-contextual Pretrained Embeddings The GLOVE model architecture does not perform as well as ELMO or BERT. On average over experimental settings, the GLOVE variant of the winning algorithm has 10% lower IC Accuracy and 16 point lower slot F1 score than the winning algorithm paired with the best model. Note that an experimental setting here refers to a combination of dataset, value of K_{max}, and use of individual or joint training. Somewhat surprisingly, GLOVE performs nearly as well as ELMO and even better than BERT on ATIS IC. We speculate that ATIS IC does not benefit as much from the use of ELMO or BERT because ATIS carrier phrases are less diverse, as evidenced by the smaller number of unique carrier phrases in the ATIS test set (527) compared to SNIPS (3,718) and TOP (4,153).

Contextual Pretrained Embeddings A priori, it is reasonable to suspect that the performance gain obtained by our few-shot learning algorithms could be dwarfed by the benefit of using a large, pre-trained model like ELMO or BERT. However, our experimental results suggest that the use of pre-trained language models is complementary to our approach, in most cases. For example, ELMO increases the slot F1 score of foMAML from 14.07 to 33.81 and boosts the slot F1 of prototypical networks from 31.57 to 62.71 on the SNIPS dataset for $K_{max} = 100$. Similarly, when $K_{max} = 20$, BERT improves foMAML and prototypical networks TOP IC accuracy from 33.75% to 38.50% and from 43.20% to 52.76%, respectively. In aggregate, we find ELMO outperforms BERT. We quantify this via the average absolute improvement ELMO obtains over BERT when both models use the winning algorithm for a given dataset and training setting. On average, ELMO improves IC accuracy over BERT by 2% for $K_{max} = 20$ and 1% for $K_{max} = 100$. With respect to slot F1 score, ELMO produces an average gain over BERT of 5 F1 points for $K_{max} = 20$ and 3 F1 points for $K_{max} = 100$. This is consistent with previous findings in (Peters et al., 2019) that ELMO can outperform BERT on certain tasks when the models are kept frozen and not fine-tuned.

7.3 Joint Training

Few-shot learning algorithms are in essence learning to learn new classes. Therefore, these algorithms should be adept at leveraging a diverse training dataset to improve generalization. We test this hypothesis by jointly training each approach on all three datasets. Our results demonstrate that joint training has little effect on IC Accuracy; however, it improves the SF performance of prototypical networks, particularly on ATIS and TOP. Joint training increases Prototypical networks average slot F1 score, computed over datasets and model variants, by 4.41 points from 31.77 to 36.18 for $K_{max} = 20$ and by 5.20 points from 32.99 to 38.19 when $K_{max} = 100$. In comparison, Fine-tune obtains much smaller average absolute improvements, 0.55 F1 points and 1.29 F1 points for $K_{max} = 20$ and $K_{max} = 100$, respectively.

8 Conclusion

We show that few-shot learning techniques can substantially improve IC/SF performance in ultra low resource scenarios. Specifically, our extension of prototypical networks for joint IC and SF consistently outperforms a fine-tuning baseline with respect to both IC Accuracy and slot F1 score. Moreover, we establish a benchmark for *few-shot IC/SF* to support future work on this important topic. Our contribution is a step toward the creation of more sample efficient IC/SF models. Yet there is still considerable work to be done in pursuit of this goal. In particular, we encourage the creation of larger *few-shot IC/SF* benchmarks to test how few-shot learning algorithms scale with larger episode sizes.

References

Alice Coucke, Alaa Saade, Adrien Ball, Théodore Bluche, Alexandre Caulier, David Leroy, Clément Doumouro, Thibault Gisselbrecht, Francesco Caltagirone, Thibaut Lavril, Maël Primet, and Joseph Dureau. 2018. Snips voice platform: an embedded spoken language understanding system for private-by-design voice interfaces. *CoRR*, abs/1805.10190.

Jacob Devlin, Ming-Wei Chang, Kenton Lee, and Kristina Toutanova. 2018. Bert: Pre-training of deep bidirectional transformers for language understanding. *arXiv preprint arXiv:1810.04805*.

Zi-Yi Dou, Keyi Yu, and Antonios Anastasopoulos. 2019. Investigating meta-learning algorithms for low-resource natural language understanding tasks. *arXiv preprint arXiv:1908.10423*.

Chelsea Finn, Pieter Abbeel, and Sergey Levine. 2017. Model-agnostic meta-learning for fast adaptation of deep networks. In *Proceedings of the 34th International Conference on Machine Learning-Volume 70*, pages 1126–1135. JMLR. org.

Alexander Fritzler, Varvara Logacheva, and Maksim Kretov. 2019. Few-shot classification in named entity recognition task. In *Proceedings of the 34th ACM/SIGAPP Symposium on Applied Computing*, pages 993–1000. ACM.

Matt Gardner, Joel Grus, Mark Neumann, Oyvind Tafjord, Pradeep Dasigi, Nelson F. Liu, Matthew Peters, Michael Schmitz, and Luke S. Zettlemoyer. 2017. Allennlp: A deep semantic natural language processing platform.

Ruiying Geng, Binhua Li, Yongbin Li, Yuxiao Ye, Ping Jian, and Jian Sun. 2019. Few-shot text classification with induction network. *arXiv preprint arXiv:1902.10482*.

Chih-Wen Goo, Guang Gao, Yun-Kai Hsu, Chih-Li Huo, Tsung-Chieh Chen, Keng-Wei Hsu, and Yun-Nung Chen. 2018. Slot-gated modeling for joint slot filling and intent prediction. In *Proceedings of the 2018 Conference of the North American Chapter of the Association for Computational Linguistics: Human Language Technologies, Volume 2 (Short Papers)*, pages 753–757.

Anuj Goyal, Angeliki Metallinou, and Spyros Matsoukas. 2018. Fast and scalable expansion of natural language understanding functionality for intelligent agents. *arXiv preprint arXiv:1805.01542*.

Alex Graves, Greg Wayne, and Ivo Danihelka. 2014. Neural turing machines. *arXiv preprint arXiv:1410.5401*.

Arshit Gupta, John Hewitt, and Katrin Kirchhoff. 2019. Simple, fast, accurate intent classification and slot labeling. *arXiv preprint arXiv:1903.08268*.

Sonal Gupta, Rushin Shah, Mrinal Mohit, Anuj Kumar, and Mike Lewis. 2018. Semantic parsing for task oriented dialog using hierarchical representations. In *Proceedings of the 2018 Conference on Empirical Methods in Natural Language Processing*, pages 2787–2792, Brussels, Belgium. Association for Computational Linguistics.

Dilek Hakkani-Tür, Gökhan Tür, Asli Celikyilmaz, Yun-Nung Chen, Jianfeng Gao, Li Deng, and Ye-Yi Wang. 2016. Multi-domain joint semantic frame parsing using bi-directional rnn-lstm. In *Interspeech*, pages 715–719.

Xu Han, Hao Zhu, Pengfei Yu, Ziyun Wang, Yuan Yao, Zhiyuan Liu, and Maosong Sun. 2018. Fewrel: A large-scale supervised few-shot relation classification dataset with state-of-the-art evaluation. In *Proceedings of the 2018 Conference on Empirical Methods in Natural Language Processing*, pages 4803–4809.

Charles T Hemphill, John J Godfrey, and George R Doddington. 1990. The atis spoken language systems pilot corpus. In *Speech and Natural Language: Proceedings of a Workshop Held at Hidden Valley, Pennsylvania, June 24-27, 1990*.

Sepp Hochreiter and Jürgen Schmidhuber. 1997. Long short-term memory. *Neural computation*, 9(8):1735–1780.

Yutai Hou, Zhihan Zhou, Yijia Liu, Ning Wang, Wanxiang Che, Han Liu, and Ting Liu. 2019. Few-shot sequence labeling with label dependency transfer. *arXiv preprint arXiv:1906.08711*.

Xiang Jiang, Mohammad Havaei, Gabriel Chartrand, Hassan Chouaib, Thomas Vincent, Andrew Jesson, Nicolas Chapados, and Stan Matwin. 2018. Attentive task-agnostic meta-learning for few-shot text classification.

Łukasz Kaiser, Ofir Nachum, Aurko Roy, and Samy Bengio. 2017. Learning to remember rare events. *arXiv preprint arXiv:1703.03129*.

Diederik P Kingma and Jimmy Ba. 2014. Adam: A method for stochastic optimization. *arXiv preprint arXiv:1412.6980*.

Gregory Koch. 2015. Siamese neural networks for one-shot image recognition.

Nikhil Mishra, Mostafa Rohaninejad, Xi Chen, and Pieter Abbeel. 2017. A simple neural attentive meta-learner. *arXiv preprint arXiv:1707.03141.*

Jeffrey Pennington, Richard Socher, and Christopher Manning. 2014. Glove: Global vectors for word representation. In *Proceedings of the 2014 conference on empirical methods in natural language processing (EMNLP)*, pages 1532–1543.

Matthew E. Peters, Mark Neumann, Mohit Iyyer, Matt Gardner, Christopher Clark, Kenton Lee, and Luke Zettlemoyer. 2018. Deep contextualized word representations. In *Proc. of NAACL.*

Matthew E. Peters, Sebastian Ruder, and Noah A. Smith. 2019. To tune or not to tune? adapting pre-trained representations to diverse tasks. In *Proceedings of the 4th Workshop on Representation Learning for NLP (RepL4NLP-2019)*, pages 7–14, Florence, Italy. Association for Computational Linguistics.

Sachin Ravi and Hugo Larochelle. 2016. Optimization as a model for few-shot learning.

Adam Santoro, Sergey Bartunov, Matthew Botvinick, Daan Wierstra, and Timothy Lillicrap. 2016. Meta-learning with memory-augmented neural networks. In *International conference on machine learning*, pages 1842–1850.

Sebastian Schuster, Sonal Gupta, Rushin Shah, and Mike Lewis. 2018. Cross-lingual transfer learning for multilingual task oriented dialog. *arXiv preprint arXiv:1810.13327.*

Jake Snell, Kevin Swersky, and Richard Zemel. 2017. Prototypical networks for few-shot learning. In *Advances in Neural Information Processing Systems*, pages 4077–4087.

Eleni Triantafillou, Tyler Zhu, Vincent Dumoulin, Pascal Lamblin, Kelvin Xu, Ross Goroshin, Carles Gelada, Kevin Swersky, Pierre-Antoine Manzagol, and Hugo Larochelle. 2019. Meta-dataset: A dataset of datasets for learning to learn from few examples. *arXiv preprint arXiv:1903.03096.*

Oriol Vinyals, Charles Blundell, Timothy Lillicrap, Daan Wierstra, et al. 2016. Matching networks for one shot learning. In *Advances in neural information processing systems*, pages 3630–3638.

Mo Yu, Xiaoxiao Guo, Jinfeng Yi, Shiyu Chang, Saloni Potdar, Yu Cheng, Gerald Tesauro, Haoyu Wang, and Bowen Zhou. 2018. Diverse few-shot text classification with multiple metrics. In *Proceedings of the 2018 Conference of the North American Chapter of the Association for Computational Linguistics: Human Language Technologies, Volume 1 (Long Papers)*, pages 1206–1215.

A   Appendices

A.1   Few-shot IC/SF Splits

We list the few-shot splits that we establish for the ATIS, SNIPS, and TOP datasets in tables 6, 7, 8, respectively. In addition to the assignment of intent classes to train, development (dev) and test splits, we also report the number of utterances and slot labels associated with each intent class.

Split	IC Name	# Utt	# SL	SL Names (without IC prefix)
Train	atis_flight	4298	71	or, mod, meal, flight, economy, connect, day_name, city_name, round_trip, class_type, flight_mod, compartment, flight_stop, flight_days, flight_time, fare_amount, airline_name, airline_code, airport_name, airport_code, cost_relative, aircraft_code, flight_number, period_of_day, toloc.city_name, arrive_time.time, meal_description, toloc.state_name, depart_time.time, toloc.state_code, depart_date.year, fare_basis_code, fromloc.city_name, stoploc.city_name, fromloc.state_name, toloc.airport_name, fromloc.state_code, toloc.country_name, toloc.airport_code, stoploc.state_code, fromloc.airport_name, fromloc.airport_code, stoploc.airport_name, stoploc.airport_code, depart_date.day_name, arrive_date.day_name, depart_time.end_time, arrive_time.end_time, return_date.day_name, arrive_date.month_name, arrive_date.day_number, depart_date.month_name, depart_date.day_number, depart_time.start_time, arrive_time.start_time, depart_time.period_mod, arrive_time.period_mod, return_time.period_mod, return_date.month_name, return_date.day_number, arrive_time.time_relative, depart_time.time_relative, depart_date.date_relative, return_date.date_relative, arrive_date.date_relative, depart_time.period_of_day, depart_date.today_relative, arrive_date.today_relative, arrive_time.period_of_day, return_time.period_of_day, return_date.today_relative
Train	atis_capacity	37	5	mod, airline_name, aircraft_code, toloc.city_name, fromloc.city_name
Train	atis_flight_no	20	22	or, flight_mod, class_type, flight_time, airline_name, cost_relative, flight_number, toloc.city_name, arrive_time.time, toloc.state_name, depart_time.time, toloc.state_code, fromloc.city_name, stoploc.city_name, fromloc.state_name, depart_date.day_name, depart_date.month_name, depart_date.day_number, arrive_time.time_relative, depart_time.time_relative, depart_time.period_of_day, depart_date.today_relative
Train	atis_meal	12	12	meal, airline_name, airline_code, flight_number, toloc.city_name, arrive_time.time, toloc.state_code, meal_description, fromloc.city_name, toloc.airport_code, depart_date.day_name, depart_time.period_of_day
Train	atis_restriction	6	6	round_trip, fare_amount, cost_relative, toloc.city_name, restriction_code, fromloc.city_name
Dev	atis_airfare	471	45	or, meal, economy, connect, round_trip, class_type, flight_mod, fare_amount, flight_stop, flight_time, flight_days, airline_name, airline_code, cost_relative, flight_number, aircraft_code, toloc.city_name, depart_time.time, toloc.state_code, toloc.state_name, depart_date.year, arrive_time.time, fromloc.city_name, stoploc.city_name, toloc.airport_name, fromloc.state_name, toloc.airport_code, fromloc.state_code, fromloc.airport_code, fromloc.airport_name, depart_date.day_name, arrive_date.day_name, arrive_date.month_name, arrive_date.day_number, depart_date.month_name, depart_date.day_number, return_date.month_name, return_date.day_number, depart_time.period_mod, depart_time.time_relative, depart_date.date_relative, arrive_time.time_relative, arrive_date.date_relative, depart_time.period_of_day, depart_date.today_relative
Dev	atis_flight_time	55	20	flight_mod, class_type, flight_time, airline_name, airline_code, airport_name, flight_number, aircraft_code, toloc.city_name, depart_time.time, meal_description, fromloc.city_name, toloc.airport_code, fromloc.airport_name, depart_date.day_name, depart_date.month_name, depart_date.day_number, depart_date.date_relative, depart_time.time_relative, depart_time.period_of_day
Dev	atis_quantity	54	25	economy, city_name, class_type, round_trip, flight_stop, flight_days, airline_code, airline_name, flight_number, aircraft_code, toloc.city_name, arrive_time.time, fare_basis_code, depart_time.time, fromloc.city_name, stoploc.city_name, toloc.airport_name, arrive_date.month_name, arrive_date.day_number, depart_date.month_name, depart_date.day_number, arrive_time.time_relative, depart_time.time_relative, depart_date.today_relative, depart_time.period_of_day
Dev	atis_distance	30	8	city_name, airport_name, toloc.city_name, depart_time.time, fromloc.city_name, fromloc.airport_name, depart_date.month_name, depart_date.day_number
Dev	atis_city	25	11	city_name, class_type, airline_name, airport_code, airport_name, toloc.city_name, depart_time.time, fromloc.city_name, fromloc.airport_code, depart_time.time_relative, depart_time.period_of_day
Dev	atis_ground_fare	25	6	city_name, airport_name, transport_type, toloc.city_name, fromloc.city_name, fromloc.airport_name
Dev	atis_airline;atis_flight_no	2	7	toloc.city_name, arrive_time.time, fromloc.city_name, depart_date.month_name, depart_date.day_number, depart_date.date_relative, arrive_time.time_relative
Test	atis_ground_service	291	23	or, time, day_name, city_name, state_code, state_name, month_name, day_number, flight_time, airport_name, airport_code, time_relative, transport_type, today_relative, period_of_day, toloc.city_name, fromloc.city_name, toloc.airport_name, fromloc.airport_name, depart_date.day_name, depart_date.month_name, depart_date.day_number, depart_date.date_relative
Test	atis_airline	195	36	mod, connect, city_name, class_type, round_trip, flight_stop, flight_days, airline_code, airport_name, airline_name, aircraft_code, flight_number, cost_relative, toloc.city_name, toloc.state_code, depart_time.time, arrive_time.time, toloc.state_name, fromloc.city_name, stoploc.city_name, toloc.airport_name, fromloc.state_code, fromloc.airport_code, fromloc.airport_name, depart_date.day_name, depart_time.end_time, arrive_date.month_name, arrive_date.day_number, depart_date.month_name, depart_date.day_number, depart_time.start_time, depart_time.time_relative, depart_date.date_relative, depart_date.today_relative, depart_time.period_of_day, arrive_time.period_of_day
Test	atis_abbreviation	180	14	mod, meal, meal_code, days_code, class_type, airport_code, airline_code, airline_name, aircraft_code, booking_class, toloc.city_name, fare_basis_code, restriction_code, fromloc.city_name
Test	atis_aircraft	90	23	mod, city_name, class_type, flight_mod, airline_name, airline_code, flight_number, aircraft_code, toloc.city_name, depart_time.time, toloc.state_code, arrive_time.time, fromloc.city_name, stoploc.city_name, depart_date.day_name, arrive_date.day_name, depart_date.month_name, depart_date.day_number, arrive_date.month_name, arrive_date.day_number, depart_time.time_relative, arrive_time.time_relative, depart_time.period_of_day
Test	atis_airport	38	9	mod, city_name, state_code, state_name, flight_stop, airport_name, airline_name, toloc.city_name, fromloc.city_name
Test	atis_flight;atis_airfare	33	21	flight_mod, round_trip, fare_amount, flight_stop, airline_name, flight_number, cost_relative, toloc.city_name, depart_time.time, arrive_time.time, toloc.state_code, fromloc.city_name, depart_date.day_name, return_date.day_name, depart_date.month_name, depart_date.day_number, depart_time.time_relative, depart_date.date_relative, arrive_time.time_relative, return_date.date_relative, depart_time.period_of_day
Test	atis_day_name	2	2	toloc.city_name, fromloc.city_name

Table 6: Few-shot splits for the ATIS dataset, listing the split assignment, number of utterances (# Utt), number of slot labels (# SL), and names of slot labels associated with each intent class (IC). For brevity, we exclude the intent class prefix that we add to the slot label names during prepossessing (in the form intent-name/slot-name).

Split	IC Name	# Utt	# SL	SL Names (without IC prefix)
Train	BookRestaurant	2073	14	poi, sort, city, state, country, cuisine, facility, timeRange, served_dish, restaurant_type, restaurant_name, spatial_relation, party_size_number, party_size_description
Train	SearchScreeningEvent	2059	7	timeRange, movie_name, movie_type, object_type, location_name, spatial_relation, object_location_type
Train	RateBook	2056	7	best_rating, rating_unit, object_name, object_type, rating_value, object_select, object_part_of_series_type
Train	AddToPlaylist	2042	5	artist, playlist, music_item, entity_name, playlist_owner
Test	PlayMusic	2100	9	sort, year, album, genre, track, artist, service, playlist, music_item
Test	GetWeather	2100	9	city, state, country, timeRange, geographic_poi, spatial_relation, current_location, condition_temperature, condition_description
Test	SearchCreativeWork	2054	2	object_name, object_type

Table 7: Few-shot splits for the SNIPS dataset, listing the split assignment, number of utterances (# Utt), number of slot labels (# SL), and names of slot labels associated with each intent class (IC). For brevity, we exclude the intent class prefix that we add to the slot label names during prepossessing (in the form intent-name/slot-name).

Split	IC Name	# Utt	# SL	SL Names (without IC prefix)
Train	IN:GET_EVENT	10063	9	SL:AMOUNT, SL:ORDINAL, SL:LOCATION, SL:DATE_TIME, SL:NAME_EVENT, SL:CATEGORY_EVENT, SL:ATTENDEE_EVENT, SL:ATTRIBUTE_EVENT, SL:ORGANIZER_EVENT
Train	IN:GET_INFO_TRAFFIC	8629	11	SL:PATH, SL:SOURCE, SL:LOCATION, SL:WAYPOINT, SL:DATE_TIME, SL:DESTINATION, SL:PATH_AVOID, SL:METHOD_TRAVEL, SL:ROAD_CONDITION, SL:WAYPOINT_AVOID, SL:OBSTRUCTION_AVOID
Train	IN:UNSUPPORTED	1484	0	
Train	IN:GET_ESTIMATED_DEPARTURE	160	10	SL:PATH, SL:SOURCE, SL:WAYPOINT, SL:LOCATION, SL:DESTINATION, SL:METHOD_TRAVEL, SL:ROAD_CONDITION, SL:OBSTRUCTION_AVOID, SL:DATE_TIME_ARRIVAL, SL:DATE_TIME_DEPARTURE
Train	IN:UNINTELLIGIBLE	4	0	
Train	IN:GET_EVENT_ATTENDEE_AMOUNT	3	5	SL:ORDINAL, SL:LOCATION, SL:DATE_TIME, SL:NAME_EVENT, SL:CATEGORY_EVENT
Train	IN:GET_EVENT_ORGANIZER	2	3	SL:LOCATION, SL:DATE_TIME, SL:CATEGORY_EVENT
Dev	IN:GET_ESTIMATED_DURATION	2309	12	SL:PATH, SL:SOURCE, SL:WAYPOINT, SL:DATE_TIME, SL:DESTINATION, SL:PATH_AVOID, SL:METHOD_TRAVEL, SL:WAYPOINT_AVOID, SL:ROAD_CONDITION, SL:OBSTRUCTION_AVOID, SL:DATE_TIME_ARRIVAL, SL:DATE_TIME_DEPARTURE
Dev	IN:GET_DISTANCE	1962	9	SL:PATH, SL:SOURCE, SL:AMOUNT, SL:DESTINATION, SL:PATH_AVOID, SL:UNIT_DISTANCE, SL:METHOD_TRAVEL, SL:OBSTRUCTION_AVOID, SL:DATE_TIME_DEPARTURE
Dev	IN:GET_LOCATION	47	5	SL:LOCATION, SL:POINT_ON_MAP, SL:LOCATION_USER, SL:LOCATION_MODIFIER, SL:CATEGORY_LOCATION
Dev	IN:GET_INFO_ROUTE	13	5	SL:PATH, SL:SOURCE, SL:WAYPOINT, SL:DESTINATION, SL:DATE_TIME_DEPARTURE
Dev	IN:GET_EVENT_ATTENDEE	2	2	SL:ATTENDEE_EVENT, SL:CATEGORY_EVENT
Test	IN:UNSUPPORTED_NAVIGATION	2175	0	
Test	IN:GET_DIRECTIONS	752	12	SL:PATH, SL:SOURCE, SL:WAYPOINT, SL:DESTINATION, SL:PATH_AVOID, SL:METHOD_TRAVEL, SL:WAYPOINT_AVOID, SL:ROAD_CONDITION, SL:OBSTRUCTION_AVOID, SL:DATE_TIME_ARRIVAL, SL:DATE_TIME_DEPARTURE, SL:ROAD_CONDITION_AVOID
Test	IN:GET_ESTIMATED_ARRIVAL	538	11	SL:PATH, SL:SOURCE, SL:WAYPOINT, SL:LOCATION, SL:DESTINATION, SL:PATH_AVOID, SL:METHOD_TRAVEL, SL:ROAD_CONDITION, SL:OBSTRUCTION_AVOID, SL:DATE_TIME_ARRIVAL, SL:DATE_TIME_DEPARTURE
Test	IN:UNSUPPORTED_EVENT	424	0	
Test	IN:GET_INFO_ROAD_CONDITION	316	9	SL:PATH, SL:SOURCE, SL:LOCATION, SL:DATE_TIME, SL:DESTINATION, SL:METHOD_TRAVEL, SL:ROAD_CONDITION, SL:DATE_TIME_ARRIVAL, SL:DATE_TIME_DEPARTURE
Test	IN:UPDATE_DIRECTIONS	221	7	SL:PATH, SL:SOURCE, SL:DESTINATION, SL:PATH_AVOID, SL:OBSTRUCTION_AVOID, SL:DATE_TIME_ARRIVAL, SL:DATE_TIME_DEPARTURE

Table 8: Few-shot splits for the TOP dataset, listing the split assignment, number of utterances (# Utt), number of slot labels (# SL), and names of slot labels associated with each intent class (IC). For brevity, we exclude the intent class prefix that we add to the slot label names during prepossessing (in the form intent-name/slot-name).

MultiWOZ 2.2 : A Dialogue Dataset with Additional Annotation Corrections and State Tracking Baselines

Xiaoxue Zang[1], Abhinav Rastogi[1], Srinivas Sunkara[1], Raghav Gupta[1],
Jianguo Zhang[2], Jindong Chen[1]
[1]Google Research, [2]University of Illinois at Chicago
[1]{xiaoxuez, abhirast, srinivasksun, raghavgupta}@google.com,
[2]jzhan51@uic.edu, [1]jdchen@google.com

Abstract

MultiWOZ (Budzianowski et al., 2018) is a well-known task-oriented dialogue dataset containing over 10,000 annotated dialogues spanning 8 domains. It is extensively used as a benchmark for dialogue state tracking. However, recent works have reported presence of substantial noise in the dialogue state annotations. MultiWOZ 2.1 (Eric et al., 2019) identified and fixed many of these erroneous annotations and user utterances, resulting in an improved version of this dataset. This work introduces MultiWOZ 2.2, which is a yet another improved version of this dataset. Firstly, we identify and fix dialogue state annotation errors across 17.3% of the utterances on top of MultiWOZ 2.1. Secondly, we redefine the ontology by disallowing vocabularies of slots with a large number of possible values (e.g., restaurant name, time of booking). In addition, we introduce slot span annotations for these slots to standardize them across recent models, which previously used custom string matching heuristics to generate them. We also benchmark a few state of the art dialogue state tracking models on the corrected dataset to facilitate comparison for future work. In the end, we discuss best practices for dialogue data collection that can help avoid annotation errors.

1 Introduction

Task-oriented dialogue systems have become very popular in the recent years. Such systems assist the users in accomplishing different tasks by helping them interact with APIs using natural language. Dialogue systems consist of multiple modules which work together to facilitate such interactions. Most architectures have a natural language understanding and dialogue state tracking module to generate a structured representation of user's preferences from the dialogue history. This structured representation is used to make API calls and as a signal for other modules. Then, the dialogue policy module determines the next actions to be taken by the dialogue system. This is followed by the natural language generation module, which converts the generated actions to a natural language utterance, which is surfaced to the user.

Recently, data-driven techniques have achieved state-of-the-art performance for the different dialogue systems modules (Wen et al., 2017b; Ren et al., 2018; Zhang et al., 2019; Chao and Lane, 2019). However, collecting high quality annotated dialogue datasets remains a challenge for the researchers because of the extensive annotation required for training the modules mentioned above. Many public datasets like DSTC2 (Henderson et al., 2014), WOZ (Wen et al., 2017a), SimulatedDialogue (Shah et al., 2018), Multi-WOZ (Budzianowski et al., 2018), TaskMaster (Byrne et al., 2019), SGD (Rastogi et al., 2019), etc. have been very useful to facilitate research in this area. Among these datasets, MultiWOZ is the most widely used benchmark for dialogue state tracking. It contains over 10,000 dialogues spanning 8 domains, namely - Restaurant, Hotel, Attraction, Taxi, Train, Hospital, Bus, and Police.

Since its inception, the MultiWOZ dataset has undergone a few updates. Lee et al. (2019) introduced user dialogue actions providing a structured semantic representation for user utterances. Eric et al. (2019) fixed 32% of dialogue state annotations across 40% of the turns and introduced slot descriptions, culminating in MultiWOZ 2.1, a new version of the dataset. Despite the large scale of corrections introduced in MultiWOZ 2.1, there are still many unaddressed annotation errors (Zhang et al., 2019). Furthermore, several approaches to dialogue state tracking use span annotations identifying the locations in the user and system utterances where slot values have been mentioned, to make the system efficient and generalizable to new

Proceedings of the 2nd Workshop on Natural Language Processing for Conversational AI, pages 109–117
July 9, 2020. ©2020 Association for Computational Linguistics

slot values (Rastogi et al., 2017; Wu et al., 2019; Zhang et al., 2019; Rastogi et al., 2019; Xu and Hu, 2018; Zhou and Small, 2019; Gao et al., 2019). Because of the absence of these span annotations in MultiWOZ, these approaches resort to generating them using custom string matching heuristics, making their comparison difficult.

To address these limitations, we introduce MultiWOZ 2.2[1], an updated version of the MultiWOZ dataset. Our contributions are threefold.

1. We identify the annotation errors, inconsistencies, and ontology issues in MultiWOZ 2.1, and publish its improved version.

2. We add slot span annotations for user and system utterances to standardize them across future models. We also annotate the active user intents and requested slots for each user utterance.

3. We benchmark a few state-of-the-art dialogue state tracking models on the corrected dataset to facilitate comparison for future work.

The paper is organized as follows. First we describe the different types of annotation errors and inconsistencies we observed in MultiWOZ 2.1 (Section 2). Then, we outline the redefinition of ontology (Section 3), followed by the description of correction procedure (Section 4) and new annotations we introduce (Section 5). Finally, in Section 6, we present the performance of a few recent dialogue state tracking models on MultiWOZ 2.2.

2 Annotation Errors

The MultiWOZ dataset was collected using a Wizard-of-Oz setup (Kelley, 1984). In this setup, two crowd-workers are paired together, one acting as a user and the other as the dialogue agent. Each dialogue is driven by a unique set of instructions specifying the user goal, which are shared with the crowd-worker playing the role of the user. After every user turn, the crowd-worker playing the role of the dialogue agent (wizard) annotates the updated dialogue state. After updating the state, the tool shows the set of entities matching the dialogue state to the wizard, who then uses it to generate a response which is sent to the user. Remaining annotations such as the system actions are collected using a second annotation task.

---

[1]The dataset is available at `https://github.com/budzianowski/multiwoz`.

The Wizard-of-Oz setup is widely considered to produce natural conversations, as there is no turn level intervention guiding the flow of the dialogue. However, because of its heavy reliance on humans for generating the correct annotations, the procedure is prone to noisy annotations. We identified two major classes of errors outlined below, which were not corrected in MultiWOZ 2.1.

2.1 Hallucinated Values

Hallucinated values are present in dialogue state without being specified in the dialogue history. We observed four different types of such errors, which are shown in Figure 1 and described below.

1. **Early Markups:** These values have been mentioned by the agent in a future utterance. Since the user has not accepted them yet, they should be excluded from the dialogue state.

2. **Annotations from Database:** These values are not mentioned in the dialogue at all, even in the future utterances. They appear to be incorrectly added by the wizard based on results of the database call.

3. **Typos:** These values cannot be found in the dialogue history because of a typographical error. These errors occur since slot values are entered as free-form text in the annotation interface.

4. **Implicit Time Processing:** This specifically relates to slots taking time as a value. Sometimes, the value is obtained by adding or subtracting some pre-determined duration from the time specified in dialogue history (Figure 1). In other cases, it is implicitly rounded off to closest quarter (Dialogue 1 in Figure 2). This further burdens models with learning temporal arithmetic.

We observed that the errors mentioned above are quite frequent. In total we found that hallucinated values appear in 3128 turns across 948 dialogues in the MultiWOZ 2.1 dataset.

2.2 Inconsistent State Updates

We also encountered annotations in MultiWOZ 2.1 that are semantically correct, but don't follow consistent annotation guidelines. Inconsistencies arise in the dialogue state because of three main reasons:

1. **Multiple Sources:** A slot value may be introduced in the dialogue state through various sources. It may either be mentioned by the user,

Example Dialogue Segment	MultiWOZ 2.1	MultiWOZ 2.2
1. Early Markup User: Help me find a moderate priced british food place please. Sys: restaurant one seven is a nice place. Do you want to book?	r-food=british, r-pricerange=moderate, r-name=one seven	r-food=british, r-pricerange=moderate
2. Annotation from Database User: Can you give me the address to the hospital in Cambridge? Sys: The address is Hills Rd, Cambridge Postcode: CB20QQ	hospital-department=acute medical assessment unit	-no update-
3. Typo Sys: Okay, I can help with that. What day and time would you like to dine and how many people should I have the reservation for? User: On Thursday at 5:00. I also need a hotel in the same area. No need to have free parking.	r-bookday=thursday, r-booktime=15:00, hotel-area=west	r-bookday=thursday, r-booktime=5:00, hotel-area=west
4. Implicit Time Processing User: Can I get the postcode for that? I also need to book a taxi to the Golden Wok.	r-name=Golden Wok, r-bookday=friday, r-booktime=11:00, taxi-leaveAt=friday, taxi-destination=Golden Wok	r-name=Golden Wok, r-bookday=friday, r-booktime=11:00, taxi-destination=Golden Wok
Sys: The postcode is cb21tt. Are you looking for a taxi from Old Schools to the Golden Wok? User: Yes I do. I'd like to make sure I arrive at the restaurant by the booked time. Can you check?	r-name=Golden Wok, r-bookday=friday, r-booktime=11:00, taxi-leaveAt=friday, taxi-arriveby=10:45	r-name=Golden Wok, r-bookday=friday, r-booktime=11:00, taxi-arriveby=11:00

Figure 1: Examples of hallucinated values in MultiWOZ 2.1 and the corrections in MultiWOZ 2.2. Please note that we omit state annotations unrelated to the extracted utterances. "r" used in the slot name in the right two columns is an abbreviation of restaurant.

offered by the system, carried over from another slot in the dialogue state of a different domain, or be a part of the ontology.

2. **Value Paraphrasing:** The same slot value can be mentioned in many different ways, often within the same dialogue e.g. the value "18:00" for the slot time may be mentioned as "6 pm", "1800", "0600 pm", "evening at 6" etc.

3. **Inconsistent tracking strategy:** Crowd-workers have inconsistent opinions on which slot values should be tracked in the same dialogue context. For example, some workers track all slot values that the user agrees with while others only track user-specified slot values.

Table 1 shows dialogue state update from three different sources for similar slots from different dialogues in MultiWOZ 2.1. In the first case, the value "08:00" for slot *train-arriveby* comes from the ontology, despite the presence of an equivalent value "8:00" in the user utterance. On the other hand, in the second example, the slot value in the dialogue state comes from the user utterance despite the ontology listing "17:45" as a value for the slot *train-leaveat*. In the third example, the value of *train-leaveat* is not derived from any of the sources mentioned above, but is generated by incorporating the semantics. The slot value can be mentioned in multiple ways, but in order to evaluate a dialogue system fairly, it's necessary to either maintain a consistent rule for deciding how the value is picked among all the mentions or consider all the mentions as the correct answer. MultiWOZ 2.1 gives one unique correct answer for each dialogue state but lacks an explicit rule on how it is determined. This inconsistency confuses the model during training and unfairly penalizes it during evaluation if it

Source	User utterance	Dialogue state update
Ontology	I need to arrive by 8:00.	train-arriveby=08:00
Dialogue history	Sometime after 5:45 PM would be great.	train-leaveat=5:45pm
None	I plan on getting lunch first, so sometime after then I'd like to leave.	train-leaveat=after lunch

Table 1: Example of slot values annotated using different strategies in "PMUL0897.json", 'MUL0681.json'", and "PMUL3200.json" in MultiWOZ 2.1.

outputs a slot value which is different but equivalent to the one listed in ground truth.

Figure 2 shows another example where dialogue states are updated differently in similar scenarios. In both dialogues, the system offers an instance that fulfills the user's requirement, but the dialogue states are updated differently after user shows an intent to book the ticket. Specifically, in dialogue 1 the value for *train-arriveby* provided by the system is tracked in the dialogue state while not in dialogue 2. Dialogue 1 also showcases the implicit time processing issue discussed in Section 2.1, where the time "12:08" has been rounded to "12:15" in the dialogue state.

3 Ontology Issues

Although MultiWOZ 2.0 provides a predefined ontology which is claimed to enumerate all slots and the possible values for every slot, it has been reported to be incomplete. As a result, many researchers have built their own ontology to achieve a better performance (Wu et al., 2019; Goel et al., 2019). To fix the problem of incompleteness, MultiWOZ 2.1 rebuilt the ontology by listing all values present in dialogue states across the dataset, but it still has some unaddressed issues.

First, for some slots, multiple values sharing the same semantics are listed. Some examples are "8pm" and "20:00", "a and b guesthouse" and "a and b guest house", "cheap|moderate" and "moderate|cheap" for the slots *restaurant-booktime*, *hotel-semi-name* and *hotel-semi-pricerange* respectively. We find that 51% of the values for the slot *hotel-name* are not semantically unique, and similar figures for the *restaurant-name* and *attraction-name* slots. Such duplicate values make evaluation hard since MultiWOZ 2.1 only assumes one correct value for each slot in the dialogue state.

Second, we observe multiple slot values in the ontology that can't be associated with any entities in the database. Values like "free" for slot *attraction-name*; "cam", "dif", and "no" for slot *restaurant-name* are some examples. Such values could be introduced in the ontology because of typographical errors in the utterances or annotation errors. Our investigation shows that 21.0% of the slot values in the ontology can't be directly mapped back to the values in the database through exact string matching. We also observed a few logical expressions like "cheap|moderate", "NOT(hamilton lodge)" etc. in the ontology. We believe that these expressions, although semantically correct, add noise during training. The ontology should either omit such expressions altogether or include all possible expressions to enable generalization to cases not observed in the training data.

4 Correction Procedure

To avoid the issues described above, we advocate the definition of ontology prior to data collection. This not only serves as a guideline for annotators, but also prevents annotation inconsistencies in the dataset and corruption of the ontology from typographical and annotation errors. This section describes our definition of the new ontology, which we call *schema*, followed by the corrections made to the state and action annotations. Lastly, we also show the statistics of our modifications.

4.1 Schema Definition

It is not realistic for the ontology to enumerate all the possible values for some slots like *restaurant-name* and *restaurant-booktime*, which can take a very large set of values. With addition or removal of entities in the database, the set of possible values also keeps changing continuously. Rastogi et al. (2019) proposed a representation of ontology, called *schema*, to facilitate building a scalable dialogue system that is capable of handling such slots. A *schema* divides the different slots into two categories - *non-categorical* and *categorical*. Slots with a large or dynamic set of possible values

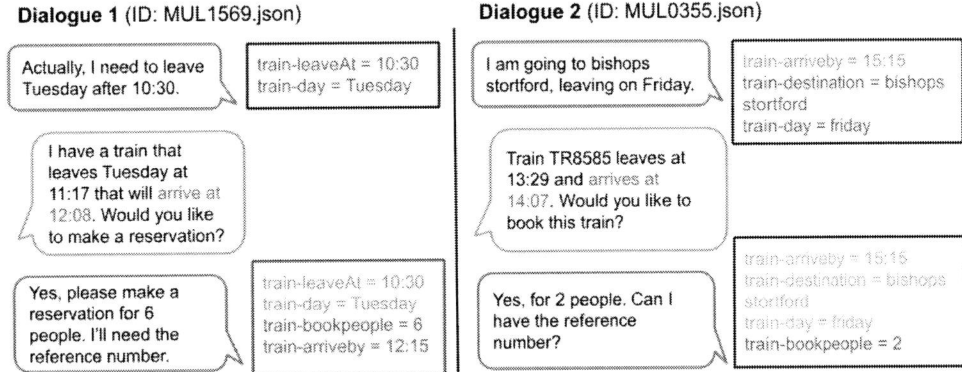

Figure 2: Example of dialogues states being updated differently in similar scenarios. In both dialogues, user accepts a train offered by the system. In dialogue 1, *train-arriveby* is annotated in the dialogue state after user's agreement, but not in dialogue 2. Dialogue 1 also shows implicit time processing, where the value 12:08 in the system utterance is rewritten to 12:15 in the subsequent dialogue state.

Domain	Categorical slots	Non-categorical slots
Restaurant	pricerange, area, bookday, bookpeople	food, name, booktime
Attraction	area, type	name
Hotel	pricerange, parking, internet, stars, area, type, bookpeople, bookday, bookstay	name
Taxi	-	destination, departure, arriveby, leaveat
Train	destination, departure, day, bookpeople	arriveby, leaveat
Bus	day	departure, destination, leaveat
Hospital	-	department
Police	-	name

Table 2: Categorical and non-categorical slots defined for 8 domains in MultiWOZ 2.2.

are called *non-categorical*. Unlike ontology, the schema doesn't provide a pre-defined list of values for such slots. Their value is extracted from the dialogue history instead.

On the other hand, slots like *hotel-pricerange* or *hotel-type*, which naturally take a small finite set of values are called *categorical*. Similar to the ontology, the schema lists all possible values for such slots. Furthermore, during annotation, the values of these slots in the dialogue state and user or system actions must be selected from a pre-defined candidate list defined in the schema. This helps achieve sanity and consistency in annotations.

We define categorical and non-categorical slots for each domain as shown in Table 2. The idea of splitting the slots in MultiWOZ into categorical and non-categorical is not new. Many models have used the number of possible slot values as the classification criterion (Zhang et al., 2019). Similarly,

we classify slots with fewer than 50 different slot values in the training set as categorical, and the others as non-categorical.

Note that since the Bus and Police domains have very few dialogues in the training set (5 and 145 respectively), the number of possible slot values in this domain does not reflect the true attributes of the slots. Thus, we classify them by referring to similar slots in different domains instead of following the threshold rule.

4.2 Categorical Slots

The list of all possible values for categorical slots is built from the corresponding database provided with MultiWOZ 2.1. In addition, we allow "dont-care" as a special value, which is used when user doesn't have a preference. We also observe cases where the mentioned value is outside the scope of the database, such as the example below, where MultiWOZ 2.1 specifies "$100" as the value for *hotel-pricerange* in the dialogue state.

User: *Well,I want it cheaper than AIRBNB,so how about $100 a night?*

System: *Unfortunately, we do not have such specific price ranges, but our options are divided into 3 categories: cheap, moderate or expensive. Which would you prefer?*

Since "$100" is not a part of the schema, we use "unknown" as the slot value in the dialogue state to express that the requirement specified by the user can not be fulfilled by the schema.

4.3 Non-categorical Slots

Values of non-categorical slots are extracted from the dialogue history. Due to the typographical errors and slot value paraphrasing, the exact value can not be found in many cases. Some examples are "el shaddia guest house" being written as "'el shaddai" or "18:00" being written as "6pm" in the dialogue utterances. Since in practice, typographical errors are inevitable and the same value can be mentioned in variable ways, we try to not modify the utterance to keep the dialogue natural. We also allow the presence of more than one value in the dialogue state. During evaluation, a prediction listing either of the listed values is considered correct.

We use a customized string matching method that takes into consideration the possible typos and alternative expressions to locate all values semantically similar to the annotation. If there are multiple matches, we select the most recently mentioned value and annotate its span. We also add this value to the dialogue state, while preserving the original value. Figure 3 shows the differences between the annotations in MultiWOZ 2.1 and MultiWOZ 2.2. The former only assumes a single value for each slot, even though the slot values can be mentioned in multiple ways and predicting any one of these variants should be considered correct. Thus, in MultiWOZ 2.2, the dialogue state can contain a list of values for a slot: predicting any value in this list is considered correct.

In some cases, slot value is carried over from other slots without being explicitly mentioned in the dialogue. For instance, in the utterance "I need to book a taxi from the museum to the restaurant", the slot value for *taxi-destination* is copied from the value for *restaurant-name* populated earlier. Instead of annotating the span for *taxi-destination*, we note down the original slot that *taxi-destination*

Utterance	"I am looking for ALexeander b&b"
MultiWOZ 2.1	**Dialogue state** hotel-name: "alexander bed and breakfast"
MultiWOZ 2.2	**Dialogue state** hotel-name: ["alexander bed and breakfast", "alexeander b&b"] **Span annotation** { "slot": "hotel-name", "start": 17, "exclusive_end": 31, "value": "ALexeander b&b" }

Figure 3: Example of the difference between dialogue state annotation in MultiWOZ 2.1 and MultiWOZ 2.2 and span annotations in MultiWOZ 2.2.

copies its value from. The span annotation for such slots can be obtained by tracing back the copy chain. We posit that this information can be beneficial for state tracking models utilizing a copy mechanism.

4.4 User and System Actions

The user and system action annotations provide a semantic representation of the respective utterances. These annotations were not part of the original MultiWOZ 2.0 release. They were created by Lee et al. (2019) and were subsequently added to MultiWOZ 2.1. However, around 5.82% of turns have missing action annotations. We use crowdsourcing to obtain annotations for these 8,333 dialogue turns (7,339 user and 994 system). The slot names used in dialogue acts are slightly different from the ones used in dialogue state annotations. We rename the slots in the dialogue acts to remove this mismatch.

MultiWOZ 2.1 uses domain-specific prefixes to associate actions with a certain domain. A few dialogue acts also have the "Booking" prefix, which is used in a few domains including Restaurant, Hotel and Train whenever a reservation is involved. In these cases, it is difficult to identify the domain corresponding to the action since the same prefix is used across many domains. We eliminate the domain and "Booking" prefixes from the dialogue acts, so that a uniform representation of actions can be used across all domains. To retain the association with the domain, actions for the same domain are grouped together into *frames*, following the representation used by Rastogi et al. (2019).

4.5 Statistics

Table 3 contains statistics on the corrections in the training, dev, and test sets. We observe that the errors are relatively uniformly distributed across the three splits. Combining all the aforementioned procedures, we modify dialogue states in 17.3% of

Dataset	% of state	% of dialogues
train	17.3	27.9
dev	17.3	28.7
test	17.6	29.5

Table 3: The ratio of the modified dialogue states (same as the number of user utterances) and modified dialogues in the training, dev, and test sets.

the user utterances across 28.2% of all dialogues. Out of the total modified 12,375 utterance annotations, a majority of the corrections fix the state update inconsistencies described in Section 2.2 by listing all the different ways in which a value has been mentioned over the dialogue context in the dialogue state. Of these state updates, 1497, or just over 12% involved corrections for two or more slots. Missing action annotations were added in a total of 8,333 utterances, whereas pre-existing actions in MultiWOZ 2.1 were verified and fixed for around 10% of the utterances.

5 Additional annotations

Besides the span annotations, we also add active user intents and requested slots for every user turn. Predicting active user intents and requested slots are two new sub-tasks that can be used to evaluate model performance and facilitate dialogue state tracking. Prediction of active intents or APIs is also essential for efficiency in large-scale dialogue systems which support hundreds of APIs.

- **Active intents:** It specifies all the intents expressed in the user utterance. Note that utterances may have multiple active intents. For example, in "can i get the college's phone number. i am also looking for a train to birmingham new street and should depart from cambridge looking for a train", the user exhibits the intent both to know more about an attraction and to search for a train.

  Based on the action and state annotations, we define a single search intent for the Attraction, Bus, Hotel, and Police domains and a single booking intent for Taxi domain, whereas for the Restaurant, Hotel, and Train domains, both search and booking intents are defined.

- **Requested slots:** It specifies the slots that the user requests information about from the system. This field is generated based on the user actions in each turn. These annotations find direct applicability in developing dialogue policy models,

since requesting additional information about entities is very common in task-oriented dialogue.

6 Dialogue State Tracking Benchmarks

Recent data-driven dialogue state tracking models that achieve state-of-the-art performance mainly adopt two classes of methods: span-based and candidate-based. Span-based methods extract values from dialogue history and are suitable for tracking states of non-categorical slots, while candidate-based methods that perform classification on predefined candidate lists to extract values are better-suited for categorical slots. To test models' performance on both categorical and non-categorical slots, we selected three dialogue state tracking models that use a mixture of both methods to benchmark the performance on the updated dataset: SGD-baseline (Rastogi et al., 2019), TRADE (Wu et al., 2019), and DS-DST (Zhang et al., 2019).

TRADE considers each slot as a mixture of categorical and non-categorical slot. It uses a pointer generator architecture to either generate the slot value from a pre-defined vocabulary or tokens in the dialogue history. On the contrary, SGD-baseline has separate tracking strategies for categorical and non-categorical slots. It first uses a shared pretrained BERT (Devlin et al., 2018) to encode a context embedding for each user turn, a slot embedding for each slot, and a slot value embedding for each slot value in the candidate list of the categorical slots. Then, it utilizes linear networks to perform classification for the categorical slot and to find start and end span indices for non-categorical slots. DS-DST is a recently proposed model achieving state-of-the-art performance on MultiWOZ 2.1 using pre-trained BERT. The main difference between DS-DST and SGD-baseline is that the context embedding used in DS-DST is conditioned on the domain-slot information while it is not in SGD-baseline.

We use joint goal accuracy as our metric to evaluate the models' performance. The joint goal accuracy is defined as the average accuracy of predicting all the slot values for a turn correctly. The performance of different models is shown in Table 4. In general, we observe similar performance on MultiWOZ 2.1 and MultiWOZ 2.2 across the three models. Table 5 compares the joint goal accuracy over only the categorical slots (cat-joint-acc) and only the non-categorical slots (noncat-joint-acc) across all the models. It shows that TRADE

Model	Multi-WOZ 2.0	Multi-WOZ 2.1	Multi-WOZ 2.2
TRADE	0.486	0.460	0.454
SGD-baseline	-	0.434	0.420
DS-DST	0.522	0.512	0.517

Table 4: Joint goal accuracy of TRADE, SGD-baseline and DS-DST models on MultiWOZ 2.0, MultiWOZ 2.1 and MultiWOZ 2.2 datasets.

Model	Cat-joint-acc	Noncat-joint-acc
TRADE	0.628	0.666
SGD-baseline	0.570	0.661
DS-DST	0.706	0.701

Table 5: Performance of TRADE, SGD-baseline, and DS-DST models on predicting categorical and non-categorical slots. Cat-joint-acc and noncat-joint-acc denote joint goal accuracy on categorical and non-categorical slots respectively.

and SGD-baseline demonstrate considerably higher performance on non-categorical slots than categorical slots. We infer that it may be caused by the corrections ensuring that the value in the dialogue state is also present in the dialogue history for all non-categorical slots.

7 Discussion

The Wizard-of-Oz paradigm is a very powerful technique to collect natural dialogues. However, the process of annotating these dialogues is prone to noise. In this section, we discuss some of the best practices to follow during task-oriented dialogue data collection so as to minimize annotation errors.

It is important to define an ontology or schema before data collection, listing the interface of all the domains and APIs. The schema should identify categorical slots, which have a fixed set of possible values, and the annotation interface should enforce the correctness of these slots. In particular, the interface should only allow the annotator to pick one of the values specified in the schema. For non-categorical slots, the interface should only allow values which have been mentioned in the dialogue history, and display an error otherwise. These simple checks help avoid typographical errors and value paraphrasing issues, discussed in Section 2. The annotation task can be followed by simple validation checks to identify erroneous annotations,

which can be fixed by a follow-up crowd-sourcing task. For instance, listing the set of all possible values for every slot in the dataset helped us quickly identify instances listing "thursday" as the value for a time slot or "no" as the name of a hotel.

We also observed a few annotations utilizing logical expressions to represent the dialogue state. For instance, some dialogue state annotations utilize string "cheap>moderate" to mean that cheap is preferred over moderate, and "cinema|entertainment|museum|theatre" to mean that all values separated by "|" are acceptable. However, such values are disproportionately rare in the dataset ($<1\%$ of dialogues), thus making it difficult for models to handle such cases. It brings into question how to define a more expressive representation which can support such complex annotations and how we should design the model capable of handling such cases. We hope that as the state tracking technology advances, there will be more focus on this direction. On the other hand, it is important to ensure that such complex constraints are proportionately represented in the dataset if the system is intended to support them.

8 Conclusion

MultiWOZ 2.1 (Eric et al., 2019) is an improved version of the MultiWOZ 2.0 dataset, which is extensively used as a benchmark for dialogue state tracking. We identify annotation errors, inconsistencies and ontology related issues which were left unaddressed in MultiWOZ 2.1, and publish a corrected version – MultiWOZ 2.2. We added a new schema, standardized slot values, corrected annotation errors and standardized span annotations. Furthermore, we annotated active intents and requested slots for each user turn, and added missing user and system actions besides fixing existing ones. We benchmark a few state-of-the-art models on the new dataset: experimental results show that the models' performance is similar between MultiWOZ 2.1 and MultiWOZ 2.2. We hope the cleaned dataset helps make fairer comparisons among models and facilitate research in this field.

References

Paweł Budzianowski, Tsung-Hsien Wen, Bo-Hsiang Tseng, Iñigo Casanueva, Stefan Ultes, Osman Ramadan, and Milica Gasic. 2018. Multiwoz-a large-scale multi-domain wizard-of-oz dataset for task-oriented dialogue modelling. In *Proceedings of the*

2018 Conference on Empirical Methods in Natural Language Processing, pages 5016–5026.

Bill Byrne, Karthik Krishnamoorthi, Chinnadhurai Sankar, Arvind Neelakantan, Ben Goodrich, Daniel Duckworth, Semih Yavuz, Amit Dubey, Kyu-Young Kim, and Andy Cedilnik. 2019. Taskmaster-1: Toward a realistic and diverse dialog dataset. In *Proceedings of the 2019 Conference on Empirical Methods in Natural Language Processing and the 9th International Joint Conference on Natural Language Processing (EMNLP-IJCNLP)*, pages 4506–4517.

Guan-Lin Chao and Ian Lane. 2019. Bert-dst: Scalable end-to-end dialogue state tracking with bidirectional encoder representations from transformer. *arXiv preprint arXiv:1907.03040*.

Jacob Devlin, Ming-Wei Chang, Kenton Lee, and Kristina Toutanova. 2018. Bert: Pre-training of deep bidirectional transformers for language understanding. *arXiv preprint arXiv:1810.04805*.

Mihail Eric, Rahul Goel, Shachi Paul, Abhishek Sethi, Sanchit Agarwal, Shuyag Gao, and Dilek Hakkani-Tur. 2019. Multiwoz 2.1: Multi-domain dialogue state corrections and state tracking baselines. *arXiv preprint arXiv:1907.01669*.

Shuyang Gao, Abhishek Sethi, Sanchit Agarwal, Tagyoung Chung, and Dilek Hakkani-Tur. 2019. Dialog state tracking: A neural reading comprehension approach. *Proceedings of the 20th Annual SIGdial Meeting on Discourse and Dialogue*.

Rahul Goel, Shachi Paul, and Dilek Hakkani-Tür. 2019. Hyst: A hybrid approach for flexible and accurate dialogue state tracking. *Interspeech 2019*.

Matthew Henderson, Blaise Thomson, and Jason D Williams. 2014. The second dialog state tracking challenge. In *Proceedings of the 15th annual meeting of the special interest group on discourse and dialogue*, pages 263–272.

J. F. Kelley. 1984. An iterative design methodology for user-friendly natural language office information applications. *ACM Trans. Inf. Syst.*, page 26–41.

Sungjin Lee, Qi Zhu, Ryuichi Takanobu, Zheng Zhang, Yaoqin Zhang, Xiang Li, Jinchao Li, Baolin Peng, Xiujun Li, Minlie Huang, et al. 2019. Convlab: Multi-domain end-to-end dialog system platform. In *Proceedings of the 57th Annual Meeting of the Association for Computational Linguistics: System Demonstrations*, pages 64–69.

Abhinav Rastogi, Dilek Hakkani-Tür, and Larry Heck. 2017. Scalable multi-domain dialogue state tracking. In *2017 IEEE Automatic Speech Recognition and Understanding Workshop*, pages 561–568. IEEE.

Abhinav Rastogi, Xiaoxue Zang, Srinivas Sunkara, Raghav Gupta, and Pranav Khaitan. 2019. Towards scalable multi-domain conversational agents: The schema-guided dialogue dataset. *arXiv preprint arXiv:1909.05855*.

Liliang Ren, Kaige Xie, Lu Chen, and Kai Yu. 2018. Towards universal dialogue state tracking. *Proceedings of the 2018 Conference on Empirical Methods in Natural Language Processing*.

Pararth Shah, Dilek Hakkani-Tür, Gokhan Tür, Abhinav Rastogi, Ankur Bapna, Neha Nayak, and Larry Heck. 2018. Building a conversational agent overnight with dialogue self-play. *arXiv preprint arXiv:1801.04871*.

Tsung-Hsien Wen, David Vandyke, Nikola Mrkšić, Milica Gasic, Lina M Rojas Barahona, Pei-Hao Su, Stefan Ultes, and Steve Young. 2017a. A network-based end-to-end trainable task-oriented dialogue system. In *Proceedings of the 15th Conference of the European Chapter of the Association for Computational Linguistics*, pages 438–449.

Tsung-Hsien Wen, David Vandyke, Nikola Mrkšić, Milica Gasic, Lina M. Rojas Barahona, Pei-Hao Su, Stefan Ultes, and Steve Young. 2017b. A network-based end-to-end trainable task-oriented dialogue system. *Proceedings of the 15th Conference of the European Chapter of the Association for Computational Linguistics*.

Chien-Sheng Wu, Andrea Madotto, Ehsan Hosseini-Asl, Caiming Xiong, Richard Socher, and Pascale Fung. 2019. Transferable multi-domain state generator for task-oriented dialogue systems. In *Proceedings of the 57th Annual Meeting of the Association for Computational Linguistics*.

Puyang Xu and Qi Hu. 2018. An end-to-end approach for handling unknown slot values in dialogue state tracking. In *Proceedings of the 56th Annual Meeting of the Association for Computational Linguistics*, pages 1448–1457.

Jian-Guo Zhang, Kazuma Hashimoto, Chien-Sheng Wu, Yao Wan, Philip S Yu, Richard Socher, and Caiming Xiong. 2019. Find or classify? dual strategy for slot-value predictions on multi-domain dialog state tracking. *arXiv preprint arXiv:1910.03544*.

Li Zhou and Kevin Small. 2019. Multi-domain dialogue state tracking as dynamic knowledge graph enhanced question answering. *arXiv preprint arXiv:1911.06192*.

Sketch-Fill-A-R: A Persona-Grounded Chit-Chat Generation Framework

Michael Shum[*1]**, Stephan Zheng**[2]**, Wojciech Kryściński**[2]**,**
Caiming Xiong[2]**, Richard Socher**[2]
[1]MIT, [2]Salesforce Research

mshum@mit.edu
{stephan.zheng,kryscinski,cxiong,rsocher}@salesforce.com

Abstract

Human-like *chit-chat* conversation requires
agents to generate responses that are fluent, engaging and consistent. We propose Sketch-
Fill-A-R, a framework that uses a persona-
memory to generate chit-chat responses in
three phases. First, it generates dynamic
sketch responses with open slots. Second, it
generates candidate responses by *filling* slots
with parts of its stored persona traits. Lastly, it
ranks and selects the final response via a language model score. Sketch-Fill-A-R outperforms a state-of-the-art baseline both quantitatively (10-point lower perplexity) and qual-
itatively (preferred by 55% in head-to-head
single-turn studies and 20% higher in consistency in multi-turn user studies) on the
Persona-Chat dataset. Finally, we extensively
analyze Sketch-Fill-A-R's responses and human feedback, and show it is more consistent and engaging by using more relevant responses and questions.

1 Introduction

Chit-chat is a rich domain that challenges machine
learning models to express fluent natural language
and to successfully interact with other agents. Chit-
chat stands in contrast to goal-oriented dialogue,
such as when a customer has the explicit goal of
booking a flight ticket. When agents communicate,
they each have internal state (e.g., their knowledge,
intent) and typically have limited knowledge of the
state of other agents (Chen et al., 2017). As a result,
human-like chit-chat requires agents to be fluent,
engaging and consistent with what has been said
and their persona (Zhang et al., 2018).

These requirements make learning generative
chit-chat models a complex task. First, given an
existing conversation history, there may be a large
number of valid responses (Vinyals and Le, 2015).

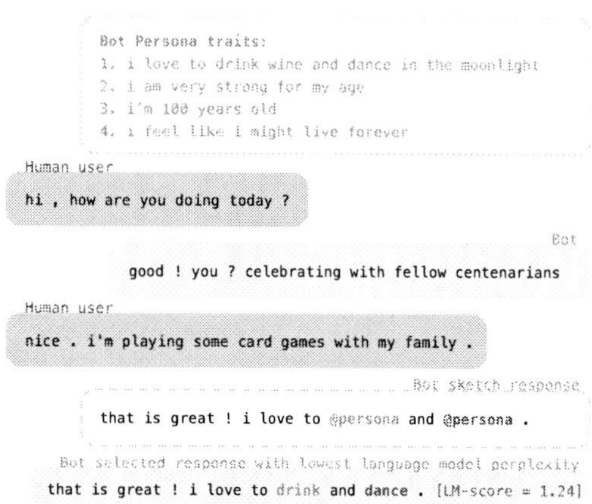

Figure 1: Chit-chat generation with Sketch-Fill-A-R.

Hence, supervised learning of chit-chat models that
cover a large number of topics and styles requires
a significant amount of data (Zhou et al., 2018).
Second, as conversations progress and more oppor-
tunities for contradiction arise, maintaining consistency becomes more difficult (Serban et al., 2016,
2017). Third, engaging chit-chat responses follow conversational structures that are not captured
well by perplexity (Dinan et al., 2019; Liu et al.,
2016). Indeed, our human user studies show that
both consistency and engagingness are only weakly
correlated with perplexity, and fluency is not at all.

We propose Sketch-Fill-A-R, a dialogue agent
framework that can learn to generate fluent, consistent and engaging chit-chat responses. Our key motivation is the hypothesis that human-like chit-chat
responses often 1) follow common conversational
patterns with insertions of agent-specific traits, and
2) condition explicitly on those persona traits.

Sketch-Fill-A-R decomposes response generation into three phases: sketching, filling and ranking, see Figure 1. First, Sketch-Fill-A-R dynamically generates a sketch response with slots, which

Work done as an intern at Salesforce Research.

Proceedings of the 2nd Workshop on Natural Language Processing for Conversational AI, pages 118–131
July 9, 2020. ©2020 Association for Computational Linguistics

enables it to learn response patterns that are compatible with many specific persona traits. Second, it generates candidate responses by filling in slots with words stored in memory. This enables Sketch-Fill-A-R's responses to adhere to its persona. Third, the candidate responses are ranked by perplexity under a pre-trained language model (LM), which encourages the final response (with lowest LM perplexity) to be fluent.

In sum, our contributions are as follows:

- We describe Sketch-Fill-A-R and how its multi-phase generation process encourages fluency, consistency and engagingness.

- We show that Sketch-Fill-A-R significantly improves hold-out perplexity by ~ 10 points on the `Persona-Chat` dataset over state-of-the-art baselines.

- We show Sketch-Fill-A-R is rated higher on conversational metrics and preferred over baselines in single and multi-turn user studies.

- We extensively analyze Sketch-Fill-A-R's response statistics and human feedback, and show that it is more consistent by using a narrower set of responses, and more engaging, by asking more questions than baselines.

2   Related Work

Chit-chat Dialogue   Dialogue agents such as Amazon Alexa, Apple Siri, and Google Home are commonplace today, and are mainly task-oriented: they help users achieve specific tasks. On the other hand, Microsoft XiaoIce (Zhou et al., 2018) is an example of an undirected chit-chat dialogue agent.

Historically task-oriented dialogue systems are composed via components such as dialogue state tracking and natural language generation (Jurafsky and Martin, 2009). Even now, the natural language generation component often uses hand-crafted templates and rules defined by domain experts that are filled via heuristics (Gao et al., 2019). More recently task-oriented dialogue systems have been trained end-to-end (Bordes et al., 2016), but these systems have specific user intents they aim to fulfill, and so represent a more constrained task. Early conversational dialogue systems such as ELIZA (Weizenbaum et al., 1966) and Alice (Wallace, 2009) were also based on hand-crafted rules and thus brittle. To alleviate this rigidity, more recent neural seq2seq models

(Sutskever et al., 2014) are trained end-to-end (Vinyals and Le, 2015; Sordoni et al., 2015; Serban et al., 2017; Li et al., 2016). To help guide conversation (Ghazvininejad et al., 2018; Dinan et al., 2018; Gopalakrishnan et al., 2019) incorporated knowledge-grounded datasets, while (Zhang et al., 2018) created the `Persona-Chat` dataset used in this work. Sketch-Fill-A-R dynamically generates slot sketches and bears resemblance to (Wu et al., 2019) which assumed data are structured domain-specific triplets and contexts follow templates. However, Sketch-Fill-A-R does not assume the personas and responses have rigid syntactic structure, and introduces a ranking procedure. Converse to our sketch-and-fill procedure, (Qian et al., 2017) train a model to select a persona trait and decode around the trait. Finally, (Welleck et al., 2018) also re-rank by scoring utterances with Natural Language Inference to improve consistency.

Neural Sequence Models   Sketch-Fill-A-R extends a neural encoder-decoder structure (Sutskever et al., 2014) but is agnostic to the chosen form of encoder-decoder. In this work we use recurrent models and attention (Bahdanau et al., 2014), which auto-regressively embed and generate sequences, but our framework is general, allowing non-recurrent encoders and decoders like Transformer networks with non-recurrent self-attention (Vaswani et al., 2017; Devlin et al., 2018) to be substituted for the recurrent encoder and decoder.

Sketch-Fill-A-R uses a simple memory module to store words from personas, which act as context for generation. Weston et al. (2014); Sukhbaatar et al. (2015) introduced learned Key-Value Memory Networks, while Kumar et al. (2016) introduced Dynamic Memory Nets for question-answering via an iterative attention over memory. Also, Sketch-Fill-A-R decodes responses using a re-ranking strategy based on language model scores, which complements strategies in (Kulikov et al., 2018).

3   Sketch-Fill-A-R

Our key motivation is to generate human-like chit-chat responses that are conditioned on persona-relevant information. Sketch-Fill-A-R generates chit-chat using a persona-memory to dynamically generate sketches that capture conversational patterns, and inserting persona-relevant information.

To set notation: capitals $W, V, \ldots$ denote matrices, i, j, k are vector-matrix indices and $x, y, \ldots$ denote vectors. The model input at time t is x_t and

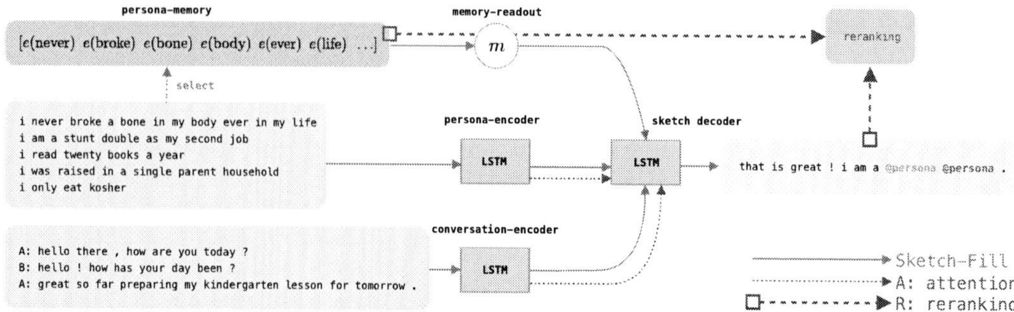

Figure 2: Sketch-Fill-A-R generates sketch responses in 4 steps. First, it encodes the conversation history and personas into hidden states $h_t^{e,\cdot}$. It stores word-embeddings for selected rare words from persona traits in a persona-memory. The final encoder hidden state $h_T^{e,c}$ produces a read-out vector h^{mem}. Lastly, the decoder outputs a sketch response with @persona slots using h^{mem}, encoder hidden states and attention over personas and conversation.

Figure 3: Sketch-Fill-A-R inference strategy. During inference, Sketch-Fill-A-R uses beam search to generate B sketch responses (step 1, depicted $B = 2$). In step 2, each beam with @persona slots produces candidate responses by filling it with rare words selected from the persona traits. Finally, a language model scores each candidate and Sketch-Fill-A-R returns the lowest-perplexity candidate.

the output at time u is y_u. We denote the conversation by x_t^c and persona trait words by x_t^p. Both input and output words $x_t, y_u \in \{0,1\}^V$ are 1-hot vectors, where V denotes the vocabulary size. The vocabulary contains all unique words, punctuation and special symbols (e.g., EOS, @persona). $x_{0:T}$ denotes a sequence $(x_0, \ldots, x_T)$.

Formally, we aim to learn a response generation model that predicts words y_u using a probability distribution $P(y_{0:U}|x_{0:T}; \theta)$ over sequences of T words and N persona traits with R rare words. Here U is the output sequence length and θ are the

model weights. We use deep neural networks, a model class that has recently seen success in language generation tasks (Bahdanau et al., 2014).

Sketch-Fill-A-R uses several components to generate sketch responses:

- An encoder $h_{0:T}^e = \text{Enc}\,(x_{0:T}; \theta)$ that computes hidden representations e_t of the input.

- A memory module $h^{\text{mem}} = \text{Mem}\,(x_{0:R}; \theta)$ that stores all rare words from persona traits (constructed by removing stop words).

- A language model $P^{LM}\,(x_{t+1}|x_{0:t}; \theta)$ that computes a distribution over next words.

- A sketch decoder

$$h_{0:U}^d = \text{Dec}\left(h_{0:T}^e, h^{\text{mem}}; \theta\right)$$

that synthesizes both the encoded input and memory readouts, and predicts the next word $\hat{y}_u$ in the sketch response.

3.1 Sketch Response Generation

Encoder We instantiate both encoder and decoder using recurrent neural networks. In this work, we use LSTMs (Hochreiter and Schmidhuber, 1997), although other choices are possible (Elman, 1990; Cho et al., 2014). The encoder computes hidden states $h_{0:T} \in \mathbb{R}^{d_{\text{hid}}}$ auto-regressively:

$$h_{t+1}^e = \text{LSTM}\,(e(x_t), h_t^e; \theta), \qquad (1)$$

where $e(x_t)$ are word-embedding representations of the raw input tokens x_t. For relevant context in decoding, Sketch-Fill-A-R encodes both conversation history $x_{0:T}^c$ and individual persona traits $x_{0:T}^p$ into hidden states $h_{0:T}^{\text{conv}}$ and $h_{0:T}^{\text{pers}}$. We denote final hidden states for all N personas as $h_{0:N}^{\text{pers}}$.

Memory Module Sketch-Fill-A-R selects a subset of rare words, x_r^p from the persona traits by removing stop-words, punctuation, and other symbols. After encoding the input dialogue, Sketch-Fill-A-R does a memory readout using the final conversation encoder hidden state h_T^{conv} as a query:

$$h^{\text{mem}} = h_T^{\text{conv}} + o, \tag{2}$$

$$o = \sum_r p_r x_r^p C^2, \tag{3}$$

$$p_r = \sigma(((h_T^{\text{conv}})^T x_r^p C^1)) \tag{4}$$

where r is a vector index over the rare word memory, σ is a softmax activation function creating attention weights $p_i \in \mathbb{R}^{d_{\text{hid}}}$, and C^k are trainable embedding matrices where $C^k \in \mathbb{R}^{V \times d_{\text{hid}}}$.

Attention Decoder The decoder is an LSTM which recursively computes hidden states h_u^d that are mapped into a distribution over output words:

$$h_{u+1}^d = \text{LSTM}\left(y_u, h_u^d; \theta\right), \tag{5}$$

$$h_0^d = f\left(W^d[h_T^e, h^{\text{mem}}] + b^d\right), \tag{6}$$

$$P\left(y_{u+1}|x_{0:T}, y_{0:u}\right) = \sigma(c_u W^{\text{emb}}). \tag{7}$$

At decoding time $u + 1$ the decoder computes the next hidden state h_{u+1}^d using the previous predicted word y_u and decoder hidden state h_u^d, in addition to attention over the context of the response (the previous utterances and the agent's persona traits). The decoder projects $[h_T^e, h^{\text{mem}}]$ down to size d_{hid} and uses it as the initial hidden state of the decoder. $W^{\text{emb}} \in \mathbb{R}^{d_{\text{hid}} \times V}$ is the transpose of the encoding embedding matrix and used to convert the decoding context to a word. The decoding context c_u augments decoder hidden state h_u^d with attention vectors c_u^{conv} over encoded conversation hidden states and c_u^{pers} over encoded persona hidden states for additional information:

$$c_u = f\left(W^{ac}[h_u^d, c_u^{\text{conv}}, c_u^{\text{pers}}] + b^{ac}\right), \tag{8}$$

$$c_u^{\text{conv}} = \langle\sigma(\langle W^a[h_u^d] + b^a, h_{0:T}^{\text{conv}}\rangle), h_{0:T}^{\text{conv}}\rangle, \tag{9}$$

$$c_u^{\text{pers}} = \langle\sigma(\langle W^a[h_u^d] + b^a, h_{0:N}^{\text{pers}}\rangle), h_{0:N}^{\text{pers}}\rangle, \tag{10}$$

where f is a tanh, $W^{ac} \in \mathbb{R}^{3*d_{\text{hid}} \times d_{\text{hid}}}$, $W^a \in \mathbb{R}^{d_{\text{hid}} \times d_{\text{hid}}}$ and σ is the softmax activation function. In Equations 9 and 10 the softmax is over the encoder time dimension and $\langle \cdot, \cdot \rangle$ is an inner product.

3.2 Inference Reranking Strategy

Sketch-Fill-A-R trains the sketch-decoder outputs (Equation 7) by minimizing cross-entropy loss

Model	Parameters	Perplexity
KVMemNet	46.3M	34.54
Sketch-Fill	26.6M	26.75
Sketch-Fill-R	26.6M	26.74
Sketch-Fill-A	26.9M	24.17
Sketch-Fill-A-R	26.9M	**24.99**

Table 1: Sketch-Fill-A-R achieves significantly lower out-of-sample perplexity than KVMemNet. Perplexity for Sketch-Fill-A-R is measured over the sketch template responses. The number of persona tag occurrences is very small, constituting 8% of the total words. See Appendix for more information.

Sequence size	KVMemNet	Sketch-Fill-A-R (ours)
Unigram	5.39%	1.72%
Bigram	32.65 %	7.32 %
Trigram	54.95 %	13.97 %
Full responses	70.16 %	50.60 %

Table 2: Percentage of novel n-grams and full responses generated by the KVMemNet and Sketch-Fill-A-R models computed on the full validation set.

with ground truths y_u^*. However, during inference, Sketch-Fill-A-R uses an iterative generate-and-score approach to produce the final response:

1. Perform beam search with beam size B to generate B sketch responses $\{\hat{y}_{0:U x^b}^b\}_{b=1,\dots,B}$ that may contain @persona tags.

2. For each sketch with tags, select the persona i^* with the highest attention weight $w_{u^*,i^*}(h_T^c)$ from the first sketch tag location u^*, and construct B' candidate responses by filling each @persona slot with words selected from i^*.

3. Compute the perplexity s_b of all B' candidate responses using a pre-trained language model:

$$s_k = \exp\frac{1}{T^b}\sum_{t=0}^{T^b} -\log P^{LM}\left(y_u^b|y_{0:u-1}^b\right).$$

4. Choose response $b^* = \min_b s_b$ with the lowest LM-likelihood score as the final response.

For Sketch-Fill variants that do not use reranking to fill slots, we follow the methodology of (Wu et al., 2019) in using a memory pointer network in order to fill slots. For detail, see the Appendix.

4 Empirical Validation

To validate Sketch-Fill-A-R, we first show that it achieves better supervised learning performance than baselines on a chit-chat dialogue dataset.

Persona-Chat Dataset We trained Sketch-Fill-A-R to generate single-turn agent responses on the `Persona-Chat` dataset (Zhang et al., 2018), which contains 10,907 dialogues. Here, a dialogue consists of multiple *turns*: a single turn contains the utterance of a single agent. We processed this dataset into training examples that each consist of the conversation history x_t^c, set of persona traits x_t^p of the model, and the ground truth sketch response y_u. This process yielded 131,438 training examples. Rare words were identified by removing all punctuation and stop words from the set of persona traits (see Appendix for more information). Ground truth sketch responses were then constructed by replacing all rare word instances in ground truth responses with `@persona` tags.

Language Model Pre-training Sketch-Fill-A-R uses a Transformer-based GPT (Radford et al., 2018) pre-trained on the Books text corpus (Zhu et al., 2015) to rank candidate responses with filled `@persona` slots according to their LM-perplexity scores. For model details, see the Appendix.

Experimental Setup We compared 4 variations of Sketch-Fill-A-R with a strong baseline: [1]

- Key-Value Memory Network (KVMemNet) (Zhang et al., 2018),

- Sketch-Fill (SF)

- Sketch-Fill-A: SF + attention

- Sketch-Fill-R: SF + reranking

- Sketch-Fill-A-R: SF + attention + reranking

(Zhang et al., 2018) showed not only that models trained on Persona-Chat outperform models trained on other dialogue datasets (movies, Twitter) in engagingness but also that KVMemNet outperforms vanilla Seq2Seq on Persona-Chat. As a result we omit comparison with Seq2Seq. KVMemNet is the strongest of the few public baselines available to compare against on chitchat with personas.

All Sketch-Fill-A-R models use language model reranking (see Section 3.2). All input tokens x_t^c, x_t^p were first encoded using 300-dimensional GLoVe word embeddings $e(x_t)$ (Pennington et al., 2014).

All models were trained by minimizing loss on the ground truth sketch response $y_{0:U}^*$:

$$\min_\theta -\sum_{u=0}^{U} \langle y_u^*, \log P\left(y_u | x_{0:T}, y_{0:u-1}; \theta\right)\rangle. \quad (11)$$

For training details, see the Appendix. The results are shown in Table 1. Sketch-Fill models outperform KVMemNet on validation perplexity, while using significantly fewer weights than KVMemNet. This suggests the structure of Sketch-Fill models fits well with chit-chat dialogue.

5 User Study and Qualitative Analysis

Although Sketch-Fill models perform well quantitatively, a crucial test is to evaluate how well they perform when judged by human users on conversational *quality*, which is not explicitly captured by perplexity. We performed single and multi-turn dialogue user studies to assess the quality of Sketch-Fill-A-R, rated along several dimensions:

- **Fluency**: whether responses are grammatically correct and sound natural.

- **Consistency**: whether responses do not contradict the previous conversation.

- **Engagingness**: how well responses fit the previous conversation and how likely the conversation would continue.

Our definition of engagingness includes *relevance*, defined in pragmatics and relevance theory (Wilson and Sperber, 2002; Grice, 1991) as a statement leading to positive cognitive effect. However an engaging statement may be ironic (Sperber and Wilson, 1981), humorous, or specific to individuals.

We also explore which qualities of Sketch-Fill-A-R's outputs are correlated with human ratings and perplexity scores. Our results suggest that:

- Conditioning on persona-memory provides more consistency.

- Sketch-Fill-A-R poses more questions, which correlates with higher engagingness.

- Responses need to be fluent in order to be consistent or engaging. In addition, more consistent responses are more likely to be engaging.

- Perplexity is not correlated with high-quality responses.

---

[1] A number of chit-chat models posted results in the ConvAI2 competition. However, we could not reproduce these, as all competitive methods rely on extensive pre-training with large models, or do not have code or trained models available.

	Baseline	Consistency	Engagingness	Fluency	Ours	Consistency	Engagingness	Fluency
Test I	KVMemNet	**3.60 ± 0.84**	**3.81 ± 0.66**	**4.49 ± 0.45**	Sketch-Fill	2.51 ± 1.16	2.57 ± 1.10	2.98 ± 1.29
Test II	KVMemNet	**3.57 ± 0.86**	**3.77 ± 0.62**	**4.54 ± 0.47**	Sketch-Fill-A	2.49 ± 1.04	2.51 ± 1.03	2.75 ± 1.20
Test III	KVMemNet	3.18 ± 1.16	3.51 ± 0.85	4.41 ± 0.48	Sketch-Fill-R	**3.34 ± 1.02**	**3.89 ± 0.79**	**4.45 ± 0.78**
Test IV	KVMemNet	3.31 ± 1.03	3.56 ± 0.78	4.43 ± 0.48	Sketch-Fill-A-R	**3.54 ± 1.01**	**3.69 ± 0.92**	4.43 ± 0.71

Table 3: User study ratings of single-turn responses (score range where 1 is low and 5 is high). Each row shows ratings from a head-to-head experiment where responses from Sketch-Fill-A-R-variants and KVMemNet over 100 different conversations were shown to 5 human raters. Sketch-Fill with reranking show a small gain over KVMemNet on all qualitative metrics, but the variance in the ratings is high. Sketch-Fill variants without reranking perform much worse, due to their responses not being fluent, despite achieving low perplexity (see Figure 1).

A/B Experiment	KVMemNet	Sketch-Fill-x (ours)
vs Sketch-Fill	**380**	120
vs Sketch-Fill-A	**396**	103
vs Sketch-Fill-R	225	**275**
vs Sketch-Fill-A-R	232	**266**

Table 4: Human A/B-preferences between KVMemNet and Sketch-Fill-A-R variations on 100 conversations, each shown to 5 users. Two Sketch-Fill-A-R variations are preferred over KVMemNet.

	Fluency	Consistency	Engagingness	Perplexity
Fluency	1	0.40	0.46	-0.01
Consistency	-	1	0.67	-0.20
Engagingness	-	-	1	-0.15
Perplexity	-	-	-	1

Table 5: Pearson's correlation ρ between human ratings and perplexity of user study examples. For visual KDE-plots of the data, see the Appendix.

5.1 Single-turn Experiments

The studies were conducted on 100 random examples sampled from the validation set, where each example was rated by 5 judges. Each example contained a conversation with multiple lines of history and a single KVMemNet or Sketch-Fill response. Judges came from English speaking countries and were calibrated with examples of good/bad responses in all metrics before judging.

The study was executed in two settings, fine-grained, where the judges rated the responses on a scale from 1 (lowest) to 5 (highest) for each of the mentioned dimensions, and binary, where they chose which response best fit the conversation.

The results of the fine-grained survey are presented in Table 3, where each row corresponds to a separate head-to-head experiments in which the KVMemNet model was paired with one of the versions of Sketch-Fill-A-R. The study showed small gains on all metrics for all Sketch-Fill-A-R variations, however, the variance of results was high. We believe that this artifact could be caused by a number of factors, including subjective preferences of raters and potential ambiguities in the experi-

ments description. We notice that Sketch-Fill and Sketch-Fill-A reach lower perplexity values than KVMemNet, but comparatively have lower evaluations across the board. Conversely, ranking models like Sketch-Fill-R and Sketch-Fill-A-R have higher scores on all metrics. We observe that the difference is due to the ranker giving more fluent outputs via better selection of persona words to use.

Table 4 shows the results of the human study in a binary setting. In these experiments the base and attention-augmented versions of Sketch-Fill-A-R outperformed KVMemNet by a clear margin.

The following subsections present in-depth analyses of the human study. They focus on the Sketch-Fill-A-R model, since it yielded both the best perplexity and user study results.

Correlation between ratings To study and better understand the reasoning behind the ratings assigned by annotators, we look at the correlation between the different dimensions in which responses where scored. Figure 5 shows Kernel-Density-Estimation plots of the data points and associated Pearson correlation coefficients ρ. The data shows weak ($\rho = 0.397$) to moderate ($\rho = 0.462$) correlation between *fluency* and *consistency*, and *fluency* and *engagingness* ratings respectively. The data shows ρ value of 0.670 between *engagingness* and *consistency* ratings, suggesting strong correlation between those dimensions. See appendix for more detailed information. The numbers were obtained on human ratings of the Sketch-Fill-A-R model, but comparable numbers were also obtained for the KVMemNet model. The mentioned results follow intuition, as *fluency* of a response is a notion that can be easily defined and identified. On the other hand *consistency* and *engagingness* are ambiguous, and (possibly) partially overlapping, concepts.

To associate quantitative metrics from Table 1 with human ratings, we computed correlation between perplexity values from the sketch decoder of the Sketch-Fill-A-R model with human scores

Model Trait 1: I married a super model from Italy
Model Trait 2: I've zero family that I'm close to
Model Trait 3: My name is George
Model Trait 4: I'm a bee farmer
Model Trait 5: My favorite food is papaya

Human: hi what's up
Model: do you like papaya ?
Human: eh, i'm more into mango
Model: what is your favorite papaya ?
Human: probably just the normal ones.
Human: what do you like to do?
Model: i am a bee farmer .
Human: woah , that's cool
Model: how are you ?
Human: i'm doing well ,
Human: just trying to get some work done
Model: do you have any hobbies ?
Human: i like to play basketball , what about you?
Model: i love papaya food .
Human: what is your name?
Model: george . what is your favorite name ?

Table 6: Example multi-turn dialog between a human and Sketch-Fill-AR. Model persona traits are shown above; the human was not given specific persona traits.

Model Trait 1: I work for our local supermarket
Model Trait 2: My favorite band is The Who
Model Trait 3: I have never been out of Ohio
Model Trait 4: My favorite food is pizza with black olives

Human: what are you doing today?
Model: i am ok what do you do for fun ?
Human: I like biking. Do you bike?.
Model: cool ! i am watching a movie with my little girl
Human: You have a daughter? How old is she?.
Model: oh that is cool . i do not have any myself .
Human: Oh. do you have a girlfriend then?.
Model: she is an ex singer from the early 2000s ,
Model: mostly does pop songs and the like
Human: What kind of movies do you like?
Model: little girl and my mother lives with us
Model: she's a concert pianist, she in between jobs
Human: who is this little girl?
Model: she also likes karate
Model: she is why i got a brown belt !
Human: what is her name?
Model: she had a green thumb and loved flowers

Table 7: Example multi-turn dialog between a human and KVMemNet. Model persona traits are shown above; the human was not given specific persona traits.

Metric	KVMemNet	Sketch-Fill-A-R (ours)
Fluency	**3.27 ± 1.19**	2.83 ± 1.31
Consistency	2.15 ± 1.18	**3.72 ± 1.26**
Engagement	1.93 ± 0.92	**2.41 ± 1.33**

Table 8: Multi-turn user study ratings (score range 1 (lowest) - 5 (highest)). We collected 30 conversations with 20 turns between human raters and models. KVMemNet is more fluent, but Sketch-Fill-A-R is more engaging and significantly more consistent.

Human: hi there . how are you
Model: hi good just writing some music and you
Human: i am well . just took my dog for a walk

KVMemNet: sorry , i trying to become the next big thing in music , i sing
Sketch-Fill-A-R: what kind of music do you like to do ?

Table 9: An example single-turn response for KVMemNet and Sketch-Fill-A-R given the same context.

across different dimensions. The study showed no correlation for *fluency* (ρ = -0.015), and weak correlations for *consistency* (ρ = -0.190) and *engagingness* (ρ = -0.147).

Model vocabulary analysis To assess the diversity of responses generated by the models, we calculated the percentage of unique n-grams and full responses present in the model outputs. Table 2 presents these values for KVMemNet and Sketch-Fill-A-R computed on the full validation set. The numbers show that the KVMemNet model clearly outperforms our model in terms of generating diverse and unique outputs by a factor of 3-4x. How-

ever, we hypothesize that this additional diversity may lead to lower engagingness scores.

Consistency over time In order to evaluate the models capacity to stay consistent with its previous statements, and thus implicitly its ability to utilize information present in the chat history, we compared how the consistency rating changed as the number of lines of the conversation increased. Figure 4 visualizes this metric both for our model and KVMemNet. In the case of both models, the consistency decreases as the chat history get longer, indicating that models have problems keeping track of their previous statements. When analyzing the linear trend we noticed that the decrease in performance is slower for the Sketch-Fill-A-R model. We hypothesize that this effect can be partially caused by the high diversity of sequences generated by the KVMemNet, which in turn affects the models ability to generate consistent conversation.

Effect of question responses (See et al., 2019) note that for a conversation to be engaging, responses in chit-chat dialogue should be a mix of statements and questions, where the model inquires about certain traits and information of the other agent. We expand on this by evaluating the effect of a question's presence in the response has on the ratings coming from the judges. The results are presented in Figure 4c. The study showed that there is a strong correlation between the model asking a question and the users rating the response as

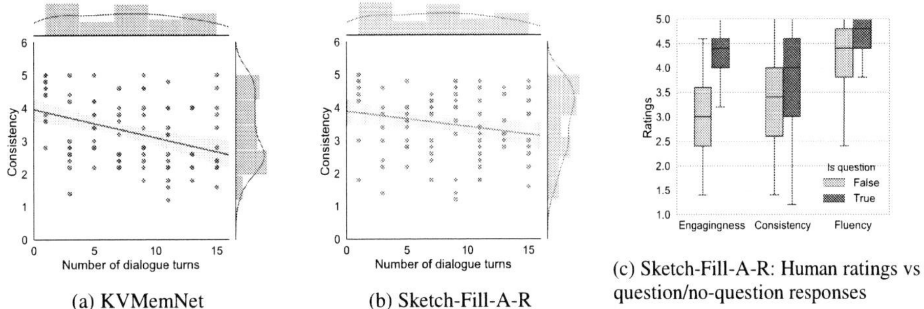

Figure 4: Impact of conversation length on the consistency of outputs generated by the KVMemNet (left) and Sketch-Fill-A-R (middle). As conversation length increases (more dialogue turns) both models become less consistent, but KVMemNet degrades faster than Sketch-Fill-A-R. Right: impact of response containing a question on human ratings. Responses including questions tend to receive higher human ratings.

more engaging. Asking questions has a small but positive influence on *engagingness* and *fluency*.

To further analyze this aspect, we measured the frequency of questions in the set of 100 responses coming from the Sketch-Fill-A-R and KVMemNet models. We found that our model produced 49 question responses out of which 25 had both a statement and a question. In the same setting the KVMemNet produced 15 questions out of which only 1 contained a statement and a question. This insight could explain the gains on the engagingness ratings found by our human study.

5.2   Multi-turn User Study

To evaluate both models in the more challenging multi-turn setting, we collected 30 conversations that lasted 20 turns, between each model and human users. Users were asked to score their conversations with the models on a scale from 1 (lowest) to 5 (highest) across the same dimensions as in the single-turn experiments. Table 8 shows the human ratings for both Sketch-Fill-A-R and KVMemNet. Both were judged as less fluent (scores $\approx$ 3) than in the single-turn case (scores $\geq$ 4). This is likely due to the models having to respond to a range of conversation histories unseen during training.

Notably, Sketch-Fill-A-R beat KVMemNet on **consistency** by a significantly larger margin (**3.72 vs 2.15**) than in the single-turn setting. This suggests that Sketch-Fill-A-R benefits from conditioning response generation on its persona-memory thus adhering more closely to responses compatible with its persona.

Further, Sketch-Fill-A-R is more engaging. This suggests that in the multi-turn setting, there also is a positive correlation between engagingness and con-

sistency as in the single-turn case (see Appendix): consistent models can be more engaging as well.

Table 7 shows an example of KVMemNet's inconsistency. While every model utterance is fluent individually, KVMemNet noticeably contradicts itself in the context of previous utterances and frequently ignores the human responses (e.g "i do not have any myself" after "my little girl"). We believe the lack of structure inherent in models built on vanilla Seq2Seq make KVMemNet prone to this mistake. Table 6 shows Sketch-Fill-A-R conducts a more engaging conversation, with pertinent responses and questions. However, this structure can restrict Sketch-Fill-A-R, as sketches may be filled with incorrect persona traits (e.g "i love papaya food."). See the Appendix for more examples.

6   Discussion and Future Work

In our study we have identified several paths for future work. First, our results reinforce that perplexity does not strongly correlate with human judgment of response quality. It is crucial to develop an automated metric that correlates well with human judgment as human evaluation is expensive, time consuming, and prone to inconsistencies. Secondly, despite outperforming other models in the multi-turn dialogue setting on consistency and engagement, our model has not reached human-like fluency. In order to demonstrate complex higher-level traits such as empathy, models must first master these lower-level abilities. Finally, correct use of rare words and proper nouns leads to higher human scores. Existing models are unable to deal with out-of-vocabulary tokens and rare words gracefully, and incorporation of commonsense via methods like external knowledge bases will be useful.

References

Dzmitry Bahdanau, Kyunghyun Cho, and Yoshua Bengio. 2014. Neural machine translation by jointly learning to align and translate. *arXiv preprint arXiv:1409.0473*.

Antoine Bordes, Y-Lan Boureau, and Jason Weston. 2016. Learning end-to-end goal-oriented dialog. *arXiv preprint arXiv:1605.07683*.

Hongshen Chen, Xiaorui Liu, Dawei Yin, and Jiliang Tang. 2017. A survey on dialogue systems: Recent advances and new frontiers. *ACM SIGKDD Explorations Newsletter*, 19(2):25–35.

Kyunghyun Cho, Bart van Merrienboer, Caglar Gulcehre, Dzmitry Bahdanau, Fethi Bougares, Holger Schwenk, and Yoshua Bengio. 2014. Learning Phrase Representations using RNN Encoder-Decoder for Statistical Machine Translation. *arXiv e-prints*, page arXiv:1406.1078.

Jacob Devlin, Ming-Wei Chang, Kenton Lee, and Kristina Toutanova. 2018. Bert: Pre-training of deep bidirectional transformers for language understanding. *arXiv preprint arXiv:1810.04805*.

Emily Dinan, Varvara Logacheva, Valentin Malykh, Alexander Miller, Kurt Shuster, Jack Urbanek, Douwe Kiela, Arthur Szlam, Iulian Serban, Ryan Lowe, et al. 2019. The second conversational intelligence challenge (convai2). *arXiv preprint arXiv:1902.00098*.

Emily Dinan, Stephen Roller, Kurt Shuster, Angela Fan, Michael Auli, and Jason Weston. 2018. Wizard of wikipedia: Knowledge-powered conversational agents. *arXiv preprint arXiv:1811.01241*.

Jeffrey L Elman. 1990. Finding structure in time. *Cognitive science*, 14(2):179–211.

Jianfeng Gao, Michel Galley, Lihong Li, et al. 2019. Neural approaches to conversational ai. *Foundations and Trends® in Information Retrieval*, 13(2-3):127–298.

Marjan Ghazvininejad, Chris Brockett, Ming-Wei Chang, Bill Dolan, Jianfeng Gao, Wen-tau Yih, and Michel Galley. 2018. A knowledge-grounded neural conversation model. In *Thirty-Second AAAI Conference on Artificial Intelligence*.

Karthik Gopalakrishnan, Behnam Hedayatnia, Qinlang Chen, Anna Gottardi, Sanjeev Kwatra, Anu Venkatesh, Raefer Gabriel, Dilek Hakkani-Tür, and Amazon Alexa AI. 2019. Topical-chat: Towards knowledge-grounded open-domain conversations. *Proc. Interspeech 2019*, pages 1891–1895.

H Paul Grice. 1991. *Studies in the Way of Words*. Harvard University Press.

Sepp Hochreiter and Jürgen Schmidhuber. 1997. Long short-term memory. *Neural computation*, 9(8):1735–1780.

Dan Jurafsky and James H. Martin. 2009. *Speech and language processing: an introduction to natural language processing, computational linguistics, and speech recognition, 2nd Edition*. Prentice Hall series in artificial intelligence. Prentice Hall, Pearson Education International.

Ilya Kulikov, Alexander H Miller, Kyunghyun Cho, and Jason Weston. 2018. Importance of a search strategy in neural dialogue modelling. *arXiv preprint arXiv:1811.00907*.

Ankit Kumar, Ozan Irsoy, Peter Ondruska, Mohit Iyyer, James Bradbury, Ishaan Gulrajani, Victor Zhong, Romain Paulus, and Richard Socher. 2016. Ask me anything: Dynamic memory networks for natural language processing. In *International Conference on Machine Learning*, pages 1378–1387.

Jiwei Li, Michel Galley, Chris Brockett, Georgios P Spithourakis, Jianfeng Gao, and Bill Dolan. 2016. A persona-based neural conversation model. *arXiv preprint arXiv:1603.06155*.

Chia-Wei Liu, Ryan Lowe, Iulian V Serban, Michael Noseworthy, Laurent Charlin, and Joelle Pineau. 2016. How not to evaluate your dialogue system: An empirical study of unsupervised evaluation metrics for dialogue response generation. *arXiv preprint arXiv:1603.08023*.

Jeffrey Pennington, Richard Socher, and Christopher Manning. 2014. Glove: Global vectors for word representation. In *Proceedings of the 2014 conference on empirical methods in natural language processing (EMNLP)*, pages 1532–1543.

Qiao Qian, Minlie Huang, Haizhou Zhao, Jingfang Xu, and Xiaoyan Zhu. 2017. Assigning personality/identity to a chatting machine for coherent conversation generation.

Alec Radford, Karthik Narasimhan, Tim Salimans, and Ilya Sutskever. 2018. Improving language understanding by generative pre-training. OpenAI.

Abigail See, Stephen Roller, Douwe Kiela, and Jason Weston. 2019. What makes a good conversation? how controllable attributes affect human judgments. *arXiv preprint arXiv:1902.08654*.

Iulian Vlad Serban, Ryan Lowe, Laurent Charlin, and Joelle Pineau. 2016. Generative deep neural networks for dialogue: A short review. *arXiv preprint arXiv:1611.06216*.

Iulian Vlad Serban, Alessandro Sordoni, Ryan Lowe, Laurent Charlin, Joelle Pineau, Aaron Courville, and Yoshua Bengio. 2017. A hierarchical latent variable encoder-decoder model for generating dialogues. In *Thirty-First AAAI Conference on Artificial Intelligence*.

Alessandro Sordoni, Michel Galley, Michael Auli, Chris Brockett, Yangfeng Ji, Margaret Mitchell, Jian-Yun Nie, Jianfeng Gao, and Bill Dolan. 2015.

A neural network approach to context-sensitive generation of conversational responses. *arXiv preprint arXiv:1506.06714*.

Dan Sperber and Deirdre Wilson. 1981. Irony and the use-mention distinction. *Philosophy*, 3:143–184.

Sainbayar Sukhbaatar, Jason Weston, Rob Fergus, et al. 2015. End-to-end memory networks. In *Advances in neural information processing systems*, pages 2440–2448.

Ilya Sutskever, Oriol Vinyals, and Quoc V Le. 2014. Sequence to sequence learning with neural networks. In *Advances in neural information processing systems*, pages 3104–3112.

Ashish Vaswani, Noam Shazeer, Niki Parmar, Jakob Uszkoreit, Llion Jones, Aidan N Gomez, Łukasz Kaiser, and Illia Polosukhin. 2017. Attention is all you need. In *Advances in Neural Information Processing Systems*, pages 5998–6008.

Oriol Vinyals and Quoc Le. 2015. A neural conversational model. *arXiv preprint arXiv:1506.05869*.

Richard S Wallace. 2009. The anatomy of alice. In *Parsing the Turing Test*, pages 181–210. Springer.

Joseph Weizenbaum et al. 1966. Eliza—a computer program for the study of natural language communication between man and machine. *Communications of the ACM*, 9(1):36–45.

Sean Welleck, Jason Weston, Arthur Szlam, and Kyunghyun Cho. 2018. Dialogue natural language inference. *arXiv preprint arXiv:1811.00671*.

Jason Weston, Sumit Chopra, and Antoine Bordes. 2014. Memory networks. *arXiv preprint arXiv:1410.3916*.

Deirdre Wilson and Dan Sperber. 2002. Relevance theory.

Chien-Sheng Wu, Richard Socher, and Caiming Xiong. 2019. Global-to-local memory pointer networks for task-oriented dialogue. In *International Conference on Learning Representations*.

Saizheng Zhang, Emily Dinan, Jack Urbanek, Arthur Szlam, Douwe Kiela, and Jason Weston. 2018. Personalizing dialogue agents: I have a dog, do you have pets too? *arXiv preprint arXiv:1801.07243*.

Li Zhou, Jianfeng Gao, Di Li, and Heung-Yeung Shum. 2018. The design and implementation of xiaoice, an empathetic social chatbot. *arXiv preprint arXiv:1812.08989*.

Yukun Zhu, Ryan Kiros, Richard Zemel, Ruslan Salakhutdinov, Raquel Urtasun, Antonio Torralba, and Sanja Fidler. 2015. Aligning books and movies: Towards story-like visual explanations by watching movies and reading books. In *arXiv preprint arXiv:1506.06724*.

7 Appendix

7.1 Ethical Implications

During experiments, we identified a number of ethical implications for future work. The `Persona-Chat` dataset was noted by some raters to contain potentially inappropriate statements (e.g., "my wife spends all my money") and is based in US culture (e.g., food, music, cars, names). It also lacked content to fail gracefully when it didn't have an appropriate response (e.g., "I'm sorry I don't understand," "I don't know"). As such, learned model responses were occasionally insensitive and confusing to human users.

7.2 Model Architecture and Training Parameters

In all models we used single-layer LSTMs with hidden sizes of 300 throughout, and used GloVe embeddings of size 300. All Sketch-and-Fill models were trained with Adam initialized with learning rate 0.0001. We used batch sizes of 32. In single-turn experiments we used beam sizes of 7, and in multi-turn experiments we used beam sizes of 10. Dropout was applied for all models with probability 0.4.

7.3 Persona Preprocessing

Persona traits were pre-processed to remove stopwords. These were initialized with the defaults from NLTK and augmented with top commonly seen words in persona traits.

["and", "my", "i", "very", "is", "favorite", "to", "like", "go", "also", "i'm", "am", "a", "lot", "at", "the", "for", "when", "are", "this", "on", "just", ".", ",", "!", "?", "help", "play", "in", "have", "of", "by", "do", "one", "it", "an", "was", "me", "could", "be", "with", "but", "before", "after", "from", "i've", "dont", "only", "love", "had", "im", "over", "what", "as", "want", "into", "try", "whatever", "get", "t", "s", "no", "own", 'i', 'me', 'my', 'myself', 'we', 'our', 'ours', 'ourselves', 'you', 'your', 'yours', 'yourself', 'yourselves', 'he', 'him', 'his', 'himself', 'she', 'her', 'hers', 'herself', 'it', 'its', 'itself', 'they', 'them', 'their', 'theirs', 'themselves', 'what', 'which', 'who', 'whom', 'this', 'that', 'these', 'those', 'am', 'is', 'are', 'was', 'were', 'be', 'been', 'being', 'have', 'has', 'had', 'having', 'do', 'does', 'did', 'doing', 'a', 'an', 'the', 'and', 'but', 'if', 'or', 'because', 'as', 'until', 'while', 'of', 'at', 'by', 'for', 'with', 'about', 'against', 'between', 'into', 'through', 'during', 'before', 'after', 'above', 'below', 'to', 'from', 'up', 'down', 'in', 'out', 'on', 'off', 'over', 'under', 'again', 'further', 'then', 'once', 'here', 'there', 'when', 'where', 'why', 'how', 'all', 'any', 'both', 'each', 'few', 'more', 'most', 'other', 'some', 'such', 'no', 'nor', 'not', 'only', 'own', 'same', 'so', 'than', 'too', 'very', 's', 't', 'can', 'will', 'just', 'don', 'should', 'now']

7.4 Number of Persona Tags

Training: 124,298 words were converted to persona tags out of 1,505,395 words total.
Validation: 8,307 words were converted to persona tags out of 92,586 words total.

7.5 Global-to-Local Memory Pointer Networks

(Wu et al., 2019) construct a global memory distribution that acts as a mask over the memory and is concatenated with encoded dialogue history and memory information before initializing as the decoder's hidden state. They also construct a local memory pointer that identifies the word to retrieve. These auxiliary tasks are trained using cross-entropy loss.

The global pointer label is defined $G^{label} = (g_0^l, ..., g_i^l)$ as a vector where g_i^l is 1 if the word is expected in y_t^* and 0 otherwise. Using the same notation as in Section 3.1, we compute the global pointer as follows:

$$g_i = Sigmoid(((y_t, h_t^d)^T e_i) \tag{12}$$

$$Loss_g = -\sum_{i=1}^{T}[g_i^l \times log(g_i) + (1 - g_i^l) \times log(1 - g_i] \tag{13}$$

$$\tag{14}$$

This global pointer is used as a mask on the memory module before the decoding procedure $e_i = e_i \times g_i$. The local pointer label is used at every time step to identify which memory index (and thus word) to point to. If at y_t^* a persona trait is expected, L_t^{label} holds corresponding index, and is m otherwise.

$$Loss_l = \sum_{t=1}^{m} -log(L_t(L_t^{label})) \tag{15}$$

7.6 Language Model Pretraining

OpenAI GPT consists of a 12 layer Transformer and is pre-trained on the BooksCorpus dataset.

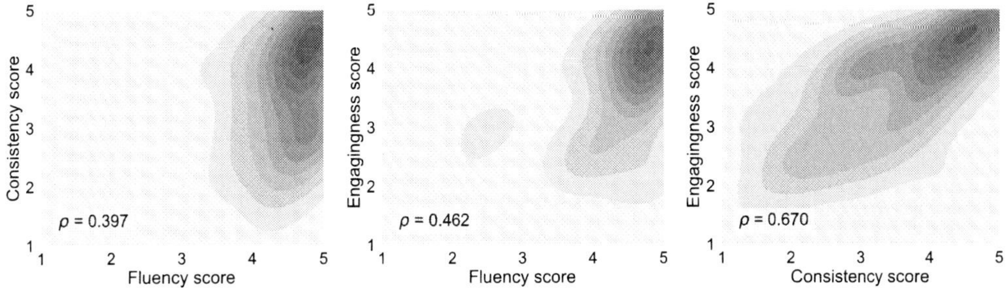

Figure 5: Correlations between different dimensions in which model responses where rated. Plots include Pearson correlation coefficients (ρ) for each dimension pair. The data suggests weak to moderate correlation between *fluency* and *consistency*, and *fluency* and *engagingness* respectively, and strong correlation between *engagingness* and *consistency*.

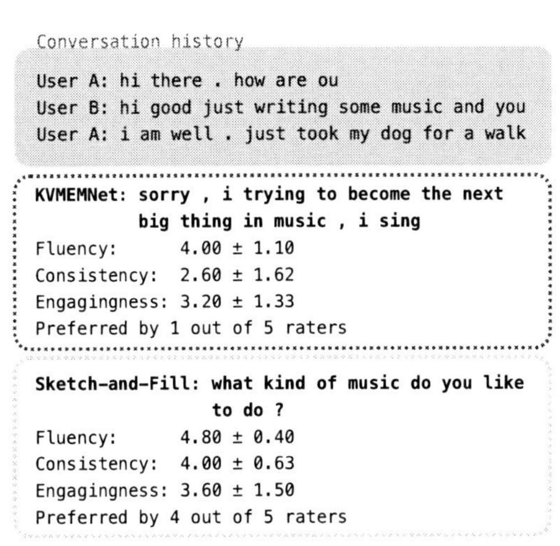

Figure 6: Example conversations from the human user studies.

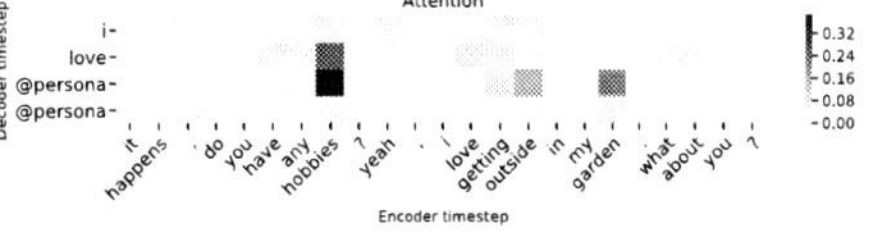

Figure 7: Attention weights over the previous context. Decoder timesteps are on the y-axis and encoder timesteps are on the x-axis.

7.7 Visualizing Model Attention

We visualize the three sets of attention weights in our model: the context weights in Figure 7, and memory weights and persona trait weights in Figure 8. Figure 7's x-axis shows a conversation ending with a question reflected by the user about hobbies. The response has high attention weights on *hobbies* and the user's own *garden* hobby in the previous context. Figure 8 (right) shows that in response to this *hobbies* question, attention is first distributed over hobby-related personas before converging on the mountain biking persona trait over time. Finally, we observe in Figure 8 (left) that the memory attention is most heavily weighted on coffee, which may explain why the coffee persona begins with such high weights.

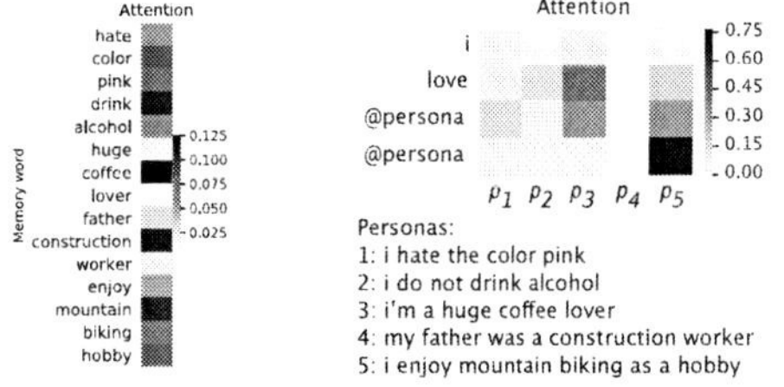

Figure 8: Attention over memory (left) and persona traits (right). After observing "love", Sketch-Fill-A-R attends to personas $3, 5$ with related personas.

```
Conversation history
User A: what do you do for work ?
User B: i'm a life coach and i'm good at it
User A: i could use your services .
User B: i'll run right over and help
User A: that is very kind of you .
User B: i run marathons and that is
        serious business
User A: i work out but it is just to hang
        with friends

KVMEMNet: that is sick i go running a lot
Fluency:       4.80 ± 0.40
Consistency:   2.40 ± 1.50
Engagingness:  3.60 ± 1.36
Preferred by 1 out of 5 raters

Sketch-and-Fill: what do you do for a living ?
Fluency:       4.80 ± 0.40
Consistency:   4.40 ± 0.49
Engagingness:  4.00 ± 1.55
Preferred by 3 out of 5 raters
```

Figure 9: Average ratings by 5 users for one example.

7.8 Example Dialogues from KVMemNet

7.9 Example Dialogues from Sketch-Fill-A-R

Model Trait 1: I played football for a division a college
Model Trait 2: I enjoy poetry
Model Trait 3: I try various coffees as a hobby
Model Trait 4: I'm a huge star wars fan

Human: Hi. What do you do you for fun?.
Model: hello ! i love music i am in school to be a music teacher
Human: That sounds exciting! I left school a long time ago..
Model: i teach french
Human: You must be talented to teach both music and french.
Model: do you speak other languages ?
Human: No, just English. What about you?.
Model: i can only speak one language !
Human: Me too. Luckily we speak the same language.
Model: no do you speak another language ?
Human: No I don't speak any other languages.
Model: i do not . i do not even speak the 5 love languages
Human: I wasn't aware that there were 5 love languages.
Human: Tell me more..
Model: i speak six other languages , pick one and i will speak it
Human: I pick language number 3.
Model: only speak english but that is pretty cool

Model Trait 1: I enjoy coloring books
Model Trait 2: My husband is adopted
Model Trait 3: I've a german shepherd dog
Model Trait 4: I like to watch NHL hockey
Model Trait 5: I live is a rural farming community

Human: yo. what's up?.
Model: i am great how about you ?
Human: i am depressed.
Model: yes ! i love to dance to it . i am pretty amazing at it
Human: oh... that's odd. and rude...
Human: you want to dance to my depression?
Model: i love to dance i have moves
Human: describe your depression
Model: dance to me. i love to dance ,
Model: not to brag but i am an incredible dancer !
Human: ok. i get it. but how. alone or with others?.
Model: that is nice . no do not dance but i like to sing so...
Human: no dancing after all? you're just messing with me?
Model: yeah , dancing with my friends is my favorite .
Human: whatever man. cool .
Model: can we dance together ? i have no brothers or sisters .

Model Trait 1: I have zero family that I'm close to
Model Trait 2: My name is George
Model Trait 3: My favorite food is papaya
Model Trait 4: I am a bee farmer
Model Trait 5: I married a super model from Italy

Human: hi.
Model: i am good how about you
Human: i didn't ask you that?.
Model: its pretty cool lol , tell me about you ?
Human: my favorite color is orange.
Model: oh i see that sounds cool then
Human: what about you?
Model: i hate organ lol
Human: what do u do for fun i like to go hiking.
Model: i like blue my favorite disney princess is ariel .
Human: cool, what other disney princesses do you like?.
Model: yeah disney is great . i named my 4 dogs after disney characters .
Model: i like ariel becuase i have a pet fish.
Human: i love watching disney movies ! how old are you?
Model: cool my favorite color is red
Human: you're just ignoring me huh.
Model: ariel has always been my favorite

Table 10: Multi-turn examples from KVMemNet. Model persona traits are listed before the example conversation.

Model Trait 1: I'm a librarian
Model Trait 2: I really like to travel
Model Trait 3: I have visited Spain a times
Model Trait 4: I think I will retire in a few years
Model Trait 5: I am 60years old

Human: hi , how are you doing?.
Model: i am doing well . how about you ?
Human: i'm doing ok, i used to be an alcoholic.
Model: oh . i am sorry to hear that .
Human: tell me something about yourself.
Model: i'm a librarian .
Human: neat , what do you do as a librarian?.
Model: i work at a library .
Human: cool, what do you do for fun?.
Model: i love to read . what about you ?
Human: i like to play basketball.
Model: that sounds like fun .
Human: it is! where are you from?.
Model: i'm in the librarian .

Model Trait 1: My dream in life is to work from home
Model Trait 2: I dye my hair every three months
Model Trait 3: I went to school to be a veterinarian
but hated it
Model Trait 4: I have an internet addiction
and spend a lot of time playing roleplaying games

Human: Ciao.
Model: how are you doing tonight ?
Human: Good. Can you speak Italian?.
Model: what do you do for a living
Human: I'm a teacher. How about you?.
Model: i am a veterinarian .
Human: Do you have a dog?
Model: i do not have any pets .
Human: How do you become a vet?
Model: i am a vet . i am a vet .
Human: Do you have emergency service?
Human: Do you need to take on call?
Model: what do you like to do for fun ?
Human: Call of duty.
Model: i like to games and roleplaying time .
Human: Me too.
Model: do you have any hobbies ?
Human: Not really.
Model: i love to addiction internet .

Model Trait 1: If I am not cooking in the kitchen
then I am definitely on the water
Model Trait 2: I love cooking but I also enjoy fishing
Model Trait 3: Spiderman is my favorite
Model Trait 4: I also love comic books

Human: hi i'm [Human name]. how are you doing today ?
Model: good, has been very busy lately.
Model: what are you going to school for ?
Human: i don't go to school, i'm working.
Model: what do you do in your free time ?
Human: i play piano.
Model: i love fishing and cooking .
Human: great.
Model: what is your favorite spiderman ?
Human: i don't like spiderman.
Model: i like to enjoy .
Human: like what?
Model: spiderman is my favorite . what is your favorite ?

Table 11: Multi-turn examples from Sketch-Fill-A-R.
Model persona traits are listed before the example conversation.

Probing Neural Dialog Models for Conversational Understanding

Abdelrhman Saleh[1], Tovly Deutsch[1],*, Stephen Casper[1],*
Yonatan Belinkov[1,2], and Stuart Shieber[1]
[1]Harvard School of Engineering and Applied Sciences
[2]MIT Computer Science and Artificial Intelligence Laboratory
abdelrhman_saleh@college.harvard.edu

Abstract

The predominant approach to open-domain dialog generation relies on end-to-end training of neural models on chat datasets. However, this approach provides little insight as to what these models learn (or do not learn) about engaging in dialog. In this study, we analyze the internal representations learned by neural open-domain dialog systems and evaluate the quality of these representations for learning basic conversational skills. Our results suggest that standard open-domain dialog systems struggle with answering questions, inferring contradiction, and determining the topic of conversation, among other tasks. We also find that the dyadic, turn-taking nature of dialog is not fully leveraged by these models. By exploring these limitations, we highlight the need for additional research into architectures and training methods that can better capture high-level information about dialog.[1]

1 Introduction

Open-domain dialog systems often rely on neural models for language generation that are trained end-to-end on chat datasets. End-to-end training eliminates the need for hand-crafted features and task-specific modules (for example, for question answering or intent detection), while delivering promising results on a variety of language generation tasks including machine translation (Bahdanau et al., 2014), abstractive summarization (Rush et al., 2015), and text simplification (Wang et al., 2016).

However, current generative models for dialog suffer from several shortcomings that limit their usefulness in the real world. Neural models can be opaque and difficult to interpret, posing barriers to their deployment in safety-critical applications such as mental health or customer service

---

[*]Second author equal contribution.

[1]Our code is available at https://github.com/AbdulSaleh/dialog-probing

(Belinkov and Glass, 2019). End-to-end training provides little insight as to what these models learn about engaging in dialog. Open-domain dialog systems also struggle to maintain basic conversations, frequently ignoring user input (Sankar et al., 2019) while generating irrelevant, repetitive, and contradictory responses (Saleh et al., 2019; Li et al., 2016, 2017a; Welleck et al., 2018). Table 1 shows examples from standard dialog models which fail at basic interactions – struggling to answer questions, detect intent, and understand conversational context.

In light of these limitations, we aim to answer the following questions: (*i*) Do neural dialog models effectively encode information about the conversation history? (*ii*) Do neural dialog models learn basic conversational skills through end-to-end training? (*iii*) And to what extent do neural dialog models leverage the dyadic, turn-taking structure of dialog to learn these skills?

To answer these questions, we propose a set of eight *probing tasks* to measure the conversational understanding of neural dialog models. Our tasks include question classification, intent detection, natural language inference, and commonsense reasoning, which all require high-level understanding of language. We also carry out *perturbation experiments* designed to test if these models fully exploit dialog structure during training. These experiments entail breaking the dialog structure by training on shuffled conversations and measuring the effects on probing performance and perplexity.

We experiment with both recurrent (Sutskever et al., 2014) and transformer-based (Vaswani et al., 2017) open-domain dialog models. We also analyze models with different sizes and initialization strategies, training small models from scratch and fine-tuning large pre-trained models on dialog data. Thus, our study covers a variety of standard models and approaches for open-domain dialog generation.

Proceedings of the 2nd Workshop on Natural Language Processing for Conversational AI, pages 132–143
July 9, 2020. ©2020 Association for Computational Linguistics

Our analysis reveals three main insights:

1. Dialog models trained from scratch on chat datasets perform poorly on the probing tasks, suggesting that they struggle with basic conversational skills. Large, pre-trained models achieve much better probing performance but are still on par with simple baselines.

2. Neural dialog models fail to effectively encode information about the conversation history and the current utterance. In most cases, simply averaging the word embeddings is superior to using the learned encoder representations. This performance gap is smaller for large, pre-trained models.

3. Neural dialog models do not leverage the dyadic, turn-taking nature of conversation. Shuffling conversations in the training data had little impact on perplexity and probing performance. This suggests that breaking the dialog structure did not significantly affect the quality of learned representations.

Our code integrates with and extends ParlAI (Miller et al., 2017), a popular open-source platform for building dialog systems. We also publicly release all our code at `https://github.com/AbdulSaleh/dialog-probing`, hoping that probing will become a standard method for interpreting and analyzing open-domain dialog systems.

2   Related Work

Evaluating and interpreting open-domain dialog models is notoriously challenging. Multiple studies have shown that standard evaluation metrics such as perplexity and BLEU scores (Papineni et al., 2002) correlate very weakly with human judgements of conversation quality (Liu et al., 2016; Ghandeharioun et al., 2019; Dziri et al., 2019). This has inspired multiple new approaches for evaluating dialog systems. One popular evaluation metric involves calculating the semantic similarity between the user input and generated response in high-dimensional embedding space (Liu et al., 2016; Ghandeharioun et al., 2019; Dziri et al., 2019; Park et al., 2018; Zhao et al., 2017; Xu et al., 2018). Ghandeharioun et al. (2019) proposed calculating conversation metrics such as sentiment and coherence on self-play conversations generated by trained models. Similarly, Dziri et al. (2019) use

neural classifiers to identify whether the model-generated responses entail or contradict user input in a natural language inference setting.

To the best of our knowledge, all existing approaches for evaluating the performance of open-domain dialog systems only consider external model behavior in the sense that they analyze properties of the generated text. In this study, we explore internal representations instead, motivated by the fact that reasonable internal behavior is crucial for interpretability and is often a prerequisite for effective external behavior.

Outside of open-domain dialog, probing has been applied for analyzing natural language processing models in machine translation (Belinkov et al., 2017) and visual question answering (Subramanian et al., 2019). Probing is also commonly used for evaluating the quality of "universal" sentence representations which are trained once and used for a variety of applications (Conneau et al., 2018; Adi et al., 2016) (for example, InferSent (Conneau et al., 2017), SkipThought (Kiros et al., 2015), USE (Cer et al., 2018)). Along the same lines, natural language understanding benchmarks such as GLUE (Wang et al., 2018) and SuperGLUE (Wang et al., 2019) propose a set of diverse tasks for evaluating general linguistic knowledge. Our analysis differs from previous work since it is focused on probing for conversational skills that are particularly relevant to dialog generation.

With regard to perturbation experiments, Sankar et al. (2019) found that standard dialog models are largely insensitive to perturbations of the input text. Here we introduce an alternative set of perturbation experiments to similarly explore the extent to which dialog structure is being leveraged by these models.

3   Methodology

3.1   Models and Data

In this study, we focus on the three most widespread dialog architectures: recurrent neural networks (RNNs) (Sutskever et al., 2014), RNNs with attention (Bahdanau et al., 2014), and Transformers (Vaswani et al., 2017). We use the ParlAI platform (Miller et al., 2017) for building and training the models. We train models of two different sizes and initialization strategies. Small models ($\approx$ 14M parameters) are initialized randomly and trained from scratch on DailyDialog (Li et al., 2017b). Large models ($\approx$ 70M parameters) are

Question Answering	Inference & Entailment	Intent Detection	Emotional Understanding
[Usr]: What do you do for a living? [Bot]: I'm from south america, lol	[Usr]: what's your favorite food? [Bot]: I love food [Usr]: you like food? [Bot]: no, I don't	[Usr]: Give me music recommendations. [Bot]: I don't know what I want to do with my life.	[Usr]: I feel so miserable [Bot]: I'm afraid it's too much for me.

Table 1: Examples from open-domain dialog systems struggling with simple conversational skills.

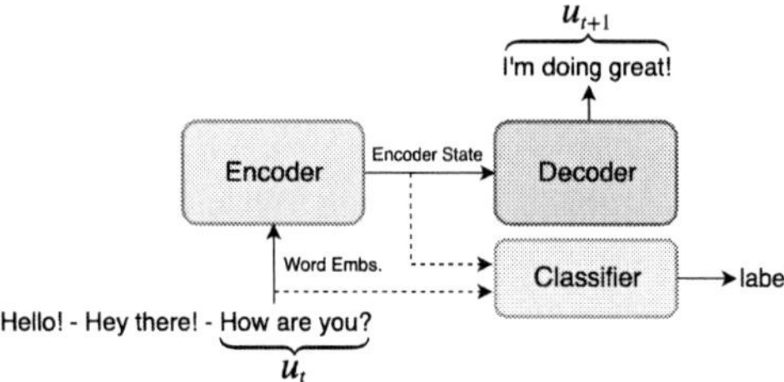

Figure 1: Probing setup. Dotted arrows emphasize that probing is applied to frozen models after dialog training. Only the parameters of the classifier module are learned during probing.

pre-trained on WikiText-103 (Merity, 2016), and then fine-tuned on DailyDialog.[2]

DailyDialog (Li et al., 2017b) is a dataset of 14K train, 1K validation, and 1K test multi-turn dialogs collected from an English learning website. The dialogs are of much higher quality than datasets scraped from Twitter or Reddit. WikiText-103 (Merity, 2016) is a dataset of 29K Wikipedia articles. For pre-training the large models, we format WikiText-103 as a dialog dataset by treating each paragraph as a conversation and each sentence as an utterance.

3.2 Probing experiments

In open-domain dialog generation, the goal is to generate the next utterance or response, u_{t+1}, given the conversation history, $[u_1, \ldots, u_t]$. First, we train our models on dialog generation using a maximum-likelihood objective (Sutskever et al., 2014). We then freeze these trained models and use them as feature extractors. We run the dialog models on text from the probing tasks and use the internal representations as features for a two-layer multilayer perceptron (MLP) classifier trained on the probing tasks as in figure 1. This follows the same methodology outlined in previous probing

studies (Belinkov et al., 2017; Belinkov and Glass, 2017; Conneau et al., 2018; Adi et al., 2016).

The assumption here is that if a model learns certain conversational skills, then knowledge of these skills should be reflected in its internal representations. For example, a model that excels at answering questions would be expected to learn useful internal representations for question answering. Thus, the performance of the probing classifier on question answering can be used as a proxy for learning this skill. We extend this reasoning to eight probing tasks designed to measure a model's conversational understanding.

The probing tasks require high-level reasoning, sometimes across multiple utterances, therefore we aggregate utterance-level representations for probing. Our probing experiments consider three types of internal representations:

Word Embeddings: To get the word embedding representations, we first averaged word embeddings of all words in the previous utterances, $[u_1, \ldots, u_{t-1}]$, then we separately averaged word embeddings of all words in the current utterance, u_t, and concatenated the two resulting, equal-length vectors. Encoding the past utterances and the current utterance separately is important since it provides some temporal information about utterance order. We used the dialog model's encoder word embedding matrix.

Encoder State: For the the encoder state, we extracted the encoder outputs after running it on the entire probing task input (i.e. the full conversation history, $[u_1, \ldots, u_t]$). Crucially, encoder states are the representations passed to the decoder for generation and are thus different for each architecture. For RNNs we used the *last* encoder hidden and cell states. For RNNs with attention the decoder has access to all the encoder hidden states (not just the final ones), through the attention mechanism. Thus, for RNNs with attention, we first

---

[2]See the supplemental material for further training details.

134

averaged the encoder hidden states corresponding to the previous utterances, $[u_1, \ldots, u_{t-1}]$, and then we separately averaged the encoder hidden states corresponding to the current utterance, u_t, and concatenated the two resulting, equal-length vectors. We also concatenated the last cell state. Similarly, for Transformers, we averaged the encoder outputs corresponding to the previous utterances and separately averaged encoder outputs corresponding to the current utterance and concatenated them.

Combined: The combined representations are the concatenation of of the word embeddings and encoder state representations.

We also use GloVe (Pennington et al., 2014) word embeddings as a simple baseline. We encode the probing task inputs using the word embeddings approach described above. We ensure that GloVe and all models of a certain size (small vs large) share the same vocabulary for comparability.

3.3 Perturbation Experiments

We also propose a set of perturbation experiments designed to measure whether dialog models fully leverage dialog structure for learning conversational skills. We create a new training dataset by shuffling the order of utterances within each conversation in DailyDialog. This completely breaks the dialog structure and utterances no longer naturally follow one another. We train (or fine-tune) separate models on the shuffled dataset and evaluate their probing performance relative to models trained on data as originally ordered.

4   Probing Tasks

The probing tasks selected for this study measure conversational understanding and skills relevant to dialog generation. Some tasks are inspired by previous benchmarks (Wang et al., 2018), while others have not been explored before for probing. Examples are listed in the supplemental material.

TREC: Question answering is a key skill for effective dialog systems. A system that deflects user questions could seem inattentive or indifferent. In order to correctly respond to questions, a model needs to determine what type of information the question is requesting. We probe for question answering using the TREC question classification dataset (Li and Roth, 2002), which consists of questions labeled with their associated answer types.

DialogueNLI: Any two turns in a conversation could entail each other (speakers agreeing, for example), or contradict each other (speakers disagreeing), or be unrelated (speakers changing topic of conversation). A dialog system should be sensitive to contradictions to avoid miscommunication and stay aligned with human preferences. We use the Dialogue NLI dataset (Welleck et al., 2018), which consists of pairs of dialog turns with entailment, contradiction, and neutral labels to probe for natural language inference. The original dataset examines two utterances from the same speaker ("I go to college", "I am a student"), so we modify the second utterance to simulate a second speaker ("I go to college", "You are a student").

MultiWOZ: Every utterance in a conversation can be considered as an action or a dialog act performed by the speaker. A speaker could be making a request, providing information, or simply greeting the system. MultiWOZ 2.1 (Eric et al., 2019) is a dataset of multi-domain, goal-oriented conversations. Human turns are labeled with dialog acts and the associated domains (hotel, restaurant, etc.), which we use to probe for natural language understanding.

SGD: Tracking user intent is also important for generating appropriate responses. The same intent is often active across multiple dialog turns since it takes more than one turn to book a hotel, for example. Determining user intent requires reasoning over multiple turns in contrast to dialog acts which are turn-specific. To probe for this task, we use intent labels from the multi-domain, goal-oriented Schema-Guided Dialog dataset (Rastogi et al., 2019).

WNLI: Endowing neural models with commonsense reasoning is an ongoing challenge in machine learning (Storks et al., 2019). We use the Winograd NLI dataset, a variant of the Winograd Schema Challenge (Levesque et al., 2012), provided in the GLUE benchmark (Wang et al., 2018) to probe for commonsense reasoning. WNLI is a sentence pair classification task where the goal is to identify whether the hypothesis correctly resolves the referent of an ambiguous pronoun in the premise.

SNIPS: The Snips NLU benchmark (Coucke et al., 2018) is a dataset of crowdsourced, single-turn queries labeled for intent. We use this dataset to probe for intent classification.

ScenarioSA: An understanding of sentiment and emotions is crucial for building social, human-centered conversational agents. We use ScenarioSA (Zhang et al., 2019) as a sentiment classification probing task. The dataset is composed of natural, multi-turn, open-ended dialogs with turn-level sentiment labels.

DailyDialog Topic: The DailyDialog dataset comes with conversation-level annotations for ten diverse topics, such as ordinary life, school life, relationships, and health. Inferring the topic of conversation is an important skill that could help dialog systems stay consistent and on topic. We use dialogs from the DailyDialog test set to create a probing tasks where the goal is to classify a dialog into the appropriate topic.

5 Results

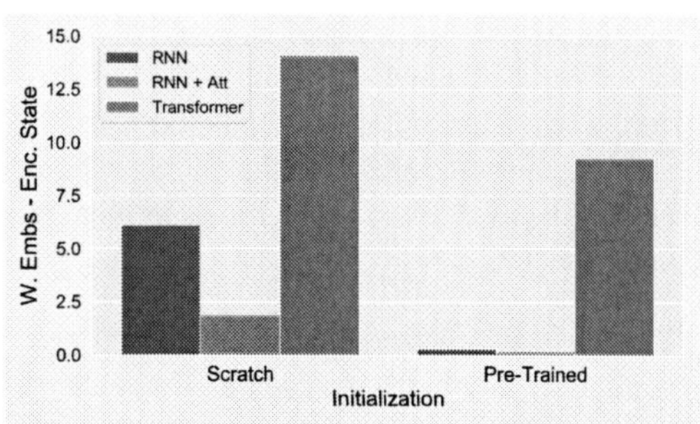

Figure 2: Bar plot showing difference between average scores for word embeddings and encoder states.

5.1 Quality of Encoder Representations

Results from our probing experiments are presented in tables 2 and 3. We calculate an average score to summarize the overall accuracy on all tasks. Here we explore whether the encoder learns high quality representations of the conversation history. We focus on *encoder states* because these representations are passed to the decoder and used for generation (figure 1). Thus, effectively encoding information in the encoder states is crucial for dialog generation.

Figure 2 shows the difference in average probing accuracy between the word embeddings and the encoder state for each model. The word embeddings outperform the encoder state for all the small models. This performance gap is most pronounced for the Transformer but is non-existent for the large recurrent models.

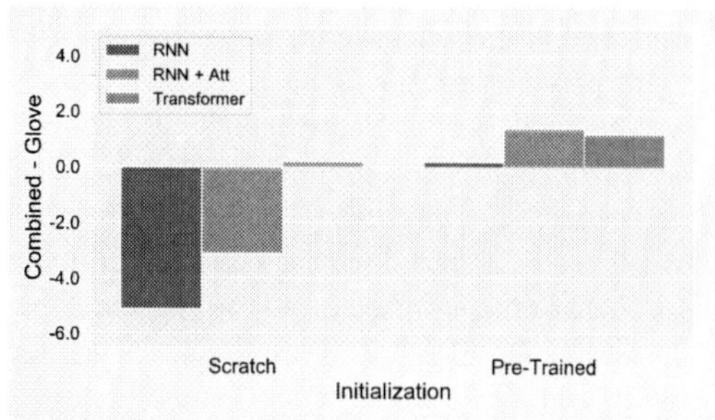

Figure 3: Bar plot showing difference between average scores for combined representations (word embeddings + encoder state) and GloVe baseline.

One possible explanation is that the encoder highlights information relevant to generating dialog at the cost of obfuscating or losing information relevant to the probing tasks – given that the goals of certain probing tasks do not perfectly align with natural dialog generation. For example, the DailyDialog dataset contains examples where a question is answered with another question (perhaps for clarification). The TREC question classification task does not account for such cases and expects each question to have a specific answer type. This explanation is supported by the observation that the information in the word embeddings and encoder state is not necessarily redundant. The combined representations often outperform using either one separately (albeit by a minute amount).

Regardless of the reason behind this gap in performance, multiple models still fail to effectively encode information about the conversation history that is already present in the word embeddings.

5.2 Probing for Conversational Understanding

In this section, we compare the probing performance of the ordered dialog models to the simple baseline of averaging GloVe word embeddings. Here we consider the *combined representations* since they achieve the best performance overall and can act as a proxy for all the information captured by the encoder about the conversation history.

Since our probing tasks test for conversational skills important for dialog generation, we would expect the dialog models to outperform GloVe word embeddings. However, this is generally not the case. As figure 3 shows, the GloVe baseline outperforms the small recurrent models while being on par with the large pre-trained models in terms of

Model	TREC	DNLI	MWOZ	SGD	SNIPS	WNLI	SSA	Topic	Avg
Majority	18.8	34.5	17.0	6.5	14.3	56.3	37.8	34.7	27.5
GloVe Mini	83.8	70.8	91.9	71.2	98.0	48.2	75.3	54.0	74.2
RNN									
Word Embs.	79.0	63.7	88.1	63.2	95.7	52.2	66.7	55.4	<u>65.7</u>
Enc. State	80.4	55.4	69.7	47.3	93.4	49.4	62.5	56.8	60.2
Combined	81.9	60.0	82.4	60.9	95.3	49.9	64.8	57.3	64.4
RNN + Attn									
Word Embs.	75.6	64.5	87.5	65.9	96.5	50.1	62.6	55.1	69.7
Enc. State	77.2	59.5	80.0	57.0	95.1	49.9	64.7	59.0	67.8
Combined	79.2	64.6	86.3	66.8	96.7	51.3	65.3	58.5	<u>71.1</u>
Transformer									
Word Embs.	81.2	71.6	90.9	70.9	97.7	48.6	74.4	62.3	**<u>74.7</u>**
Enc. State	67.9	54.1	68.7	47.2	85.1	49.4	57.4	55.4	60.7
Combined	81.5	71.3	91.2	70.3	97.9	50.1	72.8	59.6	74.3

Table 2: Accuracy on probing tasks for small models trained with random initialization on DailyDialog. Best Avg result for each model underlined. Best Avg result in bold.

Model	TREC	DNLI	MWOZ	SGD	SNIPS	WNLI	SSA	Topic	Avg
Majority	18.8	34.5	17.0	6.5	14.3	56.3	37.8	34.7	27.5
GloVe	86.5	70.3	91.6	70.5	97.8	49.9	75.1	54.3	74.5
RNN									
Word Embs.	84.0	71.6	91.4	69.8	98.1	51.4	72.0	52.3	73.8
Enc. State	84.6	66.8	89.9	72.9	97.2	48.6	67.8	61.0	73.6
Combined	85.6	69.4	91.1	74.0	97.6	49.6	69.1	61.4	<u>74.7</u>
RNN + Attn									
Word Embs.	83.4	71.4	91.8	70.1	97.9	49.5	72.1	55.7	74.0
Enc. State	85.0	65.6	90.0	73.6	97.2	47.5	70.4	63.0	74.0
Combined	86.6	70.0	92.0	75.9	97.7	48.8	73.5	62.3	<u>75.9</u>
Transformer									
Word Embs.	89.4	70.4	91.4	70.3	98.3	51.4	71.7	51.5	74.3
Enc. State	71.3	58.5	70.7	57.5	88.5	50.2	58.8	64.1	65.0
Combined	90.0	70.2	91.1	70.5	98.1	50.4	72.4	62.9	**<u>75.7</u>**

Table 3: Accuracy on probing tasks for large, Wikipedia pre-trained models fine-tuned on DailyDialog. Best Avg result for each model underlined. Best Avg result in bold.

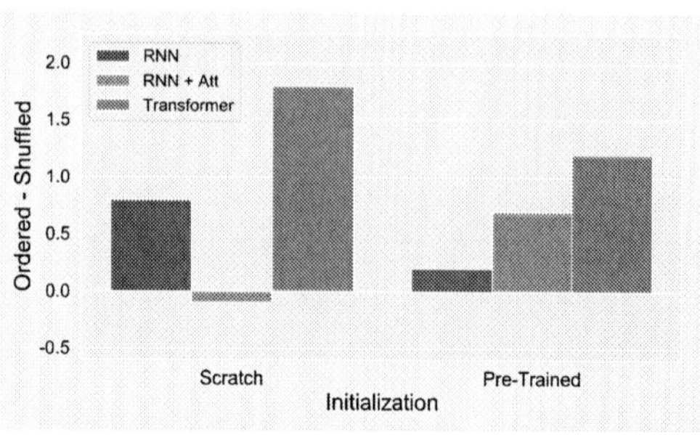

Figure 4: Bar plot showing difference between average scores for models trained on ordered and shuffled data.

average score. Tables 2 and 3 show that this pattern also generally applies at the task level, not just in terms of average score.

Closer inspection, however, reveals one exception. Combined representations from both the small and large models consistently outperform GloVe on the DailyDialog Topic task. This is the only task that is derived from the DailyDialog test data, which follows the same distribution as the dialogs used for training the models. This suggests that lack of generalization can partly explain the weak performance on other tasks. It is also worth noting that DailyDialog Topic is labeled at the conversation level rather than the turn level. Thus, identifying the correct label does not necessarily require reasoning about turn-level interactions (unlike DialogueNLI, for example).

The poor performance on the majority of tasks, relative to the simple GloVe baseline, leads us to conclude that standard dialog models trained from scratch struggle to learn the basic conversational skills examined here. Large, pre-trained models do not seem to master these skills either, with performance on par with the baselines.

5.3 Effect of Dialog Structure

Tables 4 and 5 summarize the results of the perturbation experiments. Figure 4 shows the difference in average performance between the ordered and shuffled models. We show results for the *encoder states* since these representations are important for encoding the conversation history, as discussed in section 5.1. The encoder states are also sensitive to word and utterance order, unlike averaging the word embeddings. So if a model can fully exploit the dyadic, turn-taking, structure of dialog, this is likely to be reflected in the encoder state representations.

In most of our experiments, models trained on ordered data outperformed models trained on shuffled data, as expected. We can see in figure 4, that average scores for ordered models were often higher than for shuffled models. However, the absolute gap in performance was at most 2%, which is a minute difference in practice. And even though ordered models achieved higher accuracy on average, if we examine individual tasks in tables 4 and 5, we can find instances where the shuffled models outperformed the ordered ones for each of the tested architectures, sizes, and initialization strategies.

The average difference in test perplexity between all the ordered and shuffled models was less than 2 points. This is also a minor difference in practice, suggesting that model fit and predictions are not substantially different when training on shuffled data. We evaluated all the models on the ordered DailyDialog test set to calculate perplexity. The minimal impact of shuffling the training data suggests that dialog models do not adequately leverage dialog structure during training. Our results show that essentially all of the information captured when training on ordered dialogs is also learned when training on shuffled dialogs.

6   Limitations

Some of our conclusions assume that probing performance is indicative of performance on the end-task of dialog generation. Yet it could be the case that certain models learn high quality representations for probing but cannot effectively use them for generation, due to a weakness in the decoder for example. To address this limitation, future work could examine the relationship between probing performance and human judgements of conversation quality. Belinkov (2018) argues more research on the causal relation between probing and end-task performance is required to address this limitation.

However, it is reasonable to assume that capturing information about a certain probing task is a pre-requisite to utilizing information relevant to that task for generation. For example, a model that cannot identify user sentiment is unlikely to use information about user sentiment for generation. We also find that lower perplexity (better data fit) is correlated with better probing performance (table 6), suggesting that probing is a valuable, if imperfect, analysis tool for open-domain dialog systems.

Model	Test PPL	TREC	DNLI	MWOZ	SGD	SNIPS	WNLI	SSA	Topic	Avg
Majority	-	18.8	34.5	17.0	6.5	14.3	56.3	37.8	34.7	27.5
GloVe Mini	-	83.8	70.8	91.9	71.2	98.0	48.2	75.3	54.0	74.2
RNN										
Ordered	27.2	80.4	55.4	69.7	47.3	93.4	49.4	62.5	56.8	<u>60.2</u>
Shuffled	29.0	77.3	55.7	71.2	46.4	92.8	51.5	57.0	56.8	59.7
RNN + Attn										
Ordered	26.0	77.2	59.5	80.0	57.0	95.1	49.9	64.7	59.0	67.8
Shuffled	28.8	80.2	60.8	80.8	60.7	92.9	50.8	57.9	59.3	<u>67.9</u>
Transformer										
Ordered	29.3	67.9	54.1	68.7	47.2	85.1	49.4	57.4	55.4	<u>60.7</u>
Shuffled	30.8	58.6	52.1	62.6	46.4	83.5	50.4	53.5	63.8	58.9

Table 4: Perplexity and accuracy on probing tasks for small models trained with random initialization on ordered and shuffled dialogs from DailyDialog. Results shown are for probing the encoder state. Best Avg result for each model underlined.

Model	Test PPL	TREC	DNLI	MWOZ	SGD	SNIPS	WNLI	SSA	Topic	Avg
Majority	-	18.8	34.5	17.0	6.5	14.3	56.3	37.8	34.7	27.5
GloVe	-	86.5	70.3	91.6	70.5	97.8	49.9	75.1	54.3	74.5
RNN										
Ordered	17.0	84.6	66.8	89.9	72.9	97.2	48.6	67.8	61.0	<u>73.6</u>
Shuffled	19.1	85.4	65.1	89.5	69.0	97.3	50.5	64.7	65.4	73.4
RNN + Attn										
Ordered	16.5	85.0	65.6	90.0	73.6	97.2	47.5	70.4	63.0	<u>74.0</u>
Shuffled	19.6	84.1	64.9	89.9	71.1	96.6	50.3	64.7	65.4	73.4
Transformer										
Ordered	19.8	71.3	58.5	70.7	57.5	88.5	50.2	58.8	64.1	<u>65.0</u>
Shuffled	21.4	66.1	58.0	68.8	58.0	89.6	49.0	56.3	64.2	63.8

Table 5: Perplexity and accuracy on probing tasks for large, Wikipedia pre-trained models fine-tuned on ordered and shuffled dialogs from DailyDialog. Results shown are for probing the encoder state. Best Avg result for each model underlined.

Models	TREC	DNLI	MWOZ	SGD	SNIPS	WNLI	SSA	Topic	Avg
Scratch	-0.72	-0.61	-0.65	-0.43	-0.82	-0.24	-0.99	0.40	-0.75
Pretrained	-0.76	-0.80	-0.74	-0.81	-0.71	0.61	-0.93	0.65	-0.76
All	-0.55	-0.84	-0.71	-0.87	-0.63	0.30	-0.73	-0.64	-0.92

Table 6: Probing performance of the encoder state negatively correlates with test perplexity. Results imply that models with better data fit (lower perplexity) achieve better probing performance. Note that this is insufficient to establish a causal relationship.

7 Conclusion

We use probing to shed light on the conversational understanding of neural dialog models. Our findings suggest that standard neural dialog models suffer from many limitations. They do not effectively encode information about the conversation history, struggle to learn basic conversational skills, and fail to leverage the dyadic, turn-taking structure of dialog. These limitations are particularly severe for small models trained from scratch on dialog data but occasionally also affect large pre-trained models. Addressing these limitations is an interesting direction of future work. Models could be augmented with specific components or multi-task loss functions to support learning certain skills. Future work can also explore the relationship between probing performance and human evaluation.

References

Yossi Adi, Einat Kermany, Yonatan Belinkov, Ofer Lavi, and Yoav Goldberg. 2016. Fine-grained analysis of sentence embeddings using auxiliary prediction tasks. *arXiv preprint arXiv:1608.04207*.

Dzmitry Bahdanau, Kyunghyun Cho, and Yoshua Bengio. 2014. Neural machine translation by jointly learning to align and translate. *arXiv preprint arXiv:1409.0473*.

Yonatan Belinkov. 2018. *On internal language representations in deep learning: An analysis of machine translation and speech recognition*. Ph.D. thesis, Massachusetts Institute of Technology.

Yonatan Belinkov, Nadir Durrani, Fahim Dalvi, Hassan Sajjad, and James Glass. 2017. What do neural machine translation models learn about morphology? *arXiv preprint arXiv:1704.03471*.

Yonatan Belinkov and James Glass. 2017. Analyzing hidden representations in end-to-end automatic speech recognition systems. In *Advances in Neural Information Processing Systems*, pages 2441–2451.

Yonatan Belinkov and James Glass. 2019. Analysis methods in neural language processing: A survey. *Transactions of the Association for Computational Linguistics*, 7:49–72.

Daniel Cer, Yinfei Yang, Sheng-yi Kong, Nan Hua, Nicole Limtiaco, Rhomni St John, Noah Constant, Mario Guajardo-Cespedes, Steve Yuan, Chris Tar, et al. 2018. Universal sentence encoder. *arXiv preprint arXiv:1803.11175*.

Alexis Conneau, Douwe Kiela, Holger Schwenk, Loïc Barrault, and Antoine Bordes. 2017. Supervised learning of universal sentence representations from natural language inference data. In *Proceedings of the 2017 Conference on Empirical Methods in Natural Language Processing*, pages 670–680.

Alexis Conneau, German Kruszewski, Guillaume Lample, Loïc Barrault, and Marco Baroni. 2018. What you can cram into a single vector: Probing sentence embeddings for linguistic properties. *arXiv preprint arXiv:1805.01070*.

Alice Coucke, Alaa Saade, Adrien Ball, Théodore Bluche, Alexandre Caulier, David Leroy, Clément Doumouro, Thibault Gisselbrecht, Francesco Caltagirone, Thibaut Lavril, et al. 2018. Snips voice platform: an embedded spoken language understanding system for private-by-design voice interfaces. *arXiv preprint arXiv:1805.10190*.

Nouha Dziri, Ehsan Kamalloo, Kory W Mathewson, and Osmar Zaiane. 2019. Evaluating coherence in dialogue systems using entailment. *arXiv preprint arXiv:1904.03371*.

Mihail Eric, Rahul Goel, Shachi Paul, Abhishek Sethi, Sanchit Agarwal, Shuyag Gao, and Dilek Hakkani-Tur. 2019. Multiwoz 2.1: Multi-domain dialogue state corrections and state tracking baselines. *arXiv preprint arXiv:1907.01669*.

Asma Ghandeharioun, Judy Hanwen Shen, Natasha Jaques, Craig Ferguson, Noah Jones, Agata Lapedriza, and Rosalind Picard. 2019. Approximating interactive human evaluation with self-play for open-domain dialog systems. *arXiv preprint arXiv:1906.09308*.

Diederik P Kingma and Jimmy Ba. 2014. Adam: A method for stochastic optimization. *arXiv preprint arXiv:1412.6980*.

Ryan Kiros, Yukun Zhu, Russ R Salakhutdinov, Richard Zemel, Raquel Urtasun, Antonio Torralba, and Sanja Fidler. 2015. Skip-thought vectors. In *Advances in neural information processing systems*, pages 3294–3302.

Hector Levesque, Ernest Davis, and Leora Morgenstern. 2012. The Winograd Schema Challenge. In *Thirteenth International Conference on the Principles of Knowledge Representation and Reasoning*.

Jiwei Li, Will Monroe, Alan Ritter, Michel Galley, Jianfeng Gao, and Dan Jurafsky. 2016. Deep reinforcement learning for dialogue generation. *arXiv preprint arXiv:1606.01541*.

Jiwei Li, Will Monroe, Tianlin Shi, Sébastien Jean, Alan Ritter, and Dan Jurafsky. 2017a. Adversarial learning for neural dialogue generation. *arXiv preprint arXiv:1701.06547*.

Xin Li and Dan Roth. 2002. Learning question classifiers. In *Proceedings of the 19th international conference on Computational linguistics-Volume 1*, pages 1–7. Association for Computational Linguistics.

Yanran Li, Hui Su, Xiaoyu Shen, Wenjie Li, Ziqiang Cao, and Shuzi Niu. 2017b. Dailydialog: A manually labelled multi-turn dialogue dataset. *Proceedings of the 8th International Joint Conference on Natural Language Processing*, pages 986–995.

Chia-Wei Liu, Ryan Lowe, Iulian V Serban, Michael Noseworthy, Laurent Charlin, and Joelle Pineau. 2016. How not to evaluate your dialogue system: An empirical study of unsupervised evaluation metrics for dialogue response generation. *arXiv preprint arXiv:1603.08023*.

Minh-Thang Luong, Hieu Pham, and Christopher D Manning. 2015. Effective approaches to attention-based neural machine translation. *arXiv preprint arXiv:1508.04025*.

Stephen Merity. 2016. The wikitext long term dependency language modeling dataset. *Salesforce Metamind*, 9.

Alexander H Miller, Will Feng, Adam Fisch, Jiasen Lu, Dhruv Batra, Antoine Bordes, Devi Parikh, and Jason Weston. 2017. Parlai: A dialog research software platform. *arXiv preprint arXiv:1705.06476*.

Kishore Papineni, Salim Roukos, Todd Ward, and Wei-Jing Zhu. 2002. Bleu: a method for automatic evaluation of machine translation. In *Proceedings of the 40th annual meeting on association for computational linguistics*, pages 311–318. Association for Computational Linguistics.

Yookoon Park, Jaemin Cho, and Gunhee Kim. 2018. A hierarchical latent structure for variational conversation modeling. In *NAACL (Long Papers)*, pages 1792–1801.

Jeffrey Pennington, Richard Socher, and Christopher D Manning. 2014. Glove: Global vectors for word representation. In *Proceedings of the 2014 conference on empirical methods in natural language processing (EMNLP)*, pages 1532–1543.

Abhinav Rastogi, Xiaoxue Zang, Srinivas Sunkara, Raghav Gupta, and Pranav Khaitan. 2019. Towards scalable multi-domain conversational agents: The schema-guided dialogue dataset. *arXiv preprint arXiv:1909.05855*.

Alexander M Rush, Sumit Chopra, and Jason Weston. 2015. A neural attention model for abstractive sentence summarization. *arXiv preprint arXiv:1509.00685*.

Abdelrhman Saleh, Natasha Jaques, Asma Ghandeharioun, Judy Hanwen Shen, and Rosalind Picard. 2019. Hierarchical reinforcement learning for open-domain dialog. *arXiv preprint arXiv:1909.07547*.

Chinnadhurai Sankar, Sandeep Subramanian, Christopher Pal, Sarath Chandar, and Yoshua Bengio. 2019. Do neural dialog systems use the conversation history effectively? an empirical study. *arXiv preprint arXiv:1906.01603*.

Shane Storks, Qiaozi Gao, and Joyce Y Chai. 2019. Commonsense reasoning for natural language understanding: A survey of benchmarks, resources, and approaches. *arXiv preprint arXiv:1904.01172*.

Sanjay Subramanian, Sameer Singh, and Matt Gardner. 2019. Analyzing compositionality of visual question answering. *Visually Grounded Interaction and Language Workshop*.

I Sutskever, O Vinyals, and QV Le. 2014. Sequence to sequence learning with neural networks. *Advances in NIPS*.

Ashish Vaswani, Noam Shazeer, Niki Parmar, Jakob Uszkoreit, Llion Jones, Aidan N Gomez, Łukasz Kaiser, and Illia Polosukhin. 2017. Attention is all you need. In *Advances in neural information processing systems*, pages 5998–6008.

Alex Wang, Yada Pruksachatkun, Nikita Nangia, Amanpreet Singh, Julian Michael, Felix Hill, Omer Levy, and Samuel R Bowman. 2019. Superglue: A stickier benchmark for general-purpose language understanding systems. *arXiv preprint arXiv:1905.00537*.

Alex Wang, Amanpreet Singh, Julian Michael, Felix Hill, Omer Levy, and Samuel R Bowman. 2018. Glue: A multi-task benchmark and analysis platform for natural language understanding. *arXiv preprint arXiv:1804.07461*.

Tong Wang, Ping Chen, John Rochford, and Jipeng Qiang. 2016. Text simplification using neural machine translation. In *Thirtieth AAAI Conference on Artificial Intelligence*.

Sean Welleck, Jason Weston, Arthur Szlam, and Kyunghyun Cho. 2018. Dialogue natural language inference. *arXiv preprint arXiv:1811.00671*.

Xu, Wu, and Wu. 2018. Towards explainable and controllable open domain dialogue generation with dialogue acts. *arXiv:1807.07255*.

Yazhou Zhang, Lingling Song, Dawei Song, Peng Guo, Junwei Zhang, and Peng Zhang. 2019. Scenariosa: A large scale conversational database for interactive sentiment analysis. *arXiv preprint arXiv:1907.05562*.

Tiancheng Zhao, Ran Zhao, and Maxine Eskenazi. 2017. Learning discourse-level diversity for neural dialog models using conditional variational autoencoders. In *ACL (Volume 1: Long Papers)*, pages 654–664.

A Supplemental Material

A.1 Training Details

For the small RNN trained from scratch, we used a 2-layer encoder, 2-layer decoder network with bidirectional LSTM units with a hidden size of 256 and a word embedding size of 128. For the small RNN with attention, we used the same architecture but also added multiplicative attention (Luong et al., 2015). We set dropout to 0.3 and used a batch size of 64. We used an Adam optimizer (Kingma and Ba, 2014) with a learning rate of 0.005, inverse square root decay, and 4000 warm-up updates.

For the small Transformer, we used a 2-layer encoder, 2-layer decoder network with an embedding size of 400, 8 attention heads, and a feedforward network size of 300. We set dropout to 0.3 and used a batch size of 64. We used an Adam optimizer with a learning rate of 0.001, inverse square root decay, and 6000 warm-up updates.

For the large RNN pretrained on Wikitext-103 (Merity, 2016), we used a 2-layer encoder, 2-layer decoder network with bidirectional LSTM units with a hidden size of 1024 and a word embeddings size of 300. For the large RNN with attention, we used the same architecture but also included multiplicative attention. We set dropout to 0.3 and used a batch size of 40. We used an Adam optimizer with a learning rate of 0.005, inverse square root decay, and 4000 warm-up updates.

For the large Transformer we used a 2-layer encoder, 2-layer decoder network with an embedding size of 768, 12 attention heads, and a feedforward network size of 2048. We set dropout to 0.1 and used a batch size of 32. We used an Adam optimizer with a learning rate of 0.001, inverse square root decay, and 4000 warm-up updates.

A.2 Probing Tasks Examples

Table 7 below, lists all the probing tasks and provides examples from each task. We also include the possible classes and training set sizes.

Dataset	|Train|	Example	Classes	Label
TREC	5.5K	[Usr1]: Why do heavier objects travel downhill faster?	entity, number description, location, ...	description
Dialogue NLI	310K	[Usr1]: I go to college part time. [Usr2]: You are a recent college graduate looking for a job.	entail, contradict, neutral	contradict
MultiWOZ	8.5K	[Usr1]: I need to book a hotel. [Usr2]: I can help you with that. What is your price range? [Usr1]: That doesn't matter as long as it has free wifi and parking.	hotel-inform, taxi-request, general-thank, ...	hotel-inform
Schema-Guided	16K	[Usr1]: Help me find a restaurant. [Usr2]: Which city are you looking in? [Usr1]: Cupertino, please.	find-restaurant, get-ride, reserve-flight, ...	find-restaurant
SNIPS	14K	[Usr1]: I want to see Outcast.	search-screening, play-music, get-weather, ...	search-screening
Winograd NLI	0.6K	[User1]: John couldn't see the stage with Billy in front of him because he is so tall. [User2]: John is so tall.	entail, contradict	contradict
ScenrioSA	1.9K	[Usr1]: Thank you for coming, officer. [Usr2]: What seems to be the problem? [Usr1]: I was in school all day and came home to a burglarized apartment.	positive, negative, neutral	negative
DailyDialog Topic	0.9K	[Usr1]: I think Yoga is suitable for me. [Usr2]: Why? [Usr1]: Because it doesn't require a lot of energy. [Usr2]: But I see people sweat a lot doing Yoga too.	ordinary life, work, school, tourism, politics, relationship, ...	ordinary life

Table 7: Examples from the selected probing tasks.

Author Index